The Dynamics of Innovation Clusters

NEW HORIZONS IN THE ECONOMICS OF INNOVATION

Series Editor: Christopher Freeman, *Emeritus Professor of Science Policy, SPRU – Science and Technology Policy Research, University of Sussex, UK*

Technical innovation is vital to the competitive performance of firms and of nations and for the sustained growth of the world economy. The economics of innovation is an area that has expanded dramatically in recent years and this major series, edited by one of the most distinguished scholars in the field, contributes to the debate and advances in research in this most important area.

The main emphasis is on the development and application of new ideas. The series provides a forum for original research in technology, innovation systems and management, industrial organization, technological collaboration, knowledge and innovation, research and development, evolutionary theory and industrial strategy. International in its approach, the series includes some of the best theoretical and empirical work from both well-established researchers and the new generation of scholars.

Titles in the series include:

The Dynamics of Innovation Clusters

A Study of the Food Industry

Magnus Lagnevik, Ingegerd Sjöholm, Anders Lareke and Jacob Östberg

School of Economics and Management, Institute of Economic Research, Lund University, Sweden

NEW HORIZONS IN THE ECONOMICS OF INNOVATION

Edward Elgar
Cheltenham, UK • Northampton, MA, USA

Published by
Edward Elgar Publishing Limited
Glensanda House
Montpellier Parade
Cheltenham
Glos GL50 1UA
UK

Edward Elgar Publishing, Inc.
136 West Street
Suite 202
Northampton
Massachusetts 01060
USA

Reprinted 2004
This book has been printed on demand to keep the title in print

A catalogue record for this book
is available from the British Library

Library of Congress Cataloguing in Publication Data

The dynamics of innovation clusters : a study of the food industry / Magnus
    Lagnevik... [et al.].
        p. cm. — (New horizons in the economics of innovation)
        Includes bibliographical references and index.
        1. Food industry and trade—Technological innovations—Europe. 2. Food
industry and trade—Research—Europe. 3. Processed foods—Europe—Marketing.
4. Food preference—Europe. 5. Big business—Europe. 6. Nutrition
policy—Europe. 7. Competition—Europe. I. Lagnevik, Magnus, 1949- II. Series

HD9015,A2D96   2003
664'.0068'4—dc21

2003047777

ISBN 1 84376 367 2

Printed and bound in Great Britain by
Marston Book Services Ltd, Oxfordshire

Contents

Figures

Tables

Preface

Few sectors of industry are so inextricable from people's perception of their quality of life as the food industry. Food engages, affects and provokes – it is both a source of pleasure and of fear. Given this it is strange that the food industry is characterized by both low growth and low investment in research and development. In most industrialized countries the share of household consumption occupied by food is decreasing and the level of growth of the food industry is far lower than that of traditional manufacturing industries.

This development is even more remarkable when the structural changes the industry is facing are taken into account. The ever more explicit demands of consumers are driving the process of development towards products with a greater added value, whether in terms of function or of image. Technological development has made it possible to manufacture products with an increasingly high level of added value, and competition from manufacturers with low production costs has resulted in greater demands for efficiency during the manufacturing stage.

This book poses questions about the reasons behind this development and what the food industry can do to recapture its position as a sector of industry that actively drives the process of change and renewal forward.

Research into innovation and change in the service sector in general, and in particular the food and perishables industries, is in need of development. It is precisely for this reason that this book could not come at a more opportune moment. Using innovation and cluster theory as a basis and drawing on three case studies from the Swedish food industry, the authors discuss the significance for consumers of food products with a high level of added value, as well as what is necessary to create a process which results in innovative and truly creative products.

The research programme KLIV – Kunskapsplattform för livsmedelsbranschen (Knowledge Platform for the Food Industry) – which has been the main financier of the research projects behind this book, focuses on research into consumer behaviour, innovation processes and issues concerning structure and competition. The programme is financed by the Swedish food industry and the Swedish Government.

This book is an important contribution to development in the food industry and is therefore in line with KLIV's objectives.

Bo Lindström
Programme Director KLIV

Stockholm, June 2002

Acknowledgements

This book is the result of co-operation between researchers from different disciplines. From Business Administration, Strategy and Marketing, Magnus Lagnevik, Anders Lareke and Jacob Östberg have made contributions. From Food Technology, Ingegerd Sjöholm, Federico Gomez and Charlotte Alklint made other contributions to the research project

We would like to thank all those who have contributed in various ways – in the case studies, in interviews, as respondents to questionnaires and as discussants in various seminars and informal discussions. A special thank you is directed to our colleagues and friends in the companies and research departments involved. We would like to name many, but the greatest contributions were made by Kristina Eneroth, associate professor at the Department of Business Administration and our inspiring colleagues under the leadership of Gert Göransson at Ideon Agro Food. The project is part of Lund International Food Studies, a research programme within Lund Institute of Economic Research, an excellent research institute that has provided our project with many forms of support and encouragement.

We would also like to thank those who funded this research project: K-Liv, Vinnova, Skånemejerier, the Skånska Lantmännen Foundation, the Foundation for Knowledge and Competence Development, The Swedish Agricultural University and, in parts, the European Community's ADAPT programme. They made this project possible. MarknadsTekniskt Centrum – MTC has through K-Liv been our main funding organization. They have also given us opportunities to pursue dialogue with the food industry through stimulating seminars and workshops. Thank you to Göran Liljegren, Bo Lindström and Ingela Sölvell. We would also like to thank Helen Sheppard, Eva Dagnegård and Anna Lagnevik for their valuable contributions to the editorial work.

The home base for this project is Apelgatan 11, Lund where we found a relaxing and beautiful arena for interdisciplinary creativity. We thank the Hellstrand-Sjöholm family for all their hospitality. We also thank our wives and families for their constant support.

Magnus Lagnevik, Ingegerd Sjöholm, Anders Lareke and Jacob Östberg

Lund, December 2002

1. Innovation and New Product Development in the Food Sector

How did we get into this position? The shareholders are complaining about too low return on equity. The market can never grow. You can not force people to eat more in our markets, it is therefore more probable that the market will decline – overweight is already a problem, not to mention the ongoing concentration of the business and large-scale operators leaving us with shrinking margins all the time. The pressure to rationalize is ever present and consumers are not loyal to our brands anymore. When consumers are facing shortage of money they will always buy cheap food of low quality. Is the only alternative to harvest what can be harvested, take the money and invest in some other business?

Statements resembling those above have been made by several food industry managers and employees that we have interviewed. In this book we will show that there are alternatives. We will demonstrate opportunities for the European food industry. A common theme in this book is that the recipe for success and growth involves adding value by exploiting technology and understanding consumers.

In the very last years of the previous millennium the competitive situation changed drastically in the food industry. The simultaneous occurrence of deregulation, increased international competition, shifting trends in consumer markets and the appearance of several new technologies created radically new working conditions for the food sector. A situation was created in which the conditions for innovations and new product development dramatically improved. However, the innovativeness of the food industry remained low. The main purpose of this book is to explain why, and to point out new strategies for identifying, understanding and making use of the innovation potential, and to improve the innovativeness of the food industry.

In order to gain an understanding of the innovation process, we will describe and analyse the forces at work in the creative process. This will be done with the help of strategic theory for change and innovation applied to in-depth studies of innovation processes in the food industry. We will adapt the strategic theory by focusing on innovation and adaptation to the food industry. We will confirm some earlier results from the strategic research, report some new findings and present models developed for rapid technological and market change in the food industry. Comparisons will be made with other industries. The reason for these comparisons is that the food industry is in a period of rapid development and turbulence. Other industries have recently experienced this phase of development and quite a number of interesting observations and theoretical reflections can be used to better understand and benchmark the food industry. We will also make international comparisons in order to analyse the importance of the embeddedness of the innovation processes in terms of factor conditions and unique resources, infrastructure, institutions and culture.

But first we will set the scene. In this first chapter we will describe the major changes that have created a new dynamic situation in the food industry. We will also investigate the role innovation plays in the food industry today, and what developments are desirable to create sustainably competitive food companies in a new competitive arena.

A NEW SITUATION FOR THE FOOD INDUSTRY

The food industry is by tradition local or regional, providing products from well-known recipes using traditional production technology. Consumers have appreciated this for many years.

The popular picture of olive oil production where the local farmer uses traditional grinding stones to crush the olives, then presses it more or less manually in his family-owned production facility and finally checks the oil himself before it is bottled, could be an archetype for 'high-quality food production'. The product consists of a *material and an immaterial offering*, feelings of trust, security, honesty, pureness and other associations that we may have with the product. As consumers, we like to see the kind of production described above and the method gives us a feeling of

- being close to nature,
- benefiting from personal involvement of a trustworthy individual, and
- superior products.

The fact that modern olive oil production plants provide us with

- a wider variety of well-specified products,
- guaranteed quality and taste characteristics, and
- a higher content of anti-oxidants

is probably known by many, but emotionally rejected by some. The food market is unique compared with all other markets; as consumers we eat, but we also have feelings, fears, emotions and expectations related to the food we eat. *Cooking and eating constitute an important part of our working day and social life. It takes time and has social meaning.*

The food sector is presently undergoing the greatest change that we have experienced in modern times; these changes affect consumers and their lives. As a result, consumers react to changes in a way that was not expected by the industry. Development of new products and food innovation become hazardous and exciting experiences. Those who understand the dynamics and can use their unique resources well will reap the benefits of change, while the others can only stand in the wings and watch.

International Competition

The European scene has changed in many important ways. All rounds of the World Trade Organization (WTO) negotiations have had similar outcomes, decreased entry barriers for food products in the European market, leading to more international competition and higher pressure on the Common Agricultural Policy since farmers demand compensation for reduced price levels. The expansion of the European Community directs the focus to the need for change in the agricultural policy. Maintaining present or similar compensation levels for all new member countries would be politically impossible.

Another factor driving the need for change is the recognized need for investment in urban development. The major problem areas of Europe are not the rural areas, but the big cities and their surroundings areas. The diminishing population engaged in agriculture will eventually lose out to growing urban populations regarding the attention of politicians. Therefore, the commodities markets for food in Europe can expect nothing but increased pressure to reduce costs in the future.

For Sweden, joining the European Community in 1995 had enormous effects in that national food producers found themselves in a situation of fierce international competition. Another aspect of the same change was the change in food policy. Up until the 1990s the Swedish policy had been that the country should be 85 per cent self-supplying in the food production[1] in case there was a war, or imports were cut off for some other reason. The loss of the production guarantee given by the state added to the shock of international competition in the home market.

At the same time the expansion of the home market meant that Swedish food producers could produce large volumes if they could provide food that was appealing to consumers in other countries. *The possibility of producing large volumes of niche products for international markets was an abrupt change from the traditional production of a wide assortment of products for a regional or national market.*

Structural Change

The structural change described here can be seen in three major developments:

- the globalization of retailing,
- co-operation between different actors in the value-added chain, and
- the rapid growth of the convenience market.

Rapid structural changes in the food chain affect product development and innovations. One strong force is the *globalization of retailing*, where the largest retail chains Wal-Mart, Ahold, Casino/Promodes, ITM Metro, Tesco and Carrefour all have sales in the range between US$20 and US$33 billion. They all strive to expand their operations in new markets, seeking scale economies in procurement, logistics and marketing. Since these companies often set the price level and since they have unique opportunities to compare different suppliers, the price levels of commodity products are constantly scrutinized. In order to produce standard products you must be very cost competitive. On the other hand, if you manage to develop and produce a unique product, retailers looking for new and exciting products can provide an outlet for high volumes.

Another interesting change in the value-added chain[2] *is the increasing number of products that are developed in co-operation between the different actors in the value-added chain* from plate to plough. We can find examples in meat and cold cuts, where certified farms deliver to a specific producer. For this specific type of product, the producer can co-operate with a specific retailer, using co-branding or producing for the retailers' house brand. In similar ways, breweries or whisky distillers often use barley of special origin and quality from contracted producers. In some cases, retailers provide products with a direct link to the original producer, as is the case with chicken in some markets, using a picture of the farmer on the packaging to visualize the link. This trend, to produce unique and linked products represents a counterweight to globalization and pure price competition.

A third interesting development is the *growth of the convenience market*. In order to provide convenient eating, a combination of food products and food services has become increasingly common. The largest food service companies, McDonald's, with a turnover in 1998 of US$36 billion and Tricon, with a turnover of US$20 billion, are as big as the largest global retail chains, but the demand for food services has also created a large number of small companies, catering for the needs of local consumers. Restaurants and catering firms use more prefabricated food and the traditional retailers offer more services around the products. New and different outlets challenge traditional ones. This means that we have two kinds of industrialization in the food industry. *One is in the traditional food-producing industry. The other is in the food service and convenience industry, where the goal is to industrialize the kitchen and the meal,* by offering more pre-packed, ready-to-serve, convenient meal options for the consumer.

Technological Change

The new millennium has seen rapid technological development in two important areas; development that is now having a profound impact on the food industry and the food chain. This new technological development leads to new competence and new opportunities for innovation in the food industry. New technologies change the key resources needed to compete and create a new situation in which companies with the ability to exploit these new technologies can gain sustainable competitive advantage over the companies that primarily employ established technologies. The two technological areas in question are

- information and communication technology, and
- biotechnology and bioengineering.

Information and communication technology offers the possibility to measure data and transmit information at increasingly greater speed and lower cost. For the food industry and the food chain this has resulted in new systems for logistics and handling of goods, as well as ordering systems, automatic deliveries, economic planning systems and systems for reimbursement. Major effects have already been seen in business-to-business transactions, but business-to-consumer transactions have also benefited from this new technology and have created several new businesses. Since this area of application is new, quite a number of companies have failed and gone bankrupt. Nevertheless, this area is one of the fastest growing areas in the food business and companies who learn to master the concept will no doubt have substantial business opportunities in the future.

It has also been noted that information technology (IT) offers opportunities for direct contact between producers and individual consumers. It has been concluded by several actors that this possibility may substantially alter the communication pattern and thus change the structure of the food chain.

Power will be reallocated to those who can master the information flow in an economic and efficient way.

Biotechnology is not at all new – on the contrary is it employed in many traditional production processes; wine, beer and cheese being examples. There is, however, new biotechnological knowledge based on scientific research in the fields of biology, medicine and chemistry. Molecular biology has given researchers and product developers new tools offering revolutionary opportunities. One such area is the development of techniques for DNA sequencing. Research in this area has been advanced through the huge investments that have been made in the exploration of the human genome – the HUGO project.

DNA and protein patterns in food affect the quality as well at how useful the food product is in the human metabolism. Another important area is plant science and horticultural plant engineering where food products can be genetically modified to improve crop characteristics and quality. Enzyme technology can be used to tailor-make lipids, which can give products in stable emulsions or a suitable temperature for melting. Lipids can also be modified to contain essential fatty acids. Another interesting area is the multiplication of DNA with the polymerize chain reaction (PCR) which can be used for quick and precise analysis of the microbiological status of food samples, to identify unsafe food and food of low quality.

There are also interesting *combinations of the two technologies*. The information technology also offers opportunities to identify and monitor batches of products and individual food products. In a food market where traceability is becoming increasingly important to ensure safety and quality in food products, many actors, in retailing, food production and primary production are involved in the development of projects in this area. Efforts are also being made to combine IT with breakthroughs in biotechnology in which biosensors can record the exposure of products to temperature. This, combined with transmitting chips, can offer on-line monitoring of product quality through the whole transportation and storage chain.

These are only a few examples from a very rich area of scientific development. Access to these technologies and the ability to use them in product development and product innovations may be of vital importance for food companies with the ambition of producing advanced food products, especially food products aimed at specific needs and consumers with various kinds of food intolerance.

Consumers' Changing Habits

For decades it has been said that it is important to listen to consumers. This has always been considered good advice provided that other issues were not more urgent and as long as consumers said what you expected them to. In the new millennium, however, we are facing another situation where, if we want to achieve market success, it is vital not only to listen to consumers, but also to understand in depth how and why different groups of consumers use certain food products in their daily life. Throughout this book, when we talk about consumers we refer to the end-user of the products, and when we talk about customers we refer to other actors in the value chain that might be buying a company's products.

Starting from the consumer end of the value-added chain we note that consumers are adopting new trends at an increasing speed. This is often explained by the rapid development in IT and the increased communication capabilities of the actors in the market. But globalization tendencies, immigration and travelling are also important in fuelling this development. The consumer behaviour of today is radically different from that of 1990. Consumers' demand for high-quality food and food with added value is increasing rapidly, and is mirrored by the turbulence we observe in product development and new strategies among retailers. Consequently, there is an increasing need to have a market-based product development process (Grunert et al., 1996; Lagnevik, 1996; Harmsen, 1995; Kristensen, 1992). It is also important to develop methods of measuring success in projects and programmes (Hart and Craig, 1993). The products developed must fill the need experienced by a large enough group of consumers. The perhaps most interesting aspect of the European Single Market, from a marketing point of view, is that the market is large enough to contain many different customer segments that are all large enough to be considered a potential market. These segments exist both within individual countries and across national borders. It is therefore a great advantage to be able to study the development of high-value-added products in a European context.

The food market has been the arena for a number of food scares involving dioxin, mad cow disease (BSE), listeria, poultry diseases and infected pork. It has also been the subject of substantial debate in the media and political controversies concerning food safety, additives and ingredients, cholesterol, food quality and animal welfare. Using the terminology of sociologist Ulrich Beck (1992), we are now living in a risk society, where consumers are increasingly aware of the possibilities of modern technology but, perhaps more importantly, the possible hazards.

Food consumption has become increasingly important for consumers' self-identity. What you eat is important in the sense that it shows who you are in social settings. But it also affects the perception of one's body as well as the body in a directly physiological sense. Food consumption has also become politicized in that it poses important ethical and moral questions. Monitoring your body and consumption habits has become a moral responsibility. As a result, people who eat too much, or unhealthily, feel guilty while others see it as part of their lifestyle to rebel against the norm and not to care about the nutritional qualities or the quantity of their food consumption.

There have also been some profound changes in family life; for example eating together is becoming increasingly uncommon. This development has gone furthest in the USA, while in the Mediterranean countries family meals are still common and highly valued. In the USA, many households are single households and more food is eaten outside the home than in the home. Swedish households are clearly following in the path of USA although they are still behind. Social theorist Anthony Giddens claims that individuals in late modernity have become reflexive and are consciously building a coherent lifestyle (Giddens, 1991). Food consumption is an important part of the lifestyle and the social presentation of the self. One way to analyse the changes is to study individual diversity, market segmentation, massification and structural division (Warde, 1997). Individual diversity captures the consumers' autonomy. Market segmentation has to be developed according to the new trends. The traditional groupings of consumers with similar characteristics will be replaced. A new logic is developing. Massification is the way in which the individuals adopt international trends and fads. Although we are very individually oriented, we still follow trends. Structural division helps us to identify cultural and ethnic groups and relate consumption to socio-economic living conditions.

We will devote more attention to consumer issues further on in this book. For now, we merely state that we see changing consumption patterns among consumers and that it is therefore vital to have a thorough understanding of consumers and various segments when developing new food products.

FROM COMMODITIES TO HIGH-VALUE-ADDED PRODUCTS

What we learn from the development of the food market and the food chain is that food producers on the European market need to change their strategic focus from the production of commodity products to the production and marketing of high-value-added products. Whether the value added is high or not will be judged by the consumer.

Commodity production relies on low cost. What is low cost will be increasingly defined in the international arena, where countries with low labour costs, good natural conditions for farming and an efficient production with efficient large-scale production solutions will have the advantage. The ongoing upgrading of agricultural production in Eastern Europe and some developing countries on other continents pose a troublesome future for European commodity producers, as does the continuing large-scale high-technology production in the USA, Canada and Australia.

The good news is that technological change, structural change and consumers rethinking their consumption patterns promise excellent conditions for those who want to indulge in radically new product development. To do this, many companies will have to change their strategic focus, acquire and develop new resources and competence and upgrade their marketing intelligence function. This conclusion is by no means unique to us. A number of studies point in this direction. One clear statement has been made by Traill in a study on product and process innovation in the food industry (Traill and Grunert, 1997, p. 59). His analysis of the food market and food chain leads him to the following conclusions, modestly called 'hypothesis of possible future developments'. Since the book was published we have seen clear evidence of the development predicted by Traill:

- Private-label suppliers will take advantage of the growth of retailing size throughout the Community and break down national barriers.
- The branders will increasingly emphasize European (and global) strategies, taking advantage of converging consumption patterns, Europe-wide media, lower logistics costs, lower marketing cost per unit and the elimination of legal barriers. The losers are likely to be national branders – at least those unable or unwilling to make the transition (perhaps through strategic alliances to Europe).
- If these changes take place, albeit slowly, the position of small and medium-sized enterprises (SMEs) will become increasingly vulnerable. As opportunities for supplying private-label and national branding diminish, the only remaining markets are for niche products (these could be European rather than national niches, though perhaps still relying on the original home market for the bulk of sales); and for supply to local markets where service, knowledge and particularly proximity to market will provide some protection. Local markets may be quite large, but they are a declining rather than dynamic component of modern food systems.

Our conclusions are supported by Traill's analysis. You must either be cost competitive on the European scene or develop products perceived by the consumers to have high value.

We would, however, like to *add two reflections* to Traill's conclusions. The first is that being a niche producer, which Traill describes as a last resort, is actually a very attractive option. Even small niches on large markets cover many consumers. The creation of unique high-value-added products offers opportunities for better margins. The niche segments in Europe actually provide the possibility of selling profitable products at high volumes.

The second reflection concerns Traill's reference to SMEs. In our analysis, not only SMEs, but also larger national companies have to rethink their strategy. We will later provide evidence that innovation is a troublesome activity in large companies. We have also found that innovation activities can be promoted by well-functioning industrial clusters. Therefore we will devote part of this book to cluster analysis. In clusters, both large and small companies can benefit when working on innovations.

European Union and Innovation

As far as the European Community is concerned, the need for innovation is stated already in the Ceccini report from 1988. There, two aspects of diversity in the single market are highlighted. One is that complexity must be reduced in order to promote the best-practice technology and the highest-quality products. The other aspect is that diversity must be increased in terms of new products and processes (Sloth Andersen and Braendgaard, 1992). The analysis focuses, however, on the diversity reduction aspect, since it is considered difficult to measure the effects of diversity creation as this would require a dynamic analysis which the Ceccini report does not use. The effects of diversity creation are considered to be large and positive. When the report considers these effects, the need for innovation is stated very clearly:

> Examples of this (meaning diversity creation) include product and process innovation which will modify – upwards – the entire trajectory of EC growth and welfare throughout the 1990s and beyond into the twenty-first century (Ceccini, 1988).

This line of thinking is later taken up by the EU Green Paper on Innovation (COM(95)688), where a conclusion presented in the 1994 White Paper on Innovation (1994) is highlighted.

> In the Commission's opinion, Europe's research and industrial base suffers from a series of weaknesses. The first of these weaknesses is financial. The community invests proportionately less than its competitors in research and technological development. ... .
> A second weakness is the lack of coordination at various levels of the research and technological development activities, programmes and strategies in Europe. ... The greatest weakness, however, is the comparatively limited capacity to convert scientific breakthroughs and technological achievements into industrial and commercial success.

As part of the measures taken following the Commission's conclusions a major research project on innovation was initiated, headed by the economist Charles Edquist (1997). In the Green Paper, the Commission makes a statement about the state of the industry as a whole in Europe.

> Later in this book we will address the greatest weakness at length. But first we will contend that this limited capacity to convert scientific breakthroughs and technological achievements into industrial and commercial success is clearly visible and well established in the food industry.

Similar conclusions concerning the need for innovation and development of high-value-added food products have been presented in European studies (for example Traill and Pitts, 1997), as well as Scandinavian studies (Harmsen, 1995; Lagnevik, 1996).

Furthermore, most, if not all, European countries have their own national programmes or national institutes for innovation and competitiveness in the food sector. We have come to the conclusion that most EU member countries have analysed the need for innovation in the food sector and are investing considerable amounts in this area.

Attitudes among Key Executives

As part of this research project we have carried out a survey among key people with an excellent knowledge of the food industry, the food market and strategies for the future. We interviewed those in executive positions and who had personal experience of strategic and development issues. The interviews covered many aspects of innovations and competitiveness, but we also posed a few questions in which we asked the respondents to quantify their attitudes concerning innovations. The questions that we asked were the following:

- Is innovation important for the food industry?
- Are companies in the food industry innovative?
- Is your company innovative?
- Is innovation a matter of life or death for the industry?
- Are foreign companies more innovative?

We put these questions to key people in the Swedish food sector. We also interviewed key people in the food business in the Boston area of Massachusetts, USA. The reason for this is that in our analysis of innovation in food clusters, we wished to make a comparison between the food industry in a part of the USA well known for innovative activities in general, and the 'Öresund food cluster' which is located in southern Sweden and Denmark, and is one of the most complete development clusters for the food industry in Europe. We used key actors from other high-technology industries as a reference group, so that we could relate the responses from the food industry to those from others with similar insight in other industries, such as telecom, medicine, home electronics and consumer services. We naturally put questions to the control group concerning their industry, not the food industry.

We were somewhat surprised to see strong support regarding the importance of innovation (see Figure 1.1). This may be a result of us asking people with good insight into strategy, competitiveness and innovation. The vast majority of the answers are in the range 8–10, with 10 as the most common answer. We cannot see any major differences between the Swedish and the US food industry. The answers also correspond rather well with those from other high-technology companies.

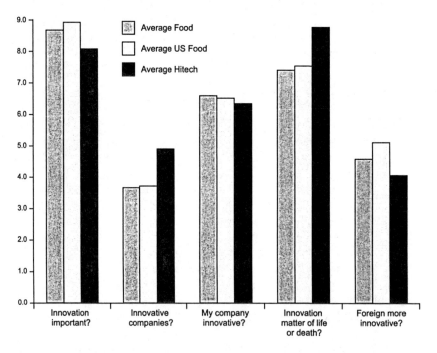

Figure 1.1   Attitudes towards innovation among experienced executives

When we asked the respondents in the food industry if they thought that the other companies in the industry were innovative, the answers were rather negative. Other high-technology industries showed more positive responses with the average of 5 on a 1–10 scale. The food companies in both Sweden and the USA ranked below 4. This means that on the whole, our respondents did not regard the food industry as innovative. All respondents regarded their own company as being more innovative than the rest of the industry. Perhaps it is natural to perceive one's own company in a more positive way than competitors, suppliers and customers.

When asked if innovation was a matter of life and death, positive responses were obtained that were almost as strong as those to the first question about the importance of innovation. We interpret this as an insight among our respondents that in the long term, new products will be necessary for the company to survive. The responses were even more positive in the other high-tech industries. This may be the result of direct experience in high-tech firms that have lost new product development races and gone bankrupt.

Foreign companies were not considered to be more innovative than domestic ones. For our interviewees, competition was not perceived as coming from somewhere else. Major innovators can be found both in the national and in the international arena. From this we conclude that major insightful actors in the food industry are aware of the need for innovation and are trying to bring it about in their own companies.

Innovation and Customer Orientation in the Primary Production

But how is the situation in primary production? Is it not true that farmers are more product-oriented and only interested in the production of large quantities? The results of our study show that the previously dominating production orientation now is giving way to thinking based on high-value-added and customer demands.

This can be illustrated by an article from a daily newspaper (*Sydsvenska dagbladet*, 16 August 2001, p. 8) The Swedish farmers' co-operatives for grain production have merged into one national organization. The news is that 125 of the biggest and most professional farms in the south of Sweden have formed their own marketing organization – Söderslätts Spannmåls-grupp. One major reason is that the new group will have a more distinct focus on the production of high-value-added crops tailor-made for specific customers.

> We will devote much effort to producing tailor-made products for the food industry. This means that we will produce the right barley for the beer industry, the best grain for the flour mills and the best wheat for Absolut Vodka. ... Our ambition is to shorten the distance to the customer. A very large organization like Svenska Lantmännen with 60,000 members will not have the speed that we can have in our organization. Moreover, also it is difficult to know exactly where the wheat comes from in a very large organization.[3]

Their ambition to produce high-value-added products in this example was so high that a number of farmers work outside their own organization in order to achieve excellence. This example illustrates that striving for unique and profitable products exists not only in retailing and food-processing companies, but also in primary production.

VERY LITTLE INNOVATION IN THE FOOD INDUSTRY

We know that the EU Commission would like more innovations, also in food production and agriculture. We know that there are EU programmes and national programmes aimed at promoting innovation. We have established that key executives have a positive attitude towards innovation and find a positive attitude in all parts of the food chain.

As a result, we would expect an industry with a substantial amount of innovation and new product development. But how much innovation is there? How many new and innovative products find their way onto the shelves in the retail outlets? This question has been dealt with in a study conducted by ECR Europe in co-operation with Ernst & Young and AC Nielsen (ECR Europe, 1999). They analysed 24,543 new products that came onto store shelves during a 13-month period. They sorted the new products into the following groups:

- *Classically innovative products.* These are breakthrough products that appear to the consumer to bring true innovation to an existing category or that create a new category. An example is ProViva Active, a product that contains healthy bacteria and other healthy components. The effect of these components is that the drink helps a tired or injured body to recover.
- *Equity transfer products.* These are products that are new to the category but recognized by the consumer. An example is Mars ice cream.
- *Line extension products.* These are new products within the same category. An example would be yoghurt with coconut flavour.
- *Me-too products.* These are products that are essentially the same as existing ones. An example might be a retailer's brand or a second coconut-flavoured yoghurt.
- *Seasonal/temporary products.* These products have a short life cycle. Examples are Easter eggs.
- *Conversion/substitution products.* These products are already marketed without adding new value to the customer. An example would be a detergent packaging size increased from 4.5 kg to 5 kg.

The study was conducted in six European countries: Finland, France, Germany, Italy, Spain and the UK. The differences between the different countries are very interesting and the size of the sample make the study reliable.

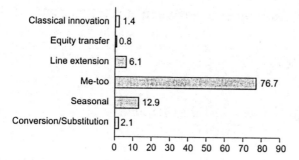

Figure 1.2   Innovations measured in food retailing

Even if we define innovation broadly as classical innovations and equity transfers, we find that only 2.2 per cent of the 24,543 launched products were innovations. The majority, 76.7 per cent were me-too products (see Figure 1.2). Returning to the formal definition above, that result means that the vast majority of all products launched in the European food stores are products that are essentially the same as existing ones. We find clear evidence that the European food industry produces very few innovations. It may be argued that the food industry has produced innovative products that have found their way onto the market through food service providers, but even if this were the case, it would only change the picture marginally. There is simply too little innovation in the food industry.

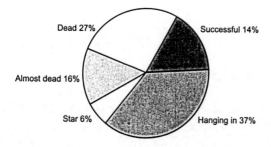

Figure 1.3   Success rate of food innovations

From the ECR study we also learned that France and Germany have a larger share of innovative products than the other countries, that is 2.7 per cent classically innovative products, while the other countries position themselves below 1 per cent. Of the truly new products launched 6 per cent are very successful after one year on the shelves while 43 per cent have less than 5 per cent distribution and can be considered to be failures (ECR Europe 1999, pp. 30–31).

Thus, the number of innovations is very small. We can furthermore deduce that when these innovations meet the consumers, they have a high death rate (see Figure 1.3). Consumers do not appreciate the majority of the few innovations that are made.

RESEARCH QUESTIONS AND THE PURPOSE OF THE STUDY

As researchers we face a situation in which there seems to be general agreement that the competitive situation is such that the food industry needs products with high added value and that the innovative capability of the industry must increase. We hear it from the EU, from national research and development planners and from the actors in the value-added chain.

Still very few innovations find their way onto the market. This leads us to consider the statement in the EU White Paper from 1994:

> The greatest weakness, however, is the comparatively limited capacity to convert scientific breakthroughs and technological achievements into industrial and commercial success.

We fully agree with this statement. We believe that the innovation process is a difficult process that is not fully understood. We have therefore investigated that process. Our main questions are:

- Why is there so little innovation in the European food industry?
- What factors stop innovation processes and what factors stimulate the dynamics of innovation?
- What can be done to stimulate innovation in the European food chain?

The purpose of our study is to provide answers to these questions.

OUR APPROACH

Our ambition is to capture the dynamics of innovation. Innovation is dependent on unique resources. These resources are costly and difficult to develop for all companies. Therefore, we have decided to study innovations inside and outside the corporation. We will seek the embeddedness of the innovation through the analysis of innovation clusters consisting of private and public actors. Furthermore we will try to capture the intricate interplay between technology and the market. We have followed three successful innovations, all the way from the research laboratory to the retail store shelves in three major case studies. The reason for these in-depth case studies is that we wanted to follow and analyse the innovation dynamics and relate that to the competitive dynamics.

The cases we have analysed are located in the Öresund food cluster. As stated earlier, the Öresund region is a very interesting development cluster for the food industry. It has unique areas of competence in the whole value-added chain. The dynamism and the urge to change are outspoken. Moreover, the cluster is interesting because it is located in two different countries – Sweden and Denmark. In order to make a comparative analysis of the role of the cluster, we have compared it with other industries and with another important development area – Boston, USA. New developments in the consumer market also demand a concerted effort to understand consumers better. This constituted part of the current project.

THE STRUCTURE OF THE BOOK

Some of the results presented in this book are of a conceptual and theoretical nature. Some are based on our own empirical research. We have included empirical results from different kinds of studies. Parts of the results have already been presented in this chapter which contains material from our own scenario studies of the future of the food industry as well as the results from questionnaire on the attitudes to innovation among top managers

In Chapter 2 we identify what is required to achieve efficient product development. We also analyse the development process and show that there are substantial differences between traditional product development and innovation processes. After a presentation of some barriers for innovation we address the need for powerful concepts and models when analysing inno-vation dynamics.

In Chapter 3 we present analytical models for studies of innovation clusters, organization and leadership of innovation as well as strategies for innovation.

In Chapter 4, the theory of consumer behaviour is accompanied by empirical results from a major study of consumers' attitudes to risk and health. We will present some insight into why consumers are reluctant to adopt radically new food products. Furthermore, we will present some tools, based on consumers' social context, that can help us to better understand food consumption behaviour.

Chapter 5 contains results from our innovation cluster studies. It starts with a presentation of the Öresund food cluster regarding the environment for the innovations that we have studied in the three cases. Some specific characteristics of the cluster will be pointed out and we will also compare them with characteristics of other clusters.

From Chapter six onwards we present the empirical material on innovation processes in food clusters. We present the ProViva Case, the Oatly Case and the Mona Carota Case. In these cases we will follow the innovation dynamics of three products and technologies, from the research lab to the store. Chapter 6 has a Methodological Appendix with some very interesting findings that we made during this research.

Chapter 7, The nature of the Innovation Processes, presents an analysis of the findings of our study. We analyse milestones in food product development, key actors, main barriers, key drivers and strategies. The role of the consumer is highlighted. We also report on leadership and organization and the interplay between market and technology as well as the interaction between research and commercial applications. We will identify the most important characteristics of the innovation process and also scrutinize the role of clusters in innovation processes. The chapter ends with critical reflections on the Ceccini report.

NOTES

1. The exact figure was debated and changed several times during the political process.
2. The definition is from Porter (1985). When we analyse the value-added chain, we perform the analysis from plate to plough. This means that we start with the consumer and the social, psychological, nutritional and economical aspects of food consumption. Then we go through the retail and wholesale activities, as well as restaurants, catering, independent distributors and so on. We also include the food processing companies and the primary production. It is important to mention this, because there is a tradition among technological researchers to define the food chain as a chain starting with primary production and ending with food-processing. Our value-added chain is different in two ways. (1) It is longer, including all activities from plate to plough. (2) We start the analysis at the opposite end from traditional analysis, with the consumer. This would be called 'going backwards in the chain' by some, following the traditional analysis. However, we see nothing backwards at all in starting with the consumer and the market for food products.
3. Statement by Kenneth Nordmark, marketing director of Söderslätts Spannmålsgrupp, previously employed for 12 years by the Scanian Farmers co-operative.

2. Product Development and Innovation

Product development is a demanding activity. Numerous studies have been performed on this subject, leading to the following general advice (Harmsen 1996, ch. 3; Grunert et al., 1996): product development is an important part of a company's strategy. When striving towards successful product development, more successful projects are found in companies where there is an explicit product development strategy, defining what type of products that should be developed. The product development strategy should also be in accordance with the general strategy of the whole company. It is also important that the product development strategy takes advantage of existing strengths and areas of competence in the organization. There should be recognition of both market-related aspects and technologically related aspects and the two should be in balance – or rather in dynamic interchange. Genuine support from top management will also strengthen product development (Harmsen, 1996, p. 121).

Upon changing from strategic to organizational considerations we find successful product development in companies where there is good co-operation between product development and marketing. Cross-functional project teams are found to be efficient. The goal should be clear, but the participants should be left with a high degree of freedom to find solutions and to try new ideas. Early screening and evaluation processes are important, as are efforts to reduce structuring and formalization in the early stages. Formalization, codification of procedures and control activities become more important as the process develops (ibid., p. 122). From a managerial point of view it is important to pay close attention to all phases of the development project. This means that upper management must have the ability to lead and organize both loosely structured processes and more strictly controlled activities.

The requirements for a successful product development process are illustrated in Figure 2.1. In short, there should be dynamic interactions between product development, marketing intelligence and production in order for product development to be successful. However, companies perceive and take advantage of market opportunities in different ways. Historical experience and the areas of core competence in the company will place a limit on the quality of the product development that can be achieved (Plichta and Harmsen, 1993). Companies differ in their ability to register and evaluate new information, that is to see and understand how this information can be related to the specific technological resources and the competence in the company. Therefore, the ability to take advantage of external market information and use it in product development differs between companies (Cohen and Levinthal, 1990, p. 128–152).

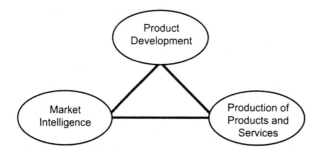

Figure 2.1   The golden triangle of product development

In the golden triangle, 'production' embodies a wide range of production-related activities; it includes the efficient everyday production activities and the development and engineering work performed to improve the production processes and increase the utilization of inputs and raw materials. The production part of the triangle represents an area in which there is a great potential for change. Many innovations and new products were invented because somebody found a new way to use existing production equipment, because new machinery or measurement equipment was available, or because unique raw materials could be obtained

It should also be noted that 'market intelligence' means the ability to use all kinds of market information, from consumers, regional and local trends, from competitors and from retailing. This ability also differs between companies. Many food-producing companies are satisfied with input and information from their immediate customers and know very little about consumers and how they use food products in their lives. In a world with increased international competition, it is also of importance to have a network including key customers in foreign markets. From these actors the company can gain information about end-user behaviour, which is necessary to compete in foreign markets. From a development perspective, the company needs such a network to gain marketing intelligence.

In the same way, a network is needed in the regional or local cluster. Through this cluster, the company can ensure the interactions necessary with suppliers of products, technologies and supplementary knowledge (Kristensen, 1992, p 107–118). In order to maintain the dynamics of the golden triangle, it is necessary for the company to balance their interaction with the two networks.

This means that the 'product development' function in a company is best performed when there is a substantial amount of interaction and exchange between production and marketing intelligence. It could even be said that the more overlap there is between the three functions, the greater the dynamic interactions. The speed of development will increase when the interaction is intense. Conditions for product development may be especially favourable *in small companies* since the few people involved are likely to interact more, and work more closely together than in a large company. Examples have been given where family-owned food-producing companies have their product development meetings at the kitchen table, and family members with knowledge about markets, products and production interact intensely in the product development process.[1]

PRODUCT DEVELOPMENT – WHY DO SO MANY COMPANIES FAIL?

Results from empirical studies show that *less than half* of food companies succeed in product development. The empirical studies we refer to here were carried out in Denmark. They are interesting because small and medium-size companies were investigated, some of which have successful international sales.

In Figure 2.2 it can be seen that 54 per cent of the companies studied had various kinds of problems in product development. We have no reason here to question the good advice given above, concerning strategy and organization for product development; however, it appears to be difficult for companies to follow that advice. The Danish study of small and medium-sized companies was performed on nine different industries: food, furniture/wood, chemistry/rubber, metal, telecom/electronics, textiles, paper/graphics, ceramics/glass and machinery. The results are relevant for several types of companies and can be regarded as generally applicable. The interesting feature of this study is that the relation of various areas of competence was also studied, using a cluster analysis. Different groups of problems are illustrated in Figure 2.2. We will devote some time to explaining how the different syndromes occur and how they affect product development in the company.

Visions, but no products is a syndrome that covers companies with strong strategic planning and a good ability to create a vision and a mission for the company. Their surveillance of the market, the customers and the suppliers also function well. However, the company does not have the ability to transform their strategies and plans into concrete action and efficient product development. As a result, the company has limited capacity to use its competence for the development of new products. The result is a weak differentiation. Another problem is that although the company is good at communicating its visions and intentions, it does not have the ability to perform according to them. Therefore, there is a discrepancy between the messages sent to the market and the products and services delivered. As a result, their marketing communication process is inefficient, and sometimes counterproductive.

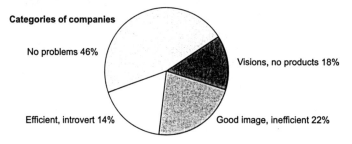

Categories of companies

No problems 46%

Visions, no products 18%

Efficient, introvert 14%

Good image, inefficient 22%

Source: Harmsen et al. (1996 p. 111).

Figure 2.2 Problems in product development

Good image but inefficient is a category where we often find companies with one or more strong products or brands that have been the 'bread and butter' for the company for several years. As a result, the company produces and sells successful products, but the products do not reflect the market relation. As a result, there are deficiencies in the development of strategies, visions and market-driven product concepts. Their traditionally strong position on the market has weakened their efforts to improve competence in production, technology and engineering and the production management leaves a lot to be desired. Loyal customers keep this company alive. The marketing intelligence function is, in the worst case, limited to surveillance of competitors. The aim of this surveillance is often to ensure that the competitors do not launch products that could harm the company's own 'golden eggs'. Since competitors, and not the end-customers, are the focus of interest, there is usually limited knowledge about why consumers buy the traditionally strong products. As a consequence, these kinds of companies often have a creative marketing department that designs sales campaigns without knowledge about what motivates the customers to buy. The result can be campaigns where the material and the immaterial offers differ, with a reduction in sales as the result. An example is a health food product which does not have any health effect on the consumer. There are constant complaints about failing customer loyalty and shrinking margins in this category of companies.

Efficient but introvert is an interesting category because food-producing companies are over-represented in this category. Typical for this group of companies is that they experience very little growth in the market. Therefore, the management does not feel any need to invest in order to increase production capacity. There is often well-established knowledge about the production process, and the production facilities are well managed. If any investments are made, they are usually aimed at increased production efficiency. There are good reasons for doing this, because the margins are low and the customers are felt to be disloyal. Mass production is the assumed key success factor, and it is very important to utilize the plant capacity to the maximum. The problem, however, is that this category of companies consists of many introvert companies. There is little knowledge about consumers, especially consumers in foreign markets. Consumer demands are interpreted in terms of direct demand from the next company in the value-added chain who buys the products. Just as in *Visions but no products*, a great deal of attention is paid to competitors, diverting attention from consumers, their consumption patterns, social meanings, hopes and fears. Product developers in this kind of company are often very proud. They are the experts on the products.

> Almost all ideas for new products originate in the Product Development Group. The Product Development Manager does not believe in encouraging people throughout the company to come up with new ideas, and he does not believe that input from research institutions can play a major role in a company like this, although some research results reach the company through its suppliers, e.g. suppliers of enzymes and cultures. Also, the members of the group agree that market research is only helpful to a very limited extent in generating ideas because if the consumers want it, it is not new. There is considerable emphasis on intuition and on the experience of the Product Development Group. Most of them have worked in various capacities in the company; there is considerable marketing expertise, but there is also considerable production expertise – 'all of us could go down and make cheese ourselves,' as the Production Manager puts it (Traill and Grunert, 1997).[2]

The effect is that there is little interaction within companies belonging to this category. The marketing competence is not used. A dynamic product development department cannot run the company, and interaction between the various parts of the company is necessary. The effect on the company is that consumer preferences are not registered, analysed or understood. Furthermore, consumer preferences do not enter the product and concept development process and, since they are not known, they cannot be used in efficient marketing.

This means that although there is a common understanding of how product development should be designed and executed, empirical studies show that many companies have considerable problems. It seems *that maintaining the dynamics between marketing intelligence, production and product development is quite a challenge*. We also have experience of companies in which this dynamic interaction was working well, but was suddenly destroyed as a result of top management decisions to reorganize or to move key actors around in the organization.

> One of the conclusions of this is that strengthening the product development function is a complicated long-term task, which can not be achieved by changing a few activities and adding a couple of new ones. There are a number of barriers to the implementation of research results in successful product development. If a company desires to change its product development (towards the golden triangle dynamics) for small and medium sized companies this is a fundamental change, and a long-term and resource-demanding process (Harmsen, 1996, p. 290).[3]

Thus, *efficient product development* is *a long-term resource-demanding strategic commitment*. In this section we have analysed what is needed to make the dynamics work. But we must now include some new aspects. In the next section we will turn from the dynamics of product development to the dynamics of innovation. There we will show that product development processes and innovation processes are different in several features. We will analyse the differences and see what extra efforts are needed to progress from product development to innovation.

INNOVATION

In the first chapter of this book we concluded that the key for future success in European food companies lies in development and new products perceived as new and interesting by consumers. We also know that technology offers many opportunities for innovation. But in what ways is innovation different from product development? That question will be dealt with in this section.

The *definition of innovation* used in this book is the following:

> An innovation is a new way to do things commercially (Porter, 1990, p. 780).

This definition is, at the same time, broad and precise. First, we acknowledge that *innovations must have a commercial application*. Thus, innovations are different from good ideas, inventions and new thinking in general. An innovation must be launched commercially.

Second, the definition focuses on the outcome of the process. We differentiate between innovations and innovation processes.

> An innovation in the economic sense is accomplished only with the first commercial transaction involving the new product, process system or device, although the word is used also to describe the process (Freeman, 1974).

In this book, an innovation is the outcome of the innovation process. Turning our attention to 'doing things', the logic behind this concept is that an innovation can have a multitude of forms. It can be a product, a service or a combination of the two. *An innovation can also be a methodology, often combined with products and services. Immaterial values may also be part of the innovation.* The essential feature is that it is something new and that it has a commercial application. The fact that the innovation is launched onto a commercial market also has the effect that the consumers, the customers and the markets are the ultimate judges of the value of the innovation, its innovativeness and the degree of innovation.

We also know that innovations are important for the company from a strategic point of view, just as we found to be the case in product development.

> The innovation process can not be separated from the company's strategic and competitive context (Afuah, 1998, p. 183).

In principle we can also distinguish between two aspects of the innovation process – the development of the product innovation and the development of the process innovation. It is quite an achievement to develop and commercialize an innovative product or service, but it is also a major challenge to develop the production process so that the product becomes functional and competitive in the long term. This can be illustrated with Edison's innovation – the electric light bulb.

> After trying hundreds of forms, they carbonised a piece of common cotton thread in a vacuum (so it would not oxidise), bent it to the shape of a horseshoe, connected it to an electric current, and mounted it in an exhausted glass bulb. Flipping on the switch, they were delighted with its glowing incandescence, which lasted through one hour, then into the night and the next day. To their great delight, the carbon filament kept burning for almost two days. Edison now had a workable 'electric candle' (Utterback, 1994, p. 62).

We can understand the joy of the inventors. The situation described above illustrates the very moment when Edison and his colleagues understood that the invention was successful. If the product had been presented to the consumers at that stage, however, it would never have entered the market. It took many years of engineering work and experimentation to develop the process part of the innovation. The experiments involved several materials, several shapes and designs, and both direct current and alternating current. This process can be understood from Table 2.1 (ibid., p. 68).

Table 2.1   Process innovation – electric light bulbs

Year	Carbon Filament	Metallic Filament	Lumens[a]	Life (hours)
1881	Carbonized bamboo		1.68	600
1884	Flashed cellulose		3.4	400
1888	Asphalted carbonized bamboo		3.0	600
1897		Refractory oxides	5.0	300 or 800[b]
1899		Osmium	5.5	1,000
1902		Tantalum	5.0	250 or 700[b]
1904	GEM (metallized carbon)		4.0	600
1904		Nonductile tungsten	7.85	800
1910		Ductile tungsten	10.0	1,000

Notes:
[a] Lumens represent efficiency per watt and are applied here to the lamp sizes most commonly used.
[b] The smaller figure applies when lamp used with direct current; the larger figure when used with alternating current.

Source: Utterback (1994, p. 68); Franklin Institute, *Incandescent Electric Lamps*, 1885; Schroeder, *The History of the Incandescent Lamp*, 1927; and Schroeder, *History of Electric Light*, 1923. All cited in Robert P. Rogers, *Staff Report on the Development and Structure of the Electric Lamp Industry* (Washington, DC: U.S. Government Printing Office, February 1980), p. 13. Reprinted by permission from Harvard Business School Press from *Mastering the Dynamics of Innovation* by James M. Utterback, Boston, MA, 1994, p. 68.

From the table we can see how intense the development of processes and materials was during a 30-year period, resulting in radically better illumination capabilities of the light bulbs, as well as a substantial increase in the number of hours that the lamps could burn. The former was of the utmost importance creating an efficient alternative to gas lighting, which was the normal method at the time; the latter was of course of great importance in creating an economically competitive alternative to gas lighting. But was there much competition? Was the electric light not simply a superior solution?

The answer is that as the years have passed, the electric alternative has proven to be superior, but we must look at the situation in the 1890s (ibid., p. 65). The inventor Carl von Welsbach had created a mantle for gas lights. The mantle was composed of filaments of cerium and thorium, and glowed brightly when heated by a gas flame. It produced a fivefold improvement in gas lighting efficiency and reduced the cost of gas lighting by almost two-thirds. The electric light was severely threatened and it was 12 years before Edison made his first profit from electric light bulbs.

This story is interesting because nowadays we all take electric lighting for granted, but when the invention was launched on the market it met with fierce competition. It was thus important for the innovators to have a strategic, long-term commitment to the innovation. This example also illustrates that the two aspects of the innovation process – the product innovation and the process innovation are intimately related and must complement each other.

We should also note that Edison was successful in obtaining patents for his products, and that this was extremely important for his commercial success. In the year 1883, the Edison Electric Light Company had 215 patents and another 307 pending (ibid., p. 66). We all know about Edison. However, very few people know of the Swan Lamp Manufacturing Company, named after the Englishman who *had constructed incandescent lamps long before Edison*, but who was less successful in protecting his intellectual property.

THREE PHASES IN THE INNOVATION PROCESS – FLUID, TRANSITIONAL AND SPECIFIC

The rate of innovative activity related to the innovation process is first high in the product innovation (see Figure 2.3). In the *fluid phase* of the innovation process, several product ideas, several actors and several technical solutions form a dynamic competitive landscape.

In the second phase, the *transitional phase* of the process, the major product solutions have competed and a dominant product design has won the battle. Some competitors have left the arena. In this transitional phase process development takes off, and there is a close linkage between product and process innovation.

In the last phase, the *specific phase* of the process, products become targets for specific users or segments, and the process is focused on maximizing value and cost efficiency for users in the segments. In the specific phase, new technology may enter the industry and create a new situation in which other key resources and key areas of competences are required for the company to be a first-class actor in the next competitive leap in the industry. *The occurrence of new technological options, invading actors from other industries and a new competitive situation is what we currently find in the European food industry.* In the following chapters we show how the rapid change in the rate of innovation due to technological and market shifts will change the competitive landscape for the food industry. Strategic behaviour in the fluid phase, the transitional phase and the specific phase are very different.

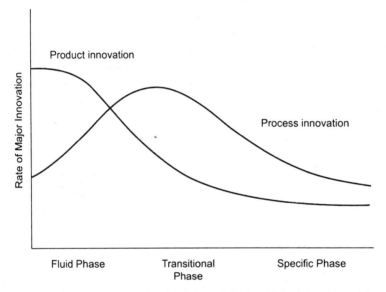

Source: Reprinted by permission from Harvard Business School Press from *Mastering the Dynamics of Innovation* by James M. Utterbac, Boston, MA, 1994, p. 91.

Figure 2.3 Product and process innovation

From Utterback's excellent study we can identify some characteristics of the innovation process.

- New innovations are often a *combination of old capabilities and new resources*.
- After an initial period of turbulence, a *dominant design emerges* and becomes the trendsetter.

- *The competitive landscape changes.* In early phases many actors compete. The emergence of a dominant design and the increased importance of process innovation reduces the number of competitors.
- The same industry will experience *several waves of change* during a longer period during which new technological and market opportunities create innovation opportunities.
- When the technological breakpoints occur and new innovations emerge, *leadership positions in industry change.* Key actors in new technologies often lose their position following periods of innovation.
- *Invasion of alien technology* from other industries often creates periods of innovation.

RADICAL INNOVATIONS – CHARACTER AND ORIGIN

An innovation can present a varying degree of challenge to key areas of competence in a company. The challenge can be analysed from two perspectives – the market perspective and the technological perspective (see Figure 2.4).

Technological competence

		Useful	Destroyed
Market competence	**Useful**	Traditional product development	Revolutionary innovation
	Destroyed	Niche innovation	Concept innovation

Figure 2.4   How revolutionary is the innovation?

An established company is designed to exploit the established technology. It has constructed a competence base with the aim of using this technology and a great deal of effort is invested in maintaining the knowledge in order to be at the forefront when it comes to using the technological knowledge within the corporation to produce a long line of products that take maximum advantage of this technology. In this way, the knowledge possessed by the company is transformed into products that correspond to consumer demands. The company has also invested in technology so that the production process can be developed, through insightful engineering, into one that has the ability to produce products of high quality in a cost-efficient way. Control systems are implemented around this core production system to ensure sustainable quality. The cost accounting systems and analytical tools, balanced scorecards, and so on, are constructed so that the key features of the technological production process are mirrored as key figures.

Likewise, the company's present success is based on its ability to understand and analyse the demands of present customers and consumers in established markets. In the specific phase, when the offer to the market is fine-tuned, the market knowledge is collected from relevant specific sources and put into a context that is relevant for present market offerings.

It can easily be understood that product development in an established company has advantages if the present technology is useful and if the present market knowledge is relevant. We then have a situation in which traditional product development processes works well. We mentioned earlier that this situation is also associated with some difficulties, and is actually problematic for many companies. In this context, however, development processes are much less demanding for the company compared with the situation in which old technology is replaced by new. In such a situation, many of the key areas of strategic competence in the company are useless, and it is necessary to gather new technological knowledge. The old technological knowledge may still be relevant, but has to be combined with a new area of competence or a new kind of technology. This demands creation of new knowledge based on old and new input.

Market knowledge is not easily accessible, and it may take a considerable time to learn the key essentials about consumer demands and how and why the corporation's products are consumed. This knowledge is also tied to specific sources and specific partners outside the corporation. Inside the corporation, the people responsible for the marketing of the products are the key bearers of knowledge. They also have superior knowledge about how to relate customer needs to technological features. It should be noted, however, that corporate market experts have expertise concerning present markets and present products. When the production is aimed at new consumers in new markets, other sources may be better informed.

When product development works well, it is also guided and supported by a consistent strategy from top corporate management. Moving into revolutionary innovation, niche innovation or concept innovation, also presents a major strategic challenge to the corporation.

For these reasons, *innovation is a more demanding activity than traditional product development*. From the perspective of running a business, it is regarded as sensible to defend established products even when new and effective alternatives are well documented.

A pattern emphasized ... is the degree to which powerful competitors not only resist innovative threats, but actually resist all efforts to understand them, preferring to further entrench their positions in the older products. This results in a surge of productivity and performance that may take the old technology to unheard-of heights. But in most cases this is a sign of impending death (Utterback, 1994, p. xxvii).

We naturally understand that established corporations with strong market positions want to defend their products against competing alternatives. But in cases where the alternatives can offer substantial cost or performance advantage due to new technology, or where user conditions and preferences have changed substantially, this defence is likely to result in a long and painful death. If the corporation has not devoted its attention to future developments, the result may be that competitors have moved faster and established a stronghold in new product market combinations. The formerly strong corporation may well see the window of opportunities start to close. Without the possibility of entering the new market, they will have to sit and see their new competitors develop profitable businesses.

Table 2.2   Origin of innovations

Revolutionary and concept innovations creating new markets		Revolutionary and niche innovations replacing established products	
From the industry	1	From the industry	11
From outside the industry	15	From outside the industry	12
Inconclusive	2	Inconclusive	5
Total	18	Total	28

Source: By permission from Harvard Business School Press from Mastering the *Dynamics of Innovation* by James M. Utterback Boston, MA, 1994, p. 206 .

Historical studies of innovations show that most innovations reach an industry through invaders from other industries.As we can see from Table 2.2, the vast majority of revolutionary innovations that create new markets come from outside the industry; 15 out of 18 cases. Regarding radical innovations that replace established products, more innovations have their origin inside the industry, but about as many have their origin in other industries. From this we can conclude that, *in situations where technologies and markets change rapidly, the main threat is not from the immediate competitors, but from companies that are not normally included in the analysis of competition.*

From this also follows the trend we have noted earlier, that after major technological shifts, new actors become the champions of the industry.

> Even the strongest product and business strategy will eventually be overturned by technical change. The central issue is not when or how, but that it will happen for sure (ibid., p. 231).

PRODUCT DEVELOPMENT AND INNOVATION – IMPORTANT DIFFERENCES

Let us now summarize the differences between traditional product development and innovation (Table 2.3), in order to distinguish between the two processes and to characterize important aspects of the two ways of creating new products and services. We find that innovation processes and product development processes; which at a first glance seem to be very similar, actually differ in such a way that they need to be dealt with differently in corporations and clusters.

Table 2.3   Differences between product development and innovation

Traditional product development	Innovation
Demands knowledge transfer	Demands knowledge integration
Works well in established organization	Demands new structure
Less demand for resources	Demands more resources, but also different resources
Limited risk for management	Higher risk, demands more courage from management

Product development means, in practical terms, that a project is defined in which the task is to develop a new product or service. The people assigned to the task then have the delicate task of developing and refining the product, using *knowledge that is transferred* from other people inside or outside the organization. The new product must be consistent with consumer demand (or at least assumed future consumer demand), it must draw on the unique areas of competence in product and production technology, and finally new user benefits must be added.

Regarding innovation, the use of knowledge is more complicated. It is not sufficient to transfer existing knowledge to a project team. On the contrary, existing knowledge and competence may even be of minor importance. The task is to understand the potential of knowledge that has been unknown to the company previously, for example a new technology. This knowledge must be understood and appreciated, its opportunities must be exploited. This knowledge must be welcomed and *integrated* with the existing key areas of competence in the company. Even if an organization is faced with the need to integrate radically new thinking, this does not mean that all previous knowledge is without value. Combining the old and the new is part of the success in innovation. We will return to knowledge integration later.

In product development processes, the mission and vision regarding the new project are often well defined and understood within the existing corporate strategy and product development strategy. Therefore, the organizational matters are rather simple; a project group must be assembled, it should have solid back-up from the management and it should be composed such that aspects of market intelligence are combined with aspects from production and product development. The corporate organization can often create a good embeddedness for such projects.

Innovation processes on the other hand have aspects that are unique. It may be a case of evaluating alternative technological solutions, finding external coalition partners or identifying opportunities for radically new product market offerings. Some of the internal resources are obsolete, either because new technological knowledge will be used or because new markets are being investigated. In such cases, the established knowledge centres can become useless. Not only that, they may become counterproductive and a threat to the development of new knowledge. The product or service developed may be so radically new that the company's basic mission and strategy must be changed in order to exploit the opportunity fully. In this situation there is an organizational challenge to allow and stimulate new thinking, to free the project from established procedures and to create a new organizational platform. This has been described in the literature for decades in terms of greenhouses, skunk works, product champions and so on (see, for example, Galbraith, 1982; Pinochet III, 1985; Lagnevik, 1989). The importance of separating new thinking from old has been well documented. In this context we should also stress the importance of bringing the new knowledge into the old organization, to change and develop the corporation so that the strategy and structure suit the strategic situation and unique competence during and after the innovation process (Lagnevik, 1989, p. 140). The organizational issue will be elaborated on in later chapters.

From a managerial point of view, developing more products and services that are in line with present areas of competence and current strategy is radically different from venturing into new technologies, with new partners and on new markets. It is imperative to decide if something really new is going to be sustainably competitive or if it is best to stick to the core business and main strategy. It is often right to pursue existing strategy and continue business as usual, but in technology and market shifts change may be the best option. If this is the case, 'wait and see' is a bad option, which will only give first mover an advantage over the others. In turbulent innovation processes, the will to act is of crucial importance and more top managers should follow the motto of the Special Air Service[4] 'He Who Dares Wins.'

HOW TO CREATE INNOVATION DYNAMICS

In this chapter we have identified the product development and innovation processes. We have presented the differences and some of the important forces at play in the development dynamics. Now, how do we succeed in manoeuvring good ideas and inventions through the process, all the way to a successful trials on the market? We will return to this question in the following chapters, but first let us look to the research literature to find good theoretical concepts and models to analyse the innovation process in more detail. We will focus our theoretical findings and contributions into a number of useful perspectives, focusing on interesting and thought-provoking findings in earlier research. We will focus on four important areas:

- Strategies for innovation
- Innovation clusters
- Leadership and organization for innovation
- Models for understanding the consumer

NOTES

1. It has been said that the Dafgård family, Swedish food producers with a number of unique products, worked in this way.
2. This quotation is used to illustrate an attitude common in introvert companies.
3. The quotation has been edited slightly.
4. The Special Air Service (SAS), an organization of well-trained, action-oriented and extremely capable British commandos.

3.   Strategic Theory and Innovation

This chapter describes interesting parts of the strategic theory and how they can be applied to research on innovation in the food industry. The intention here is to identify concepts that we believe can contribute to our frame of reference and will be important in the analysis of product and service development processes. We start with the concept of competitiveness and how sustainable competitiveness can be achieved. We have adopted the definition of competitiveness made by Agriculture Canada (1991):

> A competitive industry is one that possesses the sustained ability to profitably gain and maintain market share in domestic and/or foreign markets (Pitts and Lagnevik, 1997, p. 1).

When analysing competitiveness the focus may be on performance measures, the analysis of competitive potential or measurements of the competitive process (ibid., p.1ff). In this book we are interested in how competitive potential is converted into competitive performance, specifically the role that innovation and product development play in this dynamic process. We will therefore build our theoretical base on studies in which the upgrading of competitiveness has been analysed. We will describe how the resource-based view and the activity-based view of the firm develops into knowledge-based theory and notions of strategy as structured chaos.

The resource-based view portrays the firm as a bundle of resources and capabilities and *focuses on what the firm has.* Resources include 'anything which can be thought of as a strength or weakness in a given firm' (Wernfelt, 1984, p. 172). The resource-based view places more emphasis on the internal resources and areas of competence of the firm and less emphasis on the firm's performance in the market and working environment. A firm can gain a sustainable competitive advantage if its resources are (1) *valuable*, it must be possible to use the resources to create value for the firm; (2) *rare*, the supply of the resource must be limited; (3) it should *not be easy to imitate* them; (4) it should *not be easy to find substitutes* for the resources employed; and (5) the resources should also be well organized (Barney, 1991). We will return to these characteristics of the competitive company under the heading 'From Resource-based to Knowledge-based Strategic Theory' below.

The activity-based view of the firm focuses on what the firm does. In this view the firm is characterized by the activities it performs and the way in which it performs them (Porter, 1990, 1991, 1998a). The key concepts in the analysis are *factor conditions, demand conditions, related and supporting industries, firm strategy, structure and rivalry, government and chance.* This perspective will be of importance in the market intelligence parts of the project.

In addition to understanding the nature of the determinants of competitiveness, *we should also understand the dynamics*, that is the process of change whereby the competitive advantage is upgraded, sustained or lost and we should understand the nature of the rivalry and the interaction between the different parts of the basic model. In the dynamic process the key driving forces of competitive advantage are scale, cumulative learning, pattern of capacity utilization, timing of investment, level of vertical integration, location of the activity, institutional factors that govern activity, links between activities, the ability to share activities across business units and discretionary policies independent of other drivers (Enright, 1994, p. 9).

To further enhance the understanding of how resources can be efficiently combined in the development of new products, we will rely on contributions from competence-based strategic theory (Tsoukas, 1996; Grant, 1996). Some important contributions from chaos theory will also be included in the theoretical framework (Brown and Eisenhardt, 1998).

From Resource-based to Knowledge-based Strategic Theory

In this project we were interested in how the company interacted with and positioned itself on the market. We were also interested in the process in which the company builds up it ability to compete. Therefore, we found many useful concepts and models in resource-based strategic theory (Schumpeter, 1934; Barney, 1991). In this theory we focus on the company's resources and how they are used. We define the company as a bundle of resources, abilities and areas of competence. We define resource in the following way:

> – all assets, capabilities, organizational processes, firm attributes, information, knowledge etc. controlled by the firm that enable the firm to conceive of and implement strategies that improve its efficiency and effectiveness (Daft, 1983).

The resources that we are most interested in are the key resources for the creation of competitiveness. Resources used in our analysis are: (1) physical resources such as machinery, materials, technologies and geographic location; (2) human resources, developed by training, education, experience and judgement, abilities exhibited by the organization's employees and associates; and (3) organizational resources, a joint concept, describing formal reporting systems, formal and informal planning systems, management and leadership practices, as well as formal and informal relations between groups and individuals.

Among the resources in the companies we are especially interested in are the core areas of competence. These contribute in an exceptional way to the value of the company's products, as perceived by the consumer. This does not at all mean that the consumer must understand the core competence and its use in the production or product development process (Hamel, 1994). The resources that the company can own or control in other ways will not be meaningful in the competitiveness-creating activities until they are combined in an efficient way, in line with the company's vision and strategy. In order to make this work, people with ability/competence must co-operate in a meaningful way (Eneroth, 1997, p. 46). The combination of individuals with this ability/competence can be described as a 'knowledge set' with four dimensions (Leonard-Barton, 1992).

> Its contents are embodied in (1) employee knowledge and skills, and embedded in (2) technical systems. The process of knowledge creation and control are guided by (3) managerial systems. The fourth dimension consists of the values and norms associated with the various types of embodied and embedded knowledge and with the process of creation and control (Eneroth, 1997, p.113).

Strategy as Structured Chaos

Shona L. Brown and Kathleen M. Eisenhardt have published a contribution to research in strategy in which they address the increasing dynamics in the business environment (Brown and Eisenhardt, 1998). In their own presentation of their work in relation to previous research, the ability to create a continuous flow of advantages is stressed. It is also a theory that should have key advantages in its ability to help the organization bring about change and continual reinvention. As is shown in Table 3.1 the specific contribution to chaos theory of the research of Brown and Eisenhardt is that they start from situations with rapid, unpredictable change and define success as continual reinvention. So, in our research, the 'Competing on the Edge' approach has added to the resource-based and the knowledge-based views by incorporating rapid technological and market change as a basis for the theoretical constructs. The main differences between 'Competing on the Edge' and other important strategic approaches are summarized in Table 3.1.

Brown and Eisenhardt's book has a theoretical base in complexity theory, dealing with systems that are only partially related. The key to effective change is to remain poised on the edge of chaos. Complexity theory focuses on the interrelationship between different parts of an organization and the trade-off of less control for greater adaptation (ibid., p.14). As a consequence the book presents several balances that must be managed in order to create a strategic direction while keeping the structure open enough for continuous innovation.

Table 3.1   Competing on the Edge versus other strategy research

	Five forces	**Core competence**	**Game theory**	**Competing on the Edge**
Assumptions	Stable industry structure	Firm as bundle of competences	Industry viewed as dynamic oligopoly	Industry in rapid, unpredictable change
Goal	Defensible position	Sustainable advantage	Temporary advantage	Continuous flow of advantages
Performance driver	Industry structure	Unique firm competences	Right moves	Ability to change
Strategy	Pick an industry, pick a strategic position, fit the organization	Create a vision, build and exploit competences to realize vision	Make the 'right' competitive and collaborative moves	Gain the 'edges,' time pace, shape semicoherent strategic direction
Success	Profits	Long-term dominance	Short-term win	Continual reinvention

Source: Reprinted by permission from Harvard Business School Press from *Competing on the Edge* by Shona L. Brown and Kathleen M. Eisenhardt, Boston, MA, 1994, p. 8.

- *The Improvizational Edge* maintains the balance between too much and too little structure.
- *The Coadaptive Edge* maintains the balance between too much and too little collaboration between various parts of the company.
- *The Regenerative Edge* maintains the balance between effective reuse of past concepts and the introduction of novel ideas.
- *The Experimentation Edge* maintains the balance between the Foresight Trap and the No-sight Trap. In the Foresight Trap the development activities are planned so strictly that innovative thinking is prohibited.

In the No-sight Trap, the organization experiments so much that it loses track of its own development strategy.

One important concept which helps capture the dynamics of the innovation process is time pacing. *Time pacing* means that new products are created and introduced according to a time schedule, or to put it another way; following a predetermined development rhythm. The rhythm should be set by the company so that it reflects the speed of technologic and market change. This is the opposite of *event pacing* in which new launches follow important events, like technological breakthroughs, new regulations, new customer demand or introductions by a major competitor (ibid., p. 167). Examples are given where companies have found it to be important to pace the product development process according to some kind of change cycle in the corporate environment.

Table 3.2   Time pacing

Company	Use of time pacing
British Airways	'Five years is the maximum that you can go without refreshing the brand ... We did it [relaunched Club Europe Service] because we wanted to stay ahead so that we could continue to win premium customers.'
	BA Chairman, Sir Colin Marshall
Intel	The inventor of Moore's Law, that is the power of the computer chip would double every eighteen months. Builds a new manufacturing facility every nine months.
	'We build factories two years in advance of needing them, before we have the products to run in them, and before we know the industry is going to grow.'
	Intel CEO, Andy Grove

Source: Reprinted by permission from Harvard Business School Press from *Competing on the Edge* By Shona L. Brown and Kathleen M. Eisenhardt, Boston, MA, 1994, p. 186.

Time pacing involves two interesting management concepts (ibid. pp. 167–168). One is *transition*. Time pacing relies on planned 'choreographed' transitions from one product generation to the next, from one market to another and from one area of development to another. The other interesting concept is *rhythm*. It is important to find the right rhythm in development activities, a rhythm that is in tune with development in the market place and in the technological areas. The right time pace creates a feeling of relentless urgency in the developmental work. The pace should be such that innovative initiatives are not retarded by slow time pacing, but the pace should not be so high that bad products are being launched and development staff are worn out. A good rhythm outperforms well-choreographed event pacing, because it provides momentum. The company develops as fast and efficiently as it can. Its timing is not dependent on other actors, only on its own innovative ability.

It important when we use these concepts to realize that they have been developed from studies of extremely fast-moving companies, for example in telecom, computer software, services and so on. The food industry is by tradition not such a fast-changing sector. However, in the present situation, where the food industry is facing huge challenges in many respects, theory generated in the high-speed, high-technology world may be of benefit.

Regeneration —the Company as a DNA Spiral

Brown and Eisenhardt have developed a model of the company as a DNA spiral, in which the company has various genes linked together to an entity. Every gene represents a specific piece of knowledge, a resource and a way of doing something. The company must now establish a balance between a complexity catastrophe and an error catastrophe. *The complexity catastrophe* indicates that too little novelty is being infused into the business. The company experiences slow change and finally death. The other extreme is the *error catastrophe* in which so much novelty is infused that focus, market presence, effectiveness and new business creation suffer. This can also kill the company.

The alternative suggested by the authors is to 'wisely exploit (with genetic algorithms) the best of the past (selection), adding something new (mutation), and mixing their blend of old and new with their not-quite-new (recombinations)' (ibid., p. 111). The idea behind recombinations is to speed up natural selection by mixing up the gene pool. Genetic algorithms enhance the speed of development through both recombination and mutation. It is not directly mentioned by the authors, but our understanding is that time pacing is part of genetic algorithms. The above example illustrates how Gap Inc., who used to be a jeans retailer, turned into a global distributor through mutations and recombinations (Figure 3.1). The old Gap store concept and the retailing skills were retained. New store locations were chosen in airports. New merchandise such as nail polish, sunglasses and Barbie Dolls were included in the offering to the consumer. A new name was created — Old Navy, and a new store design. Sales rose by 20 per cent and stock prices by 46 per cent.

This example just shows the *mutation* as an illustration. Gap also made two other major moves. One was *rearchitecture*, a further enhancing of older unique characteristics, leading to an upgrading of the Banana Republic clothes stores, and the other was *recombination*, which led to the creation of the Old Navy Kids store. In this language, starting several subsidiaries doing similar things means mutation using the same gene.

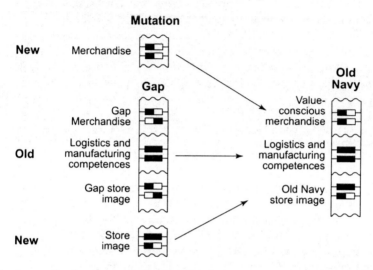

Source: Reprinted by permission from Harvard Business School Press from *Competing on the Edge* by Shona L. Brown and Kathleen M. Eisenhardt, Boston, MA, 1994, p. 112.

Figure 3.1   Mutations at Gap Inc.

Innovation Strategies and Development Traps

Another important part of the innovation problem is that the speed of development creates a situation in which it is impossible for the corporate top management to, a priori, evaluate all development alternatives and make a corporate strategic plan, which can be broken down into sub-plans to be implemented by the business areas. Instead, an efficient method of innovation is to allow experiments, large enough to learn from, but small enough not to kill the company. This must be done at the business area level, where insight, unique resources and competence as well as market knowledge are to be found. The business area level then gains responsibility for strategic development.

In this development, companies must balance between the development traps mentioned earlier. In an interesting contribution, Ahuja and Lampert (2001) later made empirical studies of development traps. They demonstrated and measured the effects of three important innovation traps. They also identified and measured the effects of three strategies to avoid the traps. According to Ahuja and Lampert there is a tendency in large corporations to favour the familiar over the unfamiliar, a tendency to prefer mature technologies at the expense of nascent ones, and a tendency to search for new product ideas and solutions in areas that are too close to existing solutions.

It is important to realize that this tendency to fall into development traps does not stem from any major malfunction of large corporations. Instead it is quite natural for a large company to exploit present products and services in a cost-efficient and profit-creating way. This creates a situation where it is quite natural to focus on the familiar, existing developments and on mature technology.

> Characterizing the problem in this fashion is useful when compared with a potential alternative characterization: that large organizations fail at breakthrough inventions because they are inept or incompetent (ibid., p. 540).

The problem from an innovation point of view, however, is that the logic behind exploiting existing ideas and concepts creates dominating ideas, rules, structures and behaviour that create development traps for the innovation process. However, large corporations can launch counter-strategies - to help avoid these traps. Ahuja and Lampert present empirical results showing that the counter-strategies are effective. Table 3.3 shows the three traps and their three counter-strategies:

The authors also make a very important comment concerning the possibility of using counter-strategies. They stress the importance of slack in the organization in order to make innovations.

> the pursuit of novel, emerging, and pioneering technologies is likely to require considerable slack resources. To go off in the search of the unknown (a.k.a. pioneering) or experiment with novel technologies is likely to demand extensive resources. Without slack, these strategies may be beyond reach. Indeed both prior research (Burgelman 1983) and anecdotal evidence suggest that cash-rich corporations can far more easily afford certain kinds of spectacular and experimental ventures (ibid., p. 541).

This is of great importance for companies operating in the Specific Phase, in Utterback's model. In tight competition between similar products in a mature market where companies fine-tune their production and sales organization so that they, with a minimum cost and a precise quality, can reach targeted consumer groups, slack is consciously reduced in the organization. Mottos like 'lean and mean' are created to support the 'no fat thinking' common in large-scale food producers, where the organization is seen as a highly motivated and goal-oriented greyhound on the racetrack. All surpluses that are generated should be delivered to the shareholders, so that they can decide how to use the financial resources.

Table 3.3   Three development traps

Development trap	Counter-strategy
The familiarity trap. Development of deeper expertise with familiar knowledge yields more immediate and likely returns. However, the reduction of experimentation and working with only familiar variables reduces the probability that a radically different approach to solve a problem will occur.	*Exploring novel technologies*, technologies that are new to the organization. This provides heterogeneity to the problem-solving competence, challenges established cognitive structures and cause-effect assumptions. The enhanced repertoire and deeper understanding can help the innovation process.
The maturity trap. Working with mature technologies that have been in existence for quite some time has the great advantage that they are well known in the industry. It is easy to get information, support and to employ people. However, relying only on mature technology means that the company abstains from greater opportunities offered by new technology.	*Experimenting with emergent technologies* can be an effective way for the organization to identify opportunities offered by new technologies, opportunities that can create new and unique solutions to problems. Using technology that one's competitors have not yet understood can be the way to gain first-mover advantage and a sustainable competitive position.
The propinquity trap. You fall into this trap when risk aversion, organizational structures and routines and convenience creates development conditions where it is only allowed to search for new solutions in the immediate neighbourhood of old solutions.	*Experimenting with pioneering technologies* can help. Instead of trying to modify available solution, pioneering technologies ignore all available solutions, focus on the basic problems and their root causes and step into the complete unknown in search of a fundamentally new solution.

Source: Ahuja and Lampert (2001).

The problem is that if we regard innovation as something that happens close to the core areas of competence, partly uncontrollable by corporate management and very difficult to evaluate, ex ante, the insight emerges that if we want companies or business units to indulge in innovation, this means that money must be allocated for that purpose, either by deliberate funding or by corporate return expectations low enough to create slack in the company. These resources can be used for experiments and anti-trap projects with high risk.

We also note the role of experiments when it comes to *pioneering technologies*. When the role of pioneering technologies is described by Ahuja and Lampert, one gets the impression that qualified people in innovative companies scan the environment for new and untested technologies in the areas of interest, and that they then choose technologies and apply them in practical experiments.

In real life, the process may be the reverse. It is quite common that development engineers and scientists perform experiments that give surprising results. When these surprising practical results occur, the developers try to find explanations in theory. Once they have found the theoretical background, a consistent design of the new product can be made. It is, for instance, a fact that John Vaught and Dave Donald who were the inventors of the Bubble Jet printer at Hewlett-Packard did not understand themselves what they had discovered when they made the first successful trials with the Bubble Jet principle. They put ink in a tube and heated it electrically with a tiny resistor.

> Vaught and Donald had discovered an entirely new way of putting ink on paper. Rather than squeezing it out of a tube, they were shooting it out in controlled bursts. It was fast and it wasn't messy. However, although the method worked, it would be some time before they, or anyone else at HP, really understood why. ... The problem was that Vaught and Donald's experiments had put them out in front of their ability, or that of anyone around them, to explain the underlying phenomenon. ... It would be some time before researchers at HP would learn that what was really going on inside the inkjet capillary tubes was a phenomenon known as vapour explosion. Liquid does not necessarily boil and turn into gas at its boiling point. If it is heated swiftly enough (modern inkjet printers heat each droplet in two-millionths of a second) it will remain liquid for a brief instant at temperatures higher than its boiling point, before exploding into vapour (Robinson and Stern, 1997, pp. 161–162).

The regeneration and development trap concepts are extremely useful because they lead to questions concerning what in the total operations of the corporation should be new and what should be retained. They also provide concepts to discuss how one radical change in the company can affect other parts of the total business, and how new ventures are related to innovation and to each other.

The Biological Metaphor – the Innovation Grows

The concepts presented above are thought-provoking and help creative thinking concerning the development process. But what is the nature of the innovation process, and how should we interpret it. One option stands out very clearly when studying handbooks on project management or innovation management. In such literature, the innovation process is described as a rational construction activity. A mechanical metaphor is used and the *innovation is assembled* piece by piece after due reflection and evaluation.

Based on the innovation processes that we have followed, we see limitations on the use of the *mechanical metaphor*. Instead we would like to propose a homology from biology, where the innovation is not assembled, but rather grows.

> A principal reason companies do not become businesses that can reinvent themselves is that their managers take rational, even mechanistic approaches to developing their businesses. These managers are often locked into the implicit assumption that a business is like a machine. They understand rational tasks like identifying markets, spotting areas of competence, and creating visions, but they miss the insight that businesses are also living things. *The distinction is absolutely fundamental. Living things grow.* They adapt and evolve with shifting competition and varying climate. Change is what living things do. In contrast, *machines run* (Brown and Eisenhardt, 1998, p. 193).

We will thus come closer to understanding the nature of innovation if we use a biological homology. The innovation grows. Brown and Eisenhardt use the picture of a prairie, which cannot be assembled, starting from a cleared plot of land. The plants and the animals are interrelated in a complex eco-system where it is impossible to tell in advance how all the components will interact in the growing system. But we do know a few things about the biological systems, which we now apply to our research area by making the following statements about innovations (ibid., p. 197).

- *Innovations are grown – not assembled.* The process is so complex that it should not be reduced to a mechanical metaphor.
- *Starting point matters.* The company history, the specific resources and areas of competence are important conditions that determine the success of the innovation process. It is also wise to start from at least some aspects well known to the company and within the core competence area.
- *Order matters.* The outcome will differ, depending on how different kinds of insight, test results, partners and resources are put into the process.
- *Missing links matter.* There are often conditions and resources that were temporally of the utmost importance for the development process, even if they are not visible in the final result. The prairie fire is of great importance for the growth of the prairie, but after a while it is quite impossible to see that a fire has occurred.

Later in this book we will show how the innovations grow in our three cases. We will see the added value of the biological homology.

A New Strategic Management

We also need to recognize that in the kind of process we have described above, the conditions for strategic management are different from traditional teachings, where corporate strategic plans, created by top management, are broken down into sub-plans and implemented in the business units. Companies that work with innovation processes are balancing on the edge of chaos, where the working day can be described as a dynamic disequilibrium. The innovation grows. Starting point matters, order matters, there should be a balance between structure and chaos, between the old and the new. Timing and rhythm are important, results can often not be anticipated, experiments large enough to learn and small enough not to kill are important.

In this situation we have to change the roles in the strategic process. The strategies must be developed at business level, while the role of the corporate government is to create joint visions and generative themes. Another important function is to learn from experimentation and to adapt the structure of the business to develop promising business ventures and to harvest the profits from established ideas. For this purpose we identify three strategic roles, *the Strategist, the Patcher and the Synthesizer.*

The Strategist is a role on business level. On this level only is there an understanding of what to do and how. It is also on the business level that you can experiment, set the rhythm and balance on the edge of chaos.

The Patcher reviews the patterns of businesses, markets and technologies, and makes new patterns. The pattern must be set up with areas with sufficient competitiveness and volume to bear the development cost.

The Synthesizer hires and fires top management. He articulates common visions and values, which should inspire people to work in the right direction, but does not present a corporate strategic plan. His words can often be summarized as *Sound Bites*, an elegant and simple rhetoric capturing complex ideas. The synthesizer also encourages and cheerleads.

Having analysed the nature of the product development and innovation processes, we will now turn to the fact that product development, as well as innovation, is no longer an activity that takes place only inside the company. Instead several actors and organizations are normally involved in innovation and product development. In the next section we penetrate innovation processes in clusters.

CLUSTERS AND INNOVATION — RESOURCES INSIDE AND OUTSIDE THE COMPANY

The development of new products, services and concepts in the retailing and catering sector is intense. More and more meals are eaten outside the home. In fact, this market shows rapid growth and has attracted much interest from the actors in the business. The catering sector is in rapid transition due to several factors. One is the retailers' strategy of increasing the value added in the retail shops. As a consequence a number of value-added services have been included in the retail assortment. Food is heated or served in a restaurant. Takeaways can be bought in the shop or ordered by telephone. Orders by Internet are also accepted.

Restaurants are facing competition from fast-food chains of various kinds. These chains represent a new type of industrial customer who assemble food products from components bought from companies that can meet the quality and price levels demanded.

A third factor influencing the catering sector specifically is the increasing ambition in private companies and public organizations, like schools and hospitals to organize service activities in a more efficient way. Company and hospital restaurant costs are being scrutinized and outsourcing of catering and other service functions is a common method of cutting overheads.

This pluralistic system containing many diverse ways of serving food outside the home and the catering sector represents an interesting mixture of very small companies and global corporations. There are two conflicting forces in the development of catering products. One is the ability to provide a service that is well suited to the consumer. The other force is the need to compete through price, which makes it necessary to use standard components and industrial production methods. At the same time, the quality and cost of transportation and logistics are important.

This change in the food chain has been well described in the research (Pellegrini, 1989, 1996; Dawson and Shaw, 1989; Henson and Northern, 1997; Lanciotti, 1997; Gabriele, 1997) and the key element is the retailers' ambition to add value to their products through increased quality, increased convenience and added service.

A review of published research results shows that empirical research on the development of new products and services in the service sector is scarce. However results have been reported from research in food-processing technology. Results from research concerning cooling, freezing and heating and the role of new technologies indicate that new food-processing technologies will create an interesting basis for innovations in the catering sector. A milestone in this research can be found in the proceedings of The International Symposium on Progress in Food Preservation Processes, 1988

(CERIA, 1988). The development in food processing, nutrition, process control, logistics, heating, cooling and freezing technology has recently created many opportunities for processes, products and services in the food sector. Thus, it is now possible, through flexible technology, to increase product quality and consumers' choice. Some of the new technological opportunities demand changes in production and distribution habits, as well as organizational solutions when providing these services. Another important aspect is the control of quality and safety in the products. In the food chain analysis and retailing literature product development in the retailing and catering sector has not been so well investigated, however. In this book our aim is to start to fill that gap and do empirical studies of some of these processes in the context of the dynamics in the food chain.

Clusters

We believe that that much can be learned by linking the study of firm strategy with that of regional clusters (Lloyd and Dicken, 1977; Goddard, 1978; Berman and Feser, 1999; Erhvervsfremme Styrelsen, 2001; OECD, 2001; Söderström, 2001). In this book 'cluster' is defined in the following way:

> A cluster is a geographically proximate group of interconnected companies and associated institutions in a particular field, linked by commonalities and comple-mentarities (Porter, 1998b,c, Porter 1990).

In a cluster we will find companies producing products and services for consumers. We will find suppliers of specialized inputs, components, machinery and services located upstream or downstream in the value-added chain, but also in related industries. In a cluster we will also find financial actors and specialized infrastructure providers. The infrastructure is commonly provided through governmental and public organizations such as universities and institutes, providing specialized training, education, information, research and technical support. A cluster also consists of institutions, providing standards, rules and cluster-specific ways of addressing co-operation and development in the cluster.

In describing and defining clusters, we can increase the precision by including the distinction between organizations and institutions and also by defining what makes a cluster work efficiently. We do this following the research on 'systems of Innovation' (Edquist, 1997; Lundvall, 1992; de la Motte and Paquet, 1998). Systems of innovation have been analysed as national, regional, local and sectoral systems of innovation. It is quite clear that the researchers in this field analyse the same object as Porter.[1] Based on this tradition we incorporate the distinction between organizations and institutions according to the following definitions:

> *Institutions* are sets of common habits, routines, established practices, rules, or laws that regulate the relations and interactions between individuals and groups (Edquist1997, p. 46).

It is important to distinguish this definition of the practices and laws that regulate cluster behaviour from government organizations, commonly referred to as 'institutions'. In our book they are not. They are organizations like other organizations, but with another ownership. It is also important to realize that the distinction between public organizations and private organizations in the real world is not a dichotomy, rather we see a spectrum of organizations in the interface between the public and the private. We can regard the 'publicness' of organizations as a position on a continuous scale.

> *Organizations* are formal structures with an explicit purpose and they are consciously created (ibid., p. 47).

Institutions are especially important for the innovation process in three ways (ibid., p. 51):

• they reduce uncertainty by providing information,
• they manage conflicts and cooperation,
• they provide incentives.

In the innovation process, especially in the early phases, there is a great deal of uncertainty. This uncertainty can be partially reduced for example by rules and laws concerning patents, other intellectual property rights and jointly defined 'rules of a fair game'. In cases of conflict there are rules governing how to solve them and there are also theoretical constructs that explain that tension is quite natural in innovation, for example between technological bases and market perspectives, as is also the case between new and old products. There may be rules and traditions that stimulate the development of new products and there may be dysfunctional institutions that create development barriers.

> Continuously changing institutions are, after all, a contradiction in terms, while institutional rigidity is, in the long run, a threat to technical change. However, it is important to move beyond these limited perspectives, and recognize that *institutions may have both promoting and retarding effects on innovation* (ibid., p. 55).

We can see the similarities very well if we compare models of Porter and de la Motte and Paquet. Porter has developed the famous Porter Diamond in which the development of competitiveness is dependent on the dynamics between the factors presented in Figure 3.2.

The basic factors interacting in competitive dynamics are:

- factor conditions,
- firm strategy, structure and rivalry,
- demand conditions, and
- relating and supporting industries.

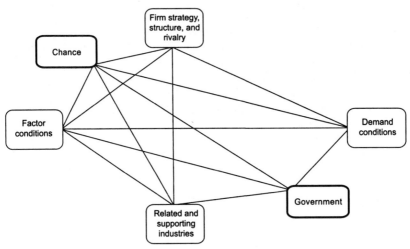

Source: Porter, 1990.

Figure 3.2   The Porter Diamond

These basic factors are affected by two others (Porter, 1990, p. 127):

- government, and
- chance.

Turning to the similarities between Porter Diamonds and Innovation Systems, the work of de la Motte and Paquet is interesting. In a book entitled 'Local and Regional Systems of Innovation' they work with the cluster concept. They state that many regions have some degree of industrial concentration, but not every concentration is a cluster. Furthermore, not all clusters are successful. Cluster success depends on more than innovation and linkages. In order to explain what it takes to make an innovation cluster successful they have developed the GEM model. The model consists of three parts, groundings, enterprises and markets – GEM. In the model we find the following elements (de La Motte and Paquet, 1998, p. 58–59):

Groundings (supply determinants)
- Resources
- Infrastructure

Enterprises (structural determinants)
- Suppliers and related industries
- Firm structure and strategies

Markets (demand determinants)
- Local markets
- Access to external markets

The similarities with Porter are striking. De la Motte and Paquet have included a distinction between local and external markets, but otherwise they describe the same phenomena. We thus conclude that there are so many similarities between the Porter clusters and Innovation Systems that the two approaches can be combined.[2]

Another tradition is represented in the Triple Helix analysis (see, for example, Hemlin, 2000), which is basically another way of describing the development cluster activities, in interaction between technology and market, between the public and private actors. Having read some good contributions in this field, we still decided to use the definitions and models from Porter clusters and Innovation Systems.

The Role of Government

The role of government is important in innovation clusters, especially the ability to make *anticipatory institutional changes* at higher subsystem levels. When the government has the ability to anticipate changes in the innovation landscape, they can undertake actions that lead to institutional change. Examples of such actions contributing to innovation are:

- creating the institutional framework for the collective supply of important capabilities and technologies,
- stimulating the emergence of bridging organizations such as innovation centres involved in soft activities such as diagnosis and referral to experts, and technological centres, involving both hard and soft functions, and

- catalytic support of initial capability generation, that is incentives to finance the transfer of technology to, and its absorption by, an intermediate organization. This also includes initial, experimental implementation of the service provision or technology transfer activities which will help the user to 'articulate demand'(Edquist, 1997, p. 368).

The appropriate role of government in creating innovation cluster dynamics is also summarized by Porter in the following way (Porter, 1998c, p. 245 –248). Governments should:

- establish a stable and predictable economic environment,
- improve the availability, quality and efficiency of general-purpose inputs and institutions,
- establish overall rules and incentives governing competition that encourage productivity growth,
- facilitate cluster development and upgrading,
- develop and implement a positive, distinctive, and long-term economic upgrading programme which mobilizes government, business, institutions and citizens. The programme should be horizontal and cluster-specific.

It is important to note that Porter, who in his writings at the beginning of the 1990s was rather sceptical towards the role that governments could play, has now moved to a position where he sees roles for governments. The important difference according to Porter is that traditional industrial policy was, in principle, a form of competition-distorting support for national industries, while cluster-based policy relates to all clusters, including relaxation of constraints and emphasizing cross-industry linkages and complementarities, thus enhancing competition.

The clusters in Europe are in competition with each other. For a cluster that experiences limited dynamics and growth, the result is a loss of business opportunities and lower affluence in the region where the cluster is located, while successful clusters lead to a gain in prosperity for a region or large parts of a country (Krugman, 1991). Therefore, an intense debate is in process concerning how to create efficient cluster-based economic policies as a way of developing industries and regions (see for example, Tson Söderberg, 2001; Ohmae, 1995; NUTEK, 2001; OECD 2001).

Clusters, Companies and Strategy

There are *three principal features* of regional clusters that influence firm strategy (Enright, 1994). The first is that the resources and capabilities vital for firms to succeed can often be found within a region rather than within a single firm. The second is that regional clusters often involve activities that are shared between firms within the cluster. The third feature is that a firm's choice of strategy can be influenced by the strategic interdependencies, rapid information flows, and the unique mixture of competition and co-operation often found in regional clusters.

There also exists a second kind of network or cluster of innovative firms. In addition to the geographically limited network centred around production, technology, unique resources and specific infrastructure, there is *also a network which is often global, including the key customers in foreign markets* (Kristensen, 1992).[3] The contribution of such partners, for example distributors, retail chains and industrial customers, can be vital to the product development process. According to a hypothesis by Langhoff (1993), the importance of a partner's supplementary areas of competence for the food company's internationalization process increases as cultural heterogeneity in the market increases (Grunert et al., 1996).

A resource-based view of regional clusters points to the fact that there are resources that are external to any single firm, but internal to the region (Herrigel in Kogut, 1993). Region-specific resources will lead to sustainable advantage when they are valuable, rare, difficult to imitate and difficult to replace. In many cases the resources of a region will be based on unique historical conditions (Saxenian, 1985; Enright in Raff and Lamoreaux, 1994). In other cases the specific resources of a region are socially complex (Piore and Sabel, 1984; Pyke et al., 1990; Fanfani and Lagnevik, 1995).

A single firm involved in product development performs its activities in a working environment where it does not possess all the necessary knowledge about consumer needs. In order to obtain a good understanding of these needs, the company must have not only a thorough understanding of the consumer, but also knowledge about the retail and service organizations further down the value-added chain, that is the companies that contribute through complementary or competing products and/or services.

Likewise, the company will possess and control some of the important technologies, resources and areas of competence – but usually not all. The company's ability to be well organized in the use of its bundle of resources thus creates *two interrelated challenges*. One is to create *effective co-ordination and creativity inside* its own organization. The other one is to create *effective co-ordination and creativity in the external networks* and clusters in which the company is participating.

Innovations in Knowledge Webs

How do we create effective co-ordination and creativity in external networks and clusters? In a recent publication, Eneroth and Malm (2001) made use of a homology from biology, where the concept of 'fitness landscapes' illustrates in a multidimensional space of peaks and valleys how well organisms and species are adapted to survive, and how the organisms change in order to become more competitive in the fitness landscape (see, for example, Kauffman, 1993). The authors introduce the concept of 'knowledge land-scape' as a metaphor to describe the strivings of companies in innovation clusters. They have analysed the landscape around the Bluetooth technology for wireless communication.

> Therefore, both established firms and a number of small start-ups experimented with various new cable replacement technologies – from improved infrared to short-range radio solutions. In terms of a *knowledge landscape* this area became difficult to navigate – not only a foggy landscape with a large number of potential hills and valleys but also rapidly changing as a result of reported progress in different technologies. It was probably also recognized that in the longer term there would only be room for one or a few technologies. That is, when the mist cleared and the landscape stabilized, there would only be one or a few high peaks. This was the situation when the Bluetooth ideas started to form in the early 1990s (Eneroth and Malm, 2001, p. 176).

What is especially interesting for us is the Eneroth and Malm knowledge landscape process when the mist eventually clears and the peaks stand clear and strong. This has a direct relation to Utterback's innovation process which we presented earlier. The *fluid phase*, as Utterback describes it, could be represented very well by the foggy turbulent landscape. As Utterback sees the process developing towards the *transitional phase*, a dominant design appears, the number of players is reduced and the innovation process is clearly focused in specific directions. The mist clears and the peaks are clearly visible.

Eneroth and Malm further address the question of efficient external net-working, making a distinction between networks and webs.

> We make a distinction between the widely used concept of network and the less common knowledge web. Simply put, knowledge webs are the development aspect of networks. If a knowledge web is to be a foundation for competitive advantages it should consist of generative relations (ibid., p. 180).

So what then is a generative relation? We learn from Eneroth and Malm that we must define efficient knowledge webs related to knowledge domains – not to specific companies. In the knowledge domain a company must decide if it wants to take a leading position and create vision strategies, or if it is to be a follower. Companies aspiring to a leadership role must have unique competences and a technological first-mover advantage. If they have the competence and the communication ability, they can provide the first quality that makes the knowledge web generative – shared visions across borders. There must be some common feeling about the way to go in the innovation process.[4]

Another quality needed is a balance between novelty and confirmation. Knowledge webs must stretch their ambitions well beyond the well known, but must not depart so far from their core areas of competence that the development project becomes rootless.

The third quality needed is a complementarity of areas of competence. Different technological areas of competence are needed, but also extensive competence in markets and the conditions for governing the application of the innovation. Summing up this gives us three key qualities necessary for the creation of innovations in clusters (Eneroth and Malm, 2001, pp. 178–180):

- a balance between novelty and confirmation in knowledge exchange – creating a greenhouse for creativity,
- a shared vision across organizational borders, and
- complementarity of areas of competence .

We now turn to the question of what kinds of knowledge are being transferred or shared within a knowledge web. In principle we can distinguish between codified knowledge, which can easily be reproduced at a low cost and transferred between distant locations on the one hand, and tacit, non-codified knowledge that is often created through common experience and direct interaction. Both kinds of knowledge are necessary in the innovation process, and this is one of the main reasons why geography matters. The degree of codification differs between different kinds of knowledge, and following Johnson and Lundvall (1994) we can distinguish further between four types of knowledge:

- *Know-what:* Knowledge of facts and transfer of codified knowledge.
- *Know-why:* Scientific knowledge about basic principles, rules and ideas.
- *Know-who:* Knowledge about specific and selective social relations. Building of trust in relations. Knowing markets and actors in the cluster and the economic value of relations with the actors.
- *Know-how:* Skills and knowledge necessary to create or do practical things – transfer of ideas so they become objects or systems in use.

These four types of knowledge differ in regard to knowledge creation and knowledge transfer. The possibility of transferring knowledge to distant locations is also different. We should also note that the key locations for the production of these four types of knowledge differ. For an example, know-why is often produced in universities and other research organizations, while know-how is often produced in, and specific to, companies. Since all four kinds of knowledge are necessary, interaction in the cluster pays off.

Evaluating Clusters

As pointed out earlier in this book with reference to Eneroth and Malm's knowledge webs, the cluster concept is often widely used and many types of network interaction can be described as a cluster in more general terms. If we want to analyse the strength and potential of a cluster we can distinguish between different clusters with a set of analysis dimensions developed by Michel J. Enright (2000b, pp. 317–21). The dimensions are as follows:

- *Geographic scope* refers to the geographical concentration of a cluster. Sporadic clusters are spread over a larger area, while localized clusters are highly concentrated to one location.
- *Density* refers to the number of, and the economic importance of, the businesses in the cluster. Dense clusters have many businesses representing a large share of the business and the market.
- *Breadth* refers to the number of horizontally related industries in the cluster. Broad clusters produce an assortment of products in several closely related industries. Narrow clusters can be found where one or very few industries and their suppliers form a cluster.
- *Activity base* refers to the number and nature of activities in the value-added chain. How much of core strategy is made in the cluster? How active are the developers and innovators in marketing and corporate co-ordination in the region?
- *Depth* refers to the reach of vertically related industries in a cluster. In deep clusters the region contains almost all suppliers along the value-added chain, while surface clusters are dependent on inputs, technology and service produced outside the region.
- *Growth potential* is related to the competitive position versus actors external to the cluster, but also to the availability of or the ability to create unique resources and knowledge needed to achieve continued growth. Enright describes the growth potential as sunrise, dawn or sunset, which should be related to the competitiveness of the cluster, for example dawn/competitive, dawn/uncompetitive.

- *Innovative capability* refers to the ability of the cluster to generate important innovations in products, processes, design, marketing, logistics and management. High innovative capability should not be confused with high-technology, since high-technology refers to the technological level and not to the innovative capability.[5]
- *Industrial organization* refers to the management structure and the interactions between the companies and organizations in the cluster, as well as the power structure between the companies and organizations.
- *Co-ordination mechanisms* refer to the inter-company relations in the cluster. Co-ordination can be hierarchical, market-type co-ordination or mixed network forms.

Using these dimensions of analysis we can proceed and characterize the clusters according to how well developed they are and how resourceful they are.

Working clusters have reached a critical mass of local knowledge, specialized work force and resources. The businesses have agglomeration advantages and as a result growing competitiveness.

Latent clusters have reached a critical mass of businesses and supporting organizations in related industries. They should be able to attain the advantages of a working cluster, but have not yet developed the level of interaction and information exchange needed to use the cluster advantages fully. This may be due to lack of knowledge, lack of joint visions or lack of trust.

Potential clusters have some of the elements needed to form an efficient cluster, but some elements need to be replaced by more efficient resources and areas of competence. This could be expressed as the existence of gaps in the competence and resource set of the cluster. At the same time, potential clusters often lack the interaction, confidence and trust required in a working cluster.

Wishful thinking clusters are clusters that have been defined as a cluster by those who wish the group of companies to work as a well-functioning cluster. These clusters are often 'appointed' by national, regional or local governments. They often lack the critical mass needed to create development and competitiveness.

With the help of Enright, we can analyse clusters to obtain a more precise understanding of their development and their qualities, and we can classify them so that the need for cluster-improving activities can be articulated. Thus, inputs aimed at improving cluster performance can be designed in an efficient way.

LEADERSHIP AND ORGANIZATION IN INNOVATION PROCESSES

When working with the resource-based strategic theory, we are interested in resources that are: (1) *valuable*, (2) *rare*, (3) *not easy to imitate*, and (4) it should *not be easy to find substitutes* for the resources employed, and (5) the resources should also be *well organized*.

Concerning the criterion 'well organized', we can deepen our understanding and the analysis with the help of Tsoukas (1996). Resources in companies are not given in advance, they are not discovered, but they are *created* by the company's activities. More important than the resource itself is how it is being used in the company's products and services. How this is done is in turn dependent on how knowledge and abilities are used in the context of planning, reporting and management systems. We can see the whole company as a *knowledge system*. This is the reason why Tsoukas and his colleagues name this variant of the resource-based strategy 'Knowledge-based Strategy'.

Following Tsoukas, we understand that no single individual can have a perfect overview of this whole system. We can exemplify this with any large food corporation. No single individual can survey and understand the very different kind of knowledge required to understand computer systems, nutritional food properties, logistics, biotechnological process aspects, consumer needs, industrial control systems, financing and agricultural policy – at least not with thorough knowledge and total insight into all the important aspects. Therefore, knowledge is distributed throughout the organization. The key issue is to make the employees and associates apply their knowledge and capabilities to vision and strategy-directed tasks in a meaningful way, so that competitiveness can be created and enhanced.

> Management, therefore, can be seen as an open-ended process of co-ordinating purposeful individuals, whose actions stem from applying their unique interpretations to the local circumstances confronting them (ibid., p. 22)

This definition is well in line with what has been suggested earlier by Lagnevik (1989):

> Summing up, we can describe leadership as a cognitive and empathic generation and distribution of creative and competitive interpretations of the key relations between the organizations and its environment.

Individuals Learn and Create in an Organizational Context

To further increase our understanding of the knowledge-based strategic theory, we will now investigate the relation between the individual and the organization. When it comes to effective use of abilities and areas of competence, we must focus on individuals and their co-operation. The concept 'organizational learning' has no meaning according to Grant (1996, p. 112):

> All learning takes place inside individual human heads, an organization learns only in two ways: (a) by learning of its members, or (b) by ingesting new members who have knowledge that the organization didn't previously have (Simon 1991). More importantly, however, is the desire to understand and organise processes through which firms access and utilise the knowledge possessed by their members (ibid., p. 113).

This process in which firms access and utilize the knowledge possessed by their members is central in our research project. We know that one of the factors that are vital for the upgrading of competitiveness is *market intelligence.* The other two factors that we will focus on are *production* and *product development.* Studies by Danish researchers have shown that in the exchange processes involving these three factors, most of the key variables that we need to understand in order to analyse the knowledge system are involved in important processes, substantial dilemmas and key creative activities.

In order to progress in our analysis we must distinguish between *knowledge transfer* and *knowledge integration* in a process of creation. If the knowledge integration process is to work efficiently, we must understand and govern four aspects of the interaction processes (ibid. p. 114):

- rules and directives – which form plans, schemes, forms and other artefacts that guide and control human actions in companies,
- sequential planning – how work sequences for the employees and associates are positioned and related to each other,
- routines – which is a concept covering how individuals manage to handle complex development processes with the help of counselling and information acquisition in situations where the rules and the sequence planning do not provide guidelines, and
- group problem solving – which is a concept covering how individuals in a group create good forms for co-operation and joint problem solving.

If these aspects are to function well, some basic requirements must be fulfilled. If the following conditions are prevailing, the context for efficient product development is supportive. If they do not exist, good reasons can be found as to why the product and service development activities fail (based on Grant, 1996).

1. A *common language* is important for the development process. This may seem trivial but is a problem in many development situations. It is difficult to be a genius and get really bright ideas if you cannot communicate them to other people. This can be seen in international companies, where inventive people with a mother tongue other than the one supported by head office are at a disadvantage. In other cases, the professional language and the cognitive base of the people involved in a project may differ considerably. Famous conflicts have been noted between engineers and marketing specialists, between development project managers and production line managers, between accountants and marketing managers, and between career scientists and career executives. It is important to note that in a large company, many languages are spoken simultaneously every day. However, an effective product and service development process demands a common language and good understanding between the individuals involved.

2. *Common symbols* in communication, such as gestures, common sayings, stories and anecdotes and the same computer software, are of key importance. These symbols facilitate a secure and empathic development context. As visitors to large companies, we often notice how key actors dress in a very similar way, meetings are conducted in similar ways in all parts of the company, the same tales about the founding fathers are told everywhere and the computer software is uniform. In fact, as visitors from the outside real world, we learn that refusal to use the common software is a sign that we have met a subculture. The same phenomenon is signalled by a strange tie, a new tale or an unusual way of treating guests. We use symbols to communicate how we see ourselves and what we believe in.

3. *Bridges between individuals with specialized knowledge* – safe arenas to meet – are of key importance. Successful development organizations devote a great deal of effort, time and money to providing such arenas. Cross-departmental teams are very common. In other cases, 'house rules' may be set up to promote exchange. Examples of such rules can be that laboratory engineers travel with the salespeople on customer tours, customers are invited to work with the company's own development engineers, employees are encouraged to participate in benchmarking networks, idea exchange arenas are created and cross-specialization promotions are encouraged.

4. *Shared experience, same meaning, shared 'silent knowledge'* and *shared skills* are of key importance to be able to actually make a new product or to really get a process working well. It is important to note that this kind

of knowledge and experience can be obtained only through active and practical work. In this respect, experienced personnel having been with the company for a long time are absolutely vital to promote a high level of skills and to 'know how to do it if you have an idea about what you want to do'. In the present climate, where there is a focus on getting new thinking into companies and changing the old ways, it seems relevant to point out the importance of senior employees and experience. In visits to very successful development companies we have found a nice blend of senior and junior employees working together.

5. Recognition of different spheres of competence is another key issue in joint development processes. *Respect for other people, respect for their professional knowledge and an openness towards contributions* from people with a background different from one's own is important. Therefore it is vital to balance the influence of various professional groups in the company and in top management. For example – a large corporation led by lawyers would probably only focus on form and structure, at the expense of market shares, profits and technological focus.

Gabriel Szulanski's (1996) study of organizational intertia is a very interesting contribution to the resource-based theory. He has performed an empirical study of why good ideas are not accepted and why good projects fail. His main result is that the N. I. H.-syndrome[5] is rejected as the main cause of organizational inertia. According to Szulanski it is not hostile attitudes towards the thinking of others, it is not protection of one's own habitat, it is not a general resistance to change which stop good projects. No, *the most common reason is that the employees of the company do not understand what to do with the idea*. They can also be uncertain about in which context the idea should be developed (ibid., p. 37). It gives quite another context and calls for another agenda if we understand that those who resist change do not do it mainly because they are envious and self-protective. They do it because they just do not understand how to use the new knowledge and the new ideas. *Consequently, it pays to guide and lead the knowledge formation process in the company.*

The important thing about all the aspects mentioned above is that *they can be guided, supported and controlled.*

Creativity and Innovation

In the innovation process, we need creativity from the individuals involved. Some actors in the innovation clusters are individuals working on their own, but the absolute majority work in an organizational context. We will now focus the question of how the organization can stimulate and encourage creativity. But first we must define a creative company:

> A company is creative when its employees do something new and potentially useful without being directly shown or taught (Robinson and Stern, 1997).[6]

There are certain key elements that should be represented in a company in order to stimulate creativity. They are:

- alignment,
- self-initiated activity,
- unofficial activity,
- serendipity,
- diverse stimuli,
- within-company communication.

Alignment is a concept that reflects the extent to which the goals, visions and interests of every employee support the visions and goals of the organization. Its importance can be illustrated clearly with its opposite – misalignment. If the members of the organization do not share the same visions and goals, it is very difficult to direct a joint process anywhere. Misalignment can be the result of bad management, bad communication or measurement and reward systems that distort the evaluations of performance so the wrong things are measured and rewarded, for example, quantity can be favoured at the expense of quality, or short-term focus can limit long-term competitiveness.

Self-initiated activity means that individuals start activities on their own initiative and drive the innovation process through thick and thin in their own interest. This element refers to the importance of recognizing entrepreneurs in the corporate context and in clusters. Much can be said about the importance of entrepreneurship and much has been said. In this book we will simply point out the importance of entrepreneurship and note that while everybody agrees about the need for entrepreneurship, organizations are still poor at understanding and supporting entrepreneurs.

Unofficial activity is necessary in the creative process. People will try things without being directed to the area. Playfulness and curiousness are important qualities in creative people. As a consequence, it is impossible to plan for, or to forecast, innovations. As an example, it can be mentioned (Robinson and Stern, 1997, pp. 149–174) that neither HP nor Canon, the two companies that dominate the world market for ink printers, planned for the introduction of bubble jet products. They were the result of experiments by entrepreneurs, experiments that came up with results that could not be theoretically understood. The invention first had to be understood by the companies, then developed and launched as an innovation. Nobody can plan ahead or assign resources in advance for such products.

You must allow mischief.[7]

Serendipity, according to the *Oxford English Dictionary*, means 'the faculty of making happy and unexpected discoveries by accident'. What can be said about this quality is that 'luck' in discovering things is not a random process. Some people are luckier than others. One reason may be that they have qualified expertise in the area that they are experimenting in. Likewise, people who are open to impressions and willing to reinterpret everyday life are luckier than others, as are those who have a bias for action. If the organization has a little slack that allows people to reflect, it will experience more serendipity.

Diverse stimuli is a concept that covers the extent to which employees are encouraged to view the corporate activity from different perspectives. Among the efficient actions that can be taken, we can mention rotating people in different job positions, exposing people to outside influences, encouraging people to compare their private perspectives with the corporate perspectives and working in multidisciplinary teams.

Within a company, the *communication function* deals with the possibility for people from different parts of the organization to meet and interact. It also deals with creating the understanding of the employee that the organization is filled with interesting resources and that – from a corporate standpoint – it is desirable that all employees use these resources in innovation processes. Since we are analysing innovations in clusters, we must add here, of course, that communication outside the company and efficient use of cluster resources are equally important.

After having covered the strategy, the clusters and the leadership and organization issues, we will now turn to the market and to the consumers to increase our understanding of the role of the consumer in the innovation process.

NOTES

1. The similarities are quite obvious. However, to conduct a formal, theoretical, explicit comparison is beyond the scope of this book. We note that Edquist (1997) in his well written and theoretically explicit book comments: 'This (comparison with other theories) means an implicit comparison between the system of innovation approach(es) and other approaches. Making this comparison explicit and systematic is a larger task than can be done in an introduction to an edited book.' Later in the book references are made to Porter (pp. 270, 320).

2. In passing, we note the little joke of de la Motte and Paquet. If Porter can produce a *diamond*, they can produce a gem.
3. This result fits well with that of de la Motte and Paquet (1998, pp. 58–59) presented above.
4. From our own empirical material we have also found examples of companies using web-participants for destructive reasons. Their mission is to confuse and misdirect knowledge webs as to which competitors have strong lead positions. The objective is to weaken the innovation process around competitive technological peaks that could threaten the company's own technological stronghold.
4. This point is also highlighted by Porter (1998, p. 85f). The term high-tech, normally used to refer to fields such as information technology and biotechnology, has distorted thinking about competition, creating the misconception that only a handful of businesses compete in sophisticated ways. In fact there is no such thing as a low-tech industry. There are only low-tech companies – that is, companies that fail to use world-class technology and practices to enhance productivity and innovation. A vibrant cluster can help any company in any industry to compete in the most sophisticated ways, using the most advanced, relevant skills and technologies.
5. *Not Invented Here syndrome.* A widespread explanation of inertia. If people have not come up with an idea or a solution themselves, they refuse to see its merits. The prime reasons are believed to be status, protection of 'habitat' and envy of the creative and successful.
6. The creativity model is based on Robinson and Stern's whole book.
7. Insight from an experienced and successful research and development (R&D) director leading several innovation processes.

4.   Consumers and Food Innovation[1]

In the introductory chapter of this book a study concerning managers' views on the importance of innovativeness was presented. One of the questions put to them was: 'Is innovation a matter of life and death for the company?' The answers to this question were all extremely positive stressing the crucial importance of innovativeness. Bearing this in mind, the answers to the question, 'Is your company innovative?' were somewhat surprising as most managers answered that they were not being innovative to any great extent.

This ambivalent attitude to what one knows to be important and what one is actually doing is not exclusively reserved for managers. If we were to ask consumers the same type of questions, for example 'Is eating healthily a matter of life and death?' and 'Are you eating healthily?', we would get exactly the same type of answers. This illustrates the fact that there is often a considerable discrepancy between what consumers rationally know when asked about something, and how this knowledge is put into practice in their day-to-day lives. Recognizing this has profound consequences regarding how we can predict consumers' responses to the high-value-added products available on the market.

In this chapter we present the views of consumers on food innovations and healthy food products. Conventionally, when consumers' perceptions of a certain product or product type are sought after one starts at the product, or industry, end of the line. One way of doing this is to engage in so-called concept testing, that is testing whether a product idea not yet developed will be marketable should a company choose to produce it. Also, an already developed product can be tested to assess how, to whom, and where a product should be marketed. This approach is based on products and definitions that are meaningful to the manufacturer, for example high-value-added products, and efforts are made to assess whether, and how, successful the products will be among consumers. The high-value-added that we are investigating here is health.[2]

In our work we started at the consumer end of the line, in an unbiased way without imposing industry-derived concepts and ideas on the consumers. Our aim was to arrive at a consumer-defined conceptualization of healthy food products. The theoretical underpinning of this chapter is based on the assumption that the choice of products and consumption form an important part of a consumer's identity. To understand the potential role of healthy food products and innovations in consumers' day-to-day lives they have to be studied in context, that is, how they fit together with other products in the consumer universe. The approach chosen was to interview consumers regarding everyday food consumption and see if and how consumers spontaneously talked about healthy and so-called value-added food products. The meaning of products is not fixed but is assigned to the products by the consumers during the full range of consumption activities. Hence, it is not sufficient to discuss the decision-making process, that is, how they choose one product over another in an in-store setting, as this is only one aspect of why certain products are successful. Rather, it is important to gain a more holistic understanding of how consumers fit the products into their everyday lives.

HEALTH IN FOCUS

Over the past decade there has been a change in the meaning structure given to food. Pasi Falk divides messages about food into four dimensions: fuel, poison, medicine and pleasure, and asserts that there has been a shift in the meaning of food emphasizing the role of the duality of medicine/poison (Falk, 1996, p. 183). It seems that no one, including food producers, farmers, TV cooks, cooking magazines, health magazines, governmental advisors, and so on, passes up an opportunity to emphasize the health-beneficial qualities a certain food product might have. Neither is any potentially harmful food allowed to pass by unnoticed – health scares of different kinds have become part of our daily life. However, it is far from clear what this concept of health, prevalent as it undoubtedly is, stands for from a consumer perspective. There is no single concept of health available to consumers, but a multitude of different claims and counterclaims made by various types of experts (see Giddens, 1991, p. 101). When considering these questions from a managerial standpoint it must be borne in mind that health is never experienced as an objective quality of food, but is rather shaped by cultural understandings that determine how health is perceived and experienced (Askegaard et al., 1999, p. 331). How consumers make sense of the various notions available regarding health is thus shaped by their cultural setting.

Over the past two or three years there has been an explosion of products claiming to be healthy in one way or another. There are a plethora of products ranging from common light, or diet, products to products making more specific claims, such as table margarine claiming to lower the cholesterol level in the blood, for example Becel produced by Unilever Best Foods.[3] An increasing demand from consumers for healthier food in general, and more convenient healthy food in particular, *supposedly* fuels the increasing supply of new 'healthy' products. This increased demand that the companies claim to be sensing did not emerge by itself, but is a result of an intricate reciprocal process of consumer research both inside and outside academia, promotional activities, media, and so on. Companies sensing this increasing demand, or just following others in the field in order not to be left behind, are becoming involved in research and development (R&D) projects aimed at developing new products with a healthy profile. Effort is also being devoted to the development of healthier food products within academia.

There is no doubt that most firms' intelligence functions are aware of the recent health trends. As was pointed out earlier,[4] if producers in the European market want to stay in the game they will have to move their strategic focus from the production of commodity products to the production and marketing of high-value-added products. Furthermore, if they want consumers to acknowledge the added value, regardless of how they niche their product, the value must be perceived by consumers as something healthy, be that as a healthy product or as a product with an absence of risk. Using the terminology of sociologist Ulrich Beck (1992) we are now living in a 'risk society' where consumers are increasingly aware of the opportunities offered by modern technology, but perhaps more importantly, the possible hazards.

HIGH-VALUE-ADDED PRODUCTS FROM A CONSUMER PERSPECTIVE

If we seriously intend to take a consumer approach it is important to avoid making premature judgements about what is valuable to consumers. 'High value-added product' is a definition coined by the food industry that does not necessarily have any counterpart in the consumer realm. For whom do we mean that the value is added when we talk about high-value-added products? Usually, when the term is used in management contexts it refers to a product that has, in some way, been diversified from other products to gain a competitive advantage. As mentioned in earlier chapters, it is important to gain sustainable advantages that cannot easily be copied by competitors. Such diversification might indeed be of value to manufacturers. However, it is often assumed that the differentiated features of the products are also of importance and of value to the consumer. One should thus be careful in assuming that the value added by the company is also the value perceived by the consumer. As has been stressed in earlier chapters of this book the value added must be recognized by the consumer in order to give a competitive advantage for the company. The question is how we can assess beforehand what consumers will value and what they will not.

When looking at products where the value added is supposed to be health-related, the situation becomes even more complicated. As stated above, we cannot take for granted that the value added by the producer is perceived as such by the consumer. Even less can we take for granted that what the producer perceives as being healthy is perceived as such by the consumer. Health is never experienced as an objective quality of food, but is shaped by cultural understandings that determine how health is understood and experienced – the concepts of health and healthiness are far from homogeneous. Not only is there a difference between how producers and consumers view health but experts may also have radically differing views. To further complicate the issue, the categories of producers and consumers are not as clear-cut as it might appear; neither are the categories of experts and laypeople. Consumers are often engaged in the production process and people working in different parts of the production are also, without doubt, consumers of food. Furthermore, experts are generally experts only in a very narrow field and would have to be considered laypeople in most other fields – the days of the omnipotent renaissance scientists are long gone.

We have to reject the notion that consumers and producers perceive what is healthy in the same way. Making these kinds of assumptions about what consumers believe to be of value and what they believe to be healthy leads to judgements of the behaviour of consumers. It is often assumed that, in a product choice situation, consumers will choose something healthy instead of something unhealthy, all other features of the products being constant. Since often they do not value the product in the way market intelligence predicted they would, their behaviour is either deemed uninformed or irrational. This view is far too limiting and does not provide us with any answers as to how consumers view healthiness and unhealthiness with regard to food.

In literature concerning new product development with a focus on healthy products (for example Chipman et al., 1995; Corney et al., 1994; Ippolito and Mathios, 1994; Kilsby and Nyström, 1998; Mazis and Raymond, 1997; Poulsen, 1999), the concepts of healthy and unhealthy are almost always dealt with in a taken-for-granted manner, as if the dichotomy of healthy and unhealthy with regard to food is a God-given one, with clear, natural boundaries. This might very well be the case from a natural science point of view, although the scientists themselves have so far not been able to reach a consensus – as a matter of fact, the history of nutritional and medical research has been characterized by many reversals and changes in opinion (Giddens, 1991; Thompson and Hirschman, 1995, p. 146). When adopting a consumer perspective, one cannot make the assumption that the same scientific understanding of health is applicable. Just because something is scientifically proven to be healthy it does not follow that it is simply a question of informing consumers so that they will understand this and realize the value of the product.

Prior studies have focused on a variety of issues including: trying to ascertain how much healthier a product must be to justify a higher price or a less appealing taste (compare Kilsby and Nyström, 1998), looking at whether adding certain substances beneficial to health will increase consumers' value perception of a product (Poulsen, 1999), experimentally testing how nutritional information is processed by consumers (Corney et al., 1994; Mazis and Raymond, 1997), evaluating how consumers react to messages about unhealthy ingredients in food (Chipman et al., 1995), and how trends in nutrition information have affected overall spending patterns (Ippolito and Mathios, 1994). Although these studies undoubtedly tell us something about how consumers view certain products or product features they do not really tell us anything about how they reason about health in their daily lives. The everyday situation of consumers includes so much else that studying various issues in isolation might not be of much value in understanding consumers.

FOOD AND IDENTITY

In modern times consumption is seen as an increasingly important tool in defining our self-identity (Firat 1998). Social theorist Anthony Giddens (1991) suggests that individuals are reflexively and consciously building a coherent lifestyle. Food consumption is an important part of this lifestyle and the social presentation of the self as what you eat has the potential of showing who you are in social settings. But what you eat also affects the perception of the body as well as the body in a directly physiological sense. Eating has also become politicized in that it can position an individual in relation to important ethical and moral questions. Monitoring the body and consumption habits has become a moral responsibility. As a result, people who eat too much or unhealthily feel guilt, while others see it as part of their lifestyle to rebel against the norm by not caring about the nutritional qualities or the quantity of their food.

Central to the idea that consumers are reflexively constructing a coherent lifestyle is that, today, people define themselves through the messages they transmit to others by the goods and practices they possess and exercise. To create and sustain a self-identity, consumers use appearances and actions in order to produce a coherent self-narrative. This narrative is in turn reflexively monitored over time and tested out under different circumstances. There are a seemingly endless number of choices that a person has to make and many of these choices, especially concerning food, are made among the huge selections of commodified products available on the market. Dealing with choice thus becomes critical, as little help is available as to which option should be selected. Increasingly, individuals are obliged to choose their identities, even a choice not to care about choosing is, and will be, interpreted as a choice. For many consumer goods this obligation to choose is indeed a risky business where the outcomes of one's choices will be scrutinized in the public eye. This is also true for food, but for food yet another factor is at play. The consumption of food is potentially risky since bad choices can lead to direct physical harm. The combination of these two risks, the risk of making a bad choice potentially harmful to one's self-identity, and the risk of making a bad choice for one's own health, makes food consumption a peculiar activity to study from theoretical points of departure. It should be noted from the very start, however, that there are no clear boundaries between the two risk areas from a consumer perspective. On the one hand, the choice of a set of alternatives regarding one's food consumption based on health is a choice that will be scrutinized in the public eye. On the other hand, choosing a lifestyle where one does not care at all about health rationales might, perhaps not surprisingly, have effects on one's health.

One way of dealing with these seemingly endless possibilities of choice is to adopt a set of guiding principles in the form of a lifestyle. In doing this, two things are accomplished. First, the 'consumption set' from which the consumer can choose is reduced by what is compatible with that lifestyle. Second, a blueprint for the narrative of the self is provided. The most vivid examples of lifestyle choices in food consumption are vegetarians and vegans who severely limit the consumption choices available. There are also other groups that provide guidelines such as religious groups and environmentalists. Despite the fact that adopting a certain lifestyle can reduce choice, consumers are still faced with a large number of choices on a day-to-day basis, especially for such a regularly occurring activity as food consumption.

When investigating how consumers view the connections between food and health it is clear that we must have a good understanding of how we are supposed to take care of our bodies. Thompson and Hirschman (1995) identified three primary sociocultural values and beliefs that follow from the ethic of control implicit in the dualistic concept of mind and body. The first one is the long-standing idealization of youthfulness. The striving to be young forever is often portrayed in the media, in commercials, and so on. In a sense, these strivings express a desire to transcend the limits of the body. The second value is the dualistic view of the individual as an essential self whose true identity is not constrained to the body in which it is housed. This is a prerequisite for the 'mind over body' ideology that has emerged. It is, to put it bluntly, the task of each individual's mind to make sure that the body is taken care of in the correct manner to prevent it from changing in unwanted ways and eventually deteriorating. To be able to exercise this type of control requires the body to be seen as a material object. Third is the ideal that knowledge not only allows the world to be controlled by the rational realm, but also liberates the transcendent self from various forces of nature. This logic is evidently present when considering the means available for exercising self-control over the body which is seen as a natural object to be controlled by reason, knowledge, and technology.

Throughout the Lutheran Western world there is also an ethic of self-control emphasizing a moralistic obligation to control the body through discipline and rationality (Greco, 1995). Rationality today encapsulates the use of knowledge for the productive purpose of managing the destructive forces of nature, especially on the body. In traditional modernist thought it is conventional to view knowledge and technology as empowering and liberating forces. In this view, the knowledge claims offered by scientific research are readily viewed as guidelines to which rational individuals should adhere (compare Giddens, 1991; Thompson and Hirschman, 1995). This technocratic legacy and the desire to control nature through technical intervention is prevalent in the medical and health-food industries, where a more fundamental change process is sought after. The ethic of self-control combined with the dominant protestant/Lutheran ethic leads to the notion that there should be no excess in eating or drinking, thus there is often some degree of asceticism combined with self-control (compare Giddens, 1991, p. 104). Obesity and bodily dysfunction have traditionally been regarded as the result of a weak mind. Throughout the history of Western culture, the state of one's body has been interpreted as a material sign of the moral character within (Thompson and Hirschman, 1995, p. 144). The pursuit of religious values often stipulates following certain kinds of physical regimes, such as asceticism, involving fasting and other forms of bodily depravation (Giddens, 1991, p. 62).

In a contemporary consumer culture, moral responsibility does not end with monitoring the physical appearance of the body. There is also a moral obligation to carefully control the foods, substances and environmental conditions to which the body is exposed (Thompson and Hirschman, 1995, p. 144). Contemporary cultural discourses, be they scientific texts or marketing promotions, that articulate an association between illness and personal responsibility, have engendered a form of self-understanding. It has become natural to experience feelings of guilt about eating incorrectly, not exercising and being overweight, and, reciprocally, to view these kinds of behaviour as signifying a lack of will, discipline and self-control (ibid.). Many consumer actions are motivated by culturally sanctioned knowledge claims regarding how consumption can be used in order to control the health and/or appearance of the body.

As has been pointed out in this section, there are a number of different rationales regarding what we should take care of and how. Numerous knowledge claims have been made by the medical and social sciences, as well as the food industry and the government. These are translated into a vast system of linguistic categories, bureaucratic documentation, normative prescriptions and the prohibition of certain activities, in sum what Giddens (1991) refers to as expert systems. There is an intricate network of cultural discourses at play concerning the authority of science and the social construction of 'good' foods, which can be freely consumed, and 'bad' foods which symbolize a threat to health. Over the past years great emphasis has been put on the connection between what we eat and the state of our health. Combining the ethic of self-control with the fact that there is an increasing emphasis on the connection between food and health has forced consumers to engage in what Beck (1992) calls nutritional engineering. This implies that, in order to eat a well-balanced diet, consumers must be very knowledgeable and up to date on what is healthy and not healthy and how these different entities should be combined. Beck sheds light on this phenomenon from the point of what should not be eaten, thus, *'Cooking and eating are becoming a kind of implicit food chemistry, a kind of witch's cauldron in reverse, meant to minimize harmful effects'* (ibid. p. 35). In this sense good food is defined negatively by the logic of risk avoidance. The aim is not so much to find positively good food as it is to avoid food that is potentially harmful.

For consumers it is virtually impossible to keep up with what is in vogue concerning food and health from day to day and from one source of information to another. The intricate web of contrasting expert systems is constantly moving and for a consumer to be able to uphold certain principles is not an easy task. In order to make sense of this stressful situation, and to achieve some degree of ease in their daily lives, consumers build up protective cocoons, which filter out potential dangers arising from the external world (Giddens, 1991). Although various issues may challenge the protective cocoons, such as the recent outbreak of BSE, they offer relative stability. The relative stability offered allows consumers to use heuristics in screening some of the information that can be used in deciding how to act. If we return to Beck's notion of risk avoidance and the notion that it is difficult for consumers to be continuously informed as to what is the most healthy solution at any time, one possible heuristic is to at least 'stay away from the bad stuff'.

HEALTH AND RISK

Screening of various media on a day-to-day basis provides sufficient evidence on the central role that health plays in contemporary society. Virtually every type of medium reports on health-related issues on a regular basis. Some of the more serious newspapers feature articles written by doctors and professors on topics such as the truth about the connection between food consumption and obesity (Rössner, 2000). *The Wall Street Journal* features a column called Health Journal every week in its Marketplace section, and *The New York Times* features a Health & Fitness Section in its Science Times section. Some tabloids, such as *Aftonbladet* in Sweden, also have special health sections, both in their printed edition and their on-line edition. These sections cover topics such as healthy fast food (Eriksson, 2000) and diet products that actually make you gain weight (Högfeldt, 2000). Also, both women's magazines, for example *Elle*, and men's magazines, for example *GQ*, feature articles on health-related issues and the topic is brought up frequently in both TV and radio shows. The topic is so frequently addressed that some general interest magazines, such as *U.S. News & World Report*, have started to write articles about how to assess the trustworthiness of so-called health information (Kulman, 2000). In a sense, things have come full circle – we not only find articles about health-related issues but also articles about how to interpret articles about health-related issues. During the past two or three years there has also been an explosion of web sites devoted to health-related issues. The number of sites has grown at such a speed that the so-called E-health industry has felt it necessary to make an attempt to regulate them and provide a 'seal of approval' for good sites (Landro, 2000).

Reading the material in these various sources provides a picture of the Western society as having a shared meaning that happiness is living a long and healthy life. This is often combined with the glorification of youthfulness and the seemingly careless, vivid, unproblematic lifestyle young people are able to live. This is true not only for the editorial material but can also be seen in commercial material. An illustration of this is a recent commercial for pension funds in Sweden (AMF-pension) that shows retirees around their seventies riding mountain bikes and boxing. The message in this, as well as numerous other commercials and magazine articles, is clearly that the goal is, in some sense, to survive life. The underlying assumption is that in order to have lived a successful life you have to arrive at retirement being healthy, wealthy and hungry for life. Even though the pension fund example given here is directed towards older people, health messages are also directed to younger people. Living a healthy life is an investment for the future. This is often a rather risky investment as it is uncertain whether even a radical change in health awareness will bring with it any short-term effects. As Pasi

Falk (1994) points out, the success of many so-called health products might be explained by the fact that their proposed healthiness cannot be disproven in the short term.

Consumers' Views on Health

In order to better understand how consumers think regarding the connections between food and health in their day-to-day lives a qualitative study has been undertaken. Utilizing a technique called ethnographic interviewing (McCracken, 1988; Spradley, 1979; Thompson and Hirschman, 1994), 20 consumers in the USA and 20 consumers in Sweden were interviewed. During the interviews a conversation was held about food in general with a specific focus on the interviewee's food consumption. The conversation was not focused specifically on health; instead the interviewer followed up on the different health-related topics that the interviewee spontaneously brought up. The logic during the analyses of the interviews was to uncover what the consumers have to take for granted to be able to speak about food in the way they did. By doing so, culturally shared values of the connections between food and health can be identified as the consumers reproduce available discourses during the interviews. In order to facilitate the presentation of the study the Greimassian square depicted in Figure 4.1 will be used.

The point of departure for Greimas' square model of the signification process is that there is a main contrariety between an assertion, 'healthy food' in this case, and its negation 'unhealthy food'. The definitions of these two categories stand in a definitional contrariety to each other; unhealthy food cannot exist without healthy food, and vice versa. In other words, the categories of healthy and unhealthy foods are merely symbols in an arbitrary relationship to a more or less abstract idea of healthiness. The meanings, in terms of healthiness, of different food products thus lie in their opposition to other products, which is consistent with semiotic theory (compare Mick, 1986).

Furthermore, the main assertions of healthy and unhealthy foods have a logical contradictory relationship to their negations, that is the categories 'not healthy food' and 'not unhealthy food'. Finally, the assertion is in a complimentary relationship to the negation of the non-assertion and consequently the non-assertion is in a similar complimentary relationship to the negation of the assertion (Askegaard and Güliz, 1997; Flosch, 1988). In this way, the two groups 'unhealthy food' and 'not healthy food' form a unit that stands for what is perceived by consumers as food that should be avoided, and 'healthy food' and 'not unhealthy food' form the other group. This might seem unnecessarily complicated at first, but we will present the different parts of the model, exemplifying them with quotes from the interviews, and show how this method dealing with the matter actually leads to a deeper understanding of consumers. It should be noted that when we discuss the interviews we do not in any way judge what the respondents said about what is healthy or unhealthy. The analysis is kept on an intratextual level and the contradictions addressed are those within a particular interview. Hence, the particular examples are idiosyncratic but the general reasoning is shared by the respondents.

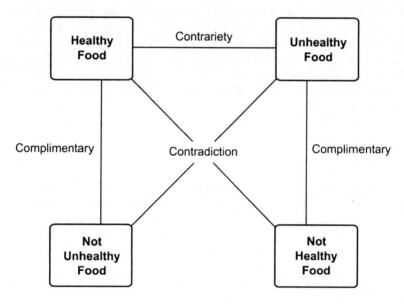

Figure 4.1 A discursive construction of the healthy and the unhealthy

Healthy Food and Unhealthy Food

There is plenty of material among the empirical data showing that the respondents think and speak of some products as healthy and others as unhealthy. What is interesting is that these categories were used mostly to categorize what should *ideally* be eaten or not. Healthy foods were spoken about as what was lacking in the diet or what the respondents thought they should be eating. In the following statement the interview had focused on the interviewee's poor eating habits and how she had been eating poorly for a while due to a hectic lifestyle. She explains that she is aware of what she should ideally be doing:

> I believe that I'm at least well aware of what is good to eat anyway, and what I
> ought to eat, and if I was a little bit more motivated right now I would probably
> prepare some good, plain food ('husmanskost')[5] and stuff (Swedish female, 26).

In this quote she talks about what she ought to eat and good, plain food is
brought up as the healthy contrariety to all the bad things she feels that she
has been eating. This respondent clearly shows that she has an ideal picture
of what she would like to consume, or more specifically what she would like
to desire. However, what she actually desires is something quite different,
which is actually the types of food she talks about as unhealthy. Consumers
tend to have an ideal picture of what they would like to consume that is not
consistent with what they actually do consume. They talk about what they
wish to desire, what is desirable. This differs from what they actually desire,
what they would want to eat if they didn't have to take the health
consequences (de Mooij, 1998).

The category of unhealthy foods is referred to when talking about foods
that are not eaten on a regular basis but rather on special occasions or as
'once in a while' treats. One respondent described how her eating habits
changed when she first moved away from home to attend university and
faced living on her own for the first time. At the beginning she tried to make
good food, like her mother. After a while she decided that she should not
pretend to be an adult, but instead indulged in all the things she desired,
thereby rebelling against her mother's strict cooking regime. Thus, she went
for what she herself referred to as the 'bad stuff':

> (I) got really sloppy, bought O'Boy[6], made toast and stuff, snabbmakaroner[7]
> (Swedish female, 26).

These foods are examples of what this particular respondent thinks of as
unhealthy foods that should be avoided. Other respondents talked about
unhealthy foods as fast food, potato crisps, sweets and chocolate and fried
foods. From the interviews we can see that the categories of healthy food and
unhealthy food are talked about in terms of what *ideally* should be eaten or
avoided. This poses an interesting question: If respondents are not regularly
eating either healthy or unhealthy food on a daily basis – what are they
actually eating?

Not Healthy Food and Not Unhealthy Food

The category of healthy food is talked about as something desirable,
something that the respondents would like to desire but do not really eat on a
regular basis. Consequently, it does not seem that the respondents are eating

what they perceive as healthy foods on a day-to-day basis. On the other hand, they did not seem to be careless 'daredevils' eating a diet consisting of what they deemed unhealthy foods. Rather, when the respondents talked about what they usually ate they talked about food such that it fitted with the category 'not unhealthy food' in Figure 4.1, that is the negation of the 'unhealthy food' category. This category consists of food that is not talked about in the positively healthy and idealized way that food in the 'healthy food' category was talked about. Neither does it consist of food that is talked about as something bad that should be avoided or eaten infrequently, as the food in the 'unhealthy food' category. When the respondents talked about the food they consumed on a day-to-day basis they did so in terms of the food being 'not too bad' or 'not unhealthy'. The respondents rarely talked about any positively healthy features but rather stressed the fact that they did contain too much fat, salt or some other ingredients that the respondents thought of as being harmful. Each respondent had a number of food features that they tried to avoid, as is expressed in the following quotes:

> Chicken is healthy since its not very fat, isn't it? And one shouldn't eat very much fried food and one really shouldn't, even though I really like salt, one shouldn't eat that either (Swedish female, 28).

> I try to avoid a lot of fried food and it's hard to avoid fried food, you know, 'cause fried hamburger, to make whatever you know. Like, I did make taco-salad this weekend and you have to fry the minced meat to make that. And I'm not really big on doing fried chicken, I'd rather roast it. And chicken is a big thing of ours. Pork chops is another thing, I try not to fry those, I try to roast them or grill them. I just, I do, I take fried foods into huge consideration (American female, 34).

On a daily basis the respondents strived towards eating food that they described as not unhealthy; for example, chicken was talked about as not unhealthy since it is not very fat and food that was not fried as not unhealthy because of precisely that – it was not fried. It becomes clear that the respondents did not eat the types of food they talked about as most beneficial for their health. The respondents often said that they were trying to eat healthier food – they tried to eat more of their 'desirables'. But for several different reasons they expressed a feeling of being stuck with having to eat things that were 'not too bad' for them, instead of things that were positively good. Thus, the 'not unhealthy food' category is related to the 'healthy food' category in that they are complementary, as depicted in Figure 4.1.

Together, these two categories make up the alternatives that are acceptable to eat: the ideal foods that the respondents say they ought to eat more of and the foods that they eat a lot of because they are, at least, not too bad. When the respondents talk about these different food products they differentiate between them in a number of ways. One of the ways that the positively healthy foods are distinguished from the not unhealthy foods is that when the respondents are talking about what they eat on a day-to-day basis they often say that they 'just' eat or drink this or that, as opposed to 'the real thing'.

> Well, usually just a cup of coffee. The kids you know, grab a doughnut some-where. It's all they've got! (American male, 32)

> I have become one of those sandwich-girls, maybe (I) cook some pasta. It is not like I'm standing there preparing casseroles or doing things in the oven (Swedish female, 26).

In both these excerpts it is clear that there is an ideal way of eating that they are not adhering to. In the first case, the interviewee has an ideal that you really should eat a proper breakfast consisting of cereal, a sandwich, orange juice, coffee, and so on. Instead he 'just' has a cup of coffee, which isn't bad in itself but which is not as good as he would like it to be. The woman in the second excerpt has an ideal of cooking a proper meal where you cook things in the oven or on top of the stove for a long time. But due to lack of time, interest and motivation she eats sandwiches or pasta instead of preparing what she sees as a proper meal.

The respondents mainly talked about their food consumption in terms of the complementary categories 'not unhealthy' and 'healthy' on the left side of Figure 4.1. However, they also talked about how they sometimes ate food that they described as being 'not healthy', that is the contradiction of the category of 'healthy food' in the figure. The food they defined as being 'not healthy' was so not because of the ingredients but rather because it was eaten at the wrong quantity or at the wrong time. Eating too much of a particular food could thus move that food from being either healthy or not unhealthy to being not healthy. One respondent gives the following description of when she goes home to eat her mother's cooking:

> or when you have been eating a lot, you know. You've been on vacation and just yummy, yummy, yummy! And then you think: No, that's it. Now it's time to go on a health-spree! (Swedish female, 28)

In this case the respondent does not describe the food itself as being unhealthy in any way. On the contrary, she later talks about her mother's cooking as being very healthy. What causes the respondent to talk about the food as being not healthy is the quantity, rather than something inherent in the food. This woman talks similarly about the food served at her workplace:

So there is always a vendor in there that we can go and buy something from. I try to stay away from them because that's way too much food. I don't wanna eat that much (American female, 52).

Again, it is not the food in itself but the quantity that is addressed. Similar tendencies can be seen for food that the respondents consume late at night or just before going to bed. As can be seen in the first quote, consumption of food described as being 'not healthy' is often accompanied by feelings of guilt, which can invoke some kind of compensatory behaviour such as a 'health-spree'. The category of 'not healthy food' should be seen as a complement to the category 'unhealthy food' on the right side of Figure 4.1; together these two categories make up the foods that the respondents try to avoid eating.

Intuitively, it might seem obvious that consumers would strive towards eating the healthiest foods available. But these interviews suggest that Ulrich Beck is quite right when he talks about nutritional engineering as a *'a witch's cauldron in reverse, meant to minimize harmful effects'* (Beck, 1992, p. 35) as was mentioned above in Chapter 1 (Consumers' Changing Habits). What he is referring to is that consumers are trying to put together a diet that does not consist of anything harmful. Clearly, on a day-to-day basis consumers define good food negatively by the logic of risk avoidance. The aim is not so much to find positively healthy food products as to avoid the bad ones. One potential explanation of this that was revealed in the interviews was that there is such a plethora of claims regarding what is healthy and what is not that it is impossible to 'keep up'. Every week something new is portrayed as being the ultimate elixir of life and many expressed a disbelief in any one thing being the ultimate solution. Rather, they tried to keep up with what was 'risky' as that posed a more immediate threat to their well-being. The result was that most respondents tried to steer clear of some things that they thought were harmful. Giddens describes this as individuals constructing protective cocoons around themselves. To be able to get on with their lives without worrying too much, they are forced to screen out many of the messages and only listen to a few. The rest of the messages bounce off the protective cocoon (Giddens, 1991). Another strategy used was to delegate responsibility to someone else by stating that if any particular food product was really as dangerous as the tabloids were saying, it would not be allowed on the shelves in the supermarket.

The notion that healthiness in food can be seen as an absence of risk fits well with Beck's notion of the risk society where 'the gain in power from techno-economic "progress" is being increasingly overshadowed by the production of risks' (Beck, 1992, p. 23). An example that came out strongly in the Swedish sample was the recent outbreak of BSE. This led most consumers to choose Swedish meat products rather than foreign ones, not because the Swedish products were seen as positively healthy but because they were at least not unhealthy. It should be noted that there was considerable confusion regarding how these precautions towards BSE should be applied as is illustrated by this quote:

> Yes, I do think quite a bit about it [BSE] it really made me change how I think when I go shopping. Now I always buy Swedish pork chops (Swedish male, 46).

Out of Control

From the discussion above we can draw the conclusion that the category of 'healthy foods' is used as an idealized category of what the respondents would like their food consumption to be. The consumers were more inclined to eat food that they described as 'not unhealthy' or even 'unhealthy'. The respondents were very aware of the debate on the connection between the state of our health and the food we eat that can be found daily in various types of media. They were also aware of the possible consequences of not adhering to the messages being disseminated, and even admitted that they felt a moral obligation to take better care of themselves.

Why is it then that consumers are not able to live up to the ideal standards they set for themselves? The most prominent theme in the interviews that helps us answer this question is that the consumers felt that they were not the ones in control of the situation. They knew what to do, how to do it, what would happen if they didn't do it, and so on, but for reasons beyond their control they could not act according to their conviction. An example is a woman who preferred to cook at home since she felt that this was the best way to keep the family together. Unfortunately, for reasons beyond her control she could not cook at home as often as she liked:

> But we eat out quite a bit, just because there are just three of us and it's so hard to cook for just three people so we find ourselves eating out a lot more than we eat here (American female, 34).

Not only was she forced to jeopardize the social aspects of the family meal, but when they were eating out she also felt that the nutritional quality of the meals deteriorated:

> But that's the, you know, it's almost like a two-part story, because when we eat here [at home] I cook healthy meals but when we eat out, that's not healthy! It's so unhealthy eating out! (American female, 34)

This woman thus put the blame for not acting according to her convictions on the size of her family. Considering the fact that we have more single households today than ever before poses an interesting question regarding how all these households are to eat. There were other examples where the respondents described feelings of powerlessness due to more internal factors. The fact that we as humans are creatures of habit is well documented, but it seems that the power of this is often underplayed, as illustrated by the following quote:

> colleagues of mine, my age or a little bit older having by-pass surgery, developing diabetes, some of those things and I think: 'Oh Jees.' you know, you know that could be me someday. So I do think about that a little bit more and that seems to be happening more frequently, or, hmm, or you know, you pick up the paper and you see somebody your own age or younger dying of a heart attack or something. It hasn't caused me to really change, but I think: 'Oh gosh, I should be doing this or I shouldn't be doing that.' I think I've had more thoughts like that too, hmm, but it, but I anticipate that it probably, in my case it will probably take something to actually to happen and then, I hope it's not too severe (American male, 52).

This quote clearly shows that consumers are not lacking information about what they should do and how they should do it. Furthermore, the respondent is painfully aware of the potential consequences of not doing what he believes he should. The respondents commonly describe the feeling of not being able to resist uncontrollable urges:

> If there is a doughnut or a roll in lie of sight it has to be consumed and I don't give a rip (American male, 32).

Again, we see that this particular respondent is well aware of the fact that he should not eat this particular doughnut or roll. He describes how he tries to shy away from situations in which he is exposed to foods that he does not want to consume. But, as he explains in the quote, if it comes into his view he does not have a choice.

One final type of justification made by the respondents is based on the implicit syntax present in the composition of meals. Certain types of food products go together with certain other types of products and one cannot be served without the other. This respondent had spoken at length about how good she thought it was to cook hamburgers on the barbecue since you could buy lean beef and you didn't have to add any cooking fat. But despite this, she could not serve a healthy meal:

> Because obviously with the little ones you have to have French fries. You know, if you're having hamburgers from the barbecue you got to have French fries to go with it.
> Interviewer: That's probably true.

But the whole house just smells like fried foods and I just don't enjoy that smell. It's like Grease City (American female, 32).

There were several other examples of respondents giving voice to being caught in the syntactical trap, for example, having to serve butter with otherwise healthy broccoli. The common theme of all the justifications made was that consumers tended to place the responsibility for their behaviour outside of their control. By doing this, they did not have to feel guilty about not living up to their own proposed standards. As has been proposed by Giddens, in late modernity, the knowledge claims offered by scientific research are readily viewed as guidelines. These guidelines can be disregarded, however, if consumers do not feel that they can act according to the guidelines.

SUMMARY

Throughout this chapter we have tried to demonstrate a number of issues related to healthy eating. Our findings are summarized below:

- Health and healthy foods are important and play a key role in con-temporary society. Consumers are becoming more aware and interested in these issues; the media are focusing on them and companies are launching and relaunching products that cater to health-aware markets.
- When studying consumers, the concept of high-value-added products has to be dealt with carefully in order not to impose a producer perspec-tive on the consumers. This becomes even more important regarding products where the added value is health related. If we want to under-stand consumers it has to be recognized that they often have ambivalent attitudes towards what they consider to be added value.
- There are many connections between consumers' food consumption and their identity. Eating habits form an important part of consumers' con-struction of a coherent narrative of the self. It has become increasingly important over recent years to actively care for one's body as physical well-being is emphasized as an important part of being successful.
- The role of food as both a potential risk and a potential means of achieving and maintaining healthiness is stressed in all sorts of media. Consumers are fed with these messages to the extent that a risk society is created in which everything is measured in terms of its potential of avoiding or posing risks.

Having laid this fundament, an alternative way of looking at consumers' views on the connections between health and food is proposed. This alternative view is based on the consumers' own use of the concepts of healthy and unhealthy foods and uncovers some of the ambivalence towards the issue.

- The categories of healthy and unhealthy foods were used as ideal types of what should and should not be eaten.
- Consumers talked about the food they ate on a daily basis as being 'not unhealthy'. They thus exhibited the kind of risk avoidance logic suggested by Beck (1992, p. 192).
- Food that normally belonged to the categories 'healthy foods' or 'not unhealthy foods' could be moved to the category 'not healthy foods' if eaten at the wrong time or in the wrong quantity. This illustrates the ephemeral character of the system.
- An implicit norm regarding what should be eaten seemed to be in effect, as consumers felt obliged to justify their deviation from this norm. They did so by explaining that the consumption of foods that they deemed less than optimal was outside their control.

This dynamic character of consumers' use of the concept of healthiness and unhealthiness with regard to food has to be recognized by companies aspiring to be successful on the market. It is clear that companies intending to cater to the market for healthy foods could gain an edge if they gave consumers a sense of regaining control over their own life. This has to be done while recognizing that traditional compositions of meals are not easily changed.

NOTES

1. This chapter is based on Jacob Östberg's doctoral thesis, "Food Consumption in Risk Society" (forthcoming 2003).
2. Other added values may be convenience, ethical qualities, or specific product quality guarantees.
3. http://www.becel.nu
4. In this book, Chapter 1, 'From Commodities to High-value-added Products'.
5. Husmanskost translates into 'homely fare' or 'good, plain food' but stands for something specific in the Swedish cuisine so we chose to use the Swedish term.
6. O'Boy is a Swedish brand of chocolate powder for milk.
7. Snabbmakaroner is a quick-cooking macaroni that only takes three minutes to cook. It has come to symbolize the stereotypical student diet, quick-cooking macaroni and ketchup.

5.   The Öresund Food Cluster

In Chapter 6 we present the key empirical findings of the study, and we introduce the three in-depth longitudinal case studies. Since all three cases originate from the same innovation cluster, we will start with a short description and analysis of the Öresund food cluster. We will present the embeddedness of the cases, and also relate the character of the cluster to that of other food clusters.

The Öresund region – Denmark and Scania in southern Sweden – is today one of the fastest developing food clusters in Europe. The cluster area is officially appointed as a highly prioritized area by both the Swedish and Danish Governments. The area is supported by the governments of the two countries regarding research, education and infrastructure. This, together with the combination of large international companies, small innovative companies, strong academic centres, professional research institutions and competitive support organizations, creates a combination of resources that can make the Öresund cluster a centre of excellence in food.

Denmark has always been a large food producer with high export volumes. A recent benchmarking study shows that, in relative terms, Denmark exports about three times more agricultural and food products than any other country in the world. The very south of Sweden – Scania – is the centre for Sweden's food industry with about 45 per cent of the food industry being located in this area.

All sectors of the food business area are found here, covering the total chain from plate to plough. Primary production, the food-processing industry, packaging, production machinery, distribution, warehousing and quality control can be found in the cluster as well as competence for product and process development, both in industry and academia.

Today the food cluster is a part of the European market. The natural and traditional market is northern Europe from the UK to Russia. And the cluster dominates the Scandinavian food market. Due to the high concentration of retailers and wholesalers in the area and the well-developed distribution system, a company located in the Öresund area can, by working with a handful of customers and supporting companies, serve almost all of the 23 million consumers in Scandinavia and the 100–200 million in the Baltic rim.

The Baltic states offer good market potential and an expanding food market parallel with the rising living standards and changing consumer patterns.

Due to the breadth and depth of the industries in the cluster it is easy for foreign investors to establish themselves in the region and be able to participate in all the R & D activities of the food cluster. Several research parks are to be found in the area. Companies are engaged in co-operation in all parts of the industry and with academia.

The combination of multinational companies, small innovative companies, cutting-edge academic centres, professional research institutions, competitive support organizations and co-operative authorities forms the key resource for the Öresund food cluster.

UNIQUE RESOURCES IN THE CLUSTER

The Öresund region is fifth in the league of high-density R&D areas in the European Union. It provides a marketplace for business and research co-operation.[1] The Öresund region has no less than 11 universities with a total of 120 000 students. The programme bringing the universities together has been dubbed the Öresund University.

The Öresund University is a voluntary co-operation between universities on both sides of the Öresund sound. The participating universities and institutes are:

- Lund University (Scandinavia's largest establishment for higher education and research with over 38,000 students),
- The University of Copenhagen, Technical University of Denmark,
- The Copenhagen Business School,
- The Royal Veterinary and Agricultural University,
- The Swedish University of Agricultural Science, Alnarp,
- The Royal Danish School of Educational Studies,
- The Royal Danish School of Pharmacy,
- Roskilde University,
- Malmö University College, and
- The Royal School of Library and Information Science.

Denmark and Sweden are among the most productive societies in terms of scientific research output per capita, as Sweden is ranked number 3 and Denmark number 6. Viewed in a regional perspective the highest concentration of scientific output in the Scandinavian countries is produced in the Öresund region. Thus the Öresund region is ranked as number 4 after

London, Paris and Moscow, as the most productive region in Europe regarding scientific research measured as the number of published publications per capita.[2]

One finds education and research concerning food at Lund University, especially at the Lund Institute of Technology of Technology (LTH), at the School of Economics and Management and the Swedish University of Agricultural Science, Alnarp (SLU) on the Swedish side. On the Danish side, the leading universities in this field are The Royal Veterinary and Agricultural University and the Technical University of Denmark. Research in the region covers all kinds of scientific knowledge in the food chain from plough to plate as well as scientific knowledge in industries related to and supporting the food chain.

In addition to the universities, a number of organizations have been created to facilitate the exchange of R&D between universities and the food industry. In the Öresund cluster we can identify 12 research organizations dedicated to R&D in the food sector and 16 organizations that have as their mission to create and support co-operation between the food industry and the universities. These are presented in a list as an appendix to this chapter. This list illustrates *that dynamic innovation clusters produce several organizations with unique resources directed at key areas of competence for this food innovation cluster.* The list also illustrates the fact that such *specialized organizations must be established with a long-term perspective. It takes many years to build up a cluster with resources that are unique and internal to the cluster, while they are external to the companies working in the cluster.*

Turning our attention to *R & D in companies*, the Öresund region has a strong position in the food branch. Many Swedish and Danish food companies have located their R&D centres in this region, as have packaging, processing and distribution plants. It is beyond the scope of this book to present a list of all these companies, but they are numerous and several of them are world-class actors, both in food and in related and supporting industries.

With the empirical material already presented as a base, we can conclude that the Öresund food cluster contains the factors and qualities needed to work as a dynamic innovation cluster. If we relate the empirical data to the GEM model of Paquet and de la Motte we find that the necessary parts are put in place.

Groundings (Supply determinants)

- *Resources*: Several unique resources. Unique knowledge. Some world class resources.
- *Infrastructure*: Well developed. Driven by the industry and supported by two national governments as well as the regional government in Scania.

Enterprises (Structural determinants)

- *Supplier and related industries*: Several world class companies in packaging, ingredients, equipment, freezing and transportation.
- *Firm structure and strategies*: Outspoken development ambitions. Coherent ambitions regarding international competition and development.

Markets (Demand determinants)

- *Local markets*: Local markets with demanding consumers in specialized areas of development like health, food safety, ethical food, organic food and animal welfare. However local markets offer too small volumes for profitable development, production and sales of high-value-added niche products. Access to external markets is necessary.
- *Access to external markets*: Most of the key players in the Öresund region are active in the European and Baltic markets – offering quantity as well as refined high-value-added products. The industry is fragmented, and many companies still have a regional or national approach (de la Motte and Paquet, 1998, pp. 58–59).

We can also be more specific in the analysis of the 'Öresund food cluster'. using the analysis dimensions developed by Enright (2000b). Using these, the outcome is as follows.

Geographic scope. Approximately half of Swedish agricultural production is located in the southern part of Sweden. Other industrial and agricultural production and development areas, for example in the west and in the Linköping and Uppsala areas, are linked to the Öresund cluster through various kinds of networks. A large part of the R&D activities are performed in the Öresund area. On the Danish side, many of the corporate headquarters as well as R&D functions are located within the region, which in principle covers most of Denmark.

Density refers to the number and the economic importance of the businesses in the cluster. The number and importance of the actors are key factors for the two nations. Strong exporting companies are located within the Öresund cluster.

Width refers to the number of horizontally related industries in the cluster. Here we find the food cluster combined with related and supporting world-class industries in packaging, ingredients, marketing and transportation. High-class research in biotechnology and information and communication technology is to be found in the region. This creates opportunities for innovation in the borderland between industries.

Activity base refers to the number and nature of activities in the value-added chain. How much of core strategy is decided in the cluster? How active are the developers and innovators in marketing and corporate co-ordination in the region? The region is interesting because unique areas of competence are available; they are present in the whole value-added chain and in many related and supporting industries. A large number of innovation projects have been launched and many have been successful.

Depth refers to the extent of vertically related industries in a cluster. The whole value-added chain from plant engineering and primary production to food production and food services is present in the cluster. Retailing and food distribution companies are present in the cluster, but some key development functions must be sought in other locations. The marketing and R&D functions are well developed, however.

Growth potential is limited in the traditional food business based on bulk production. In functional foods, convenience food and food services the growth potential is clearly higher. The same positive growth situation is apparent for organic food and certain high-quality products and services.

Innovative capability. The ability of the cluster to generate important innovations in products, processes, design, marketing, logistics and management has been demonstrated in innovation processes resulting in various kinds of functional food products and in process innovations in the areas of traceability and quality control in the value-added chain. In related industries we also see innovations in, for example. packaging, ingredients and freezing technology.

Industrial organization. There is a tradition of good co-operation between industry and regional authorities in Scania – and in the Danish case between national government and research institutions. Several organizations and knowledge webs have been developed and the dynamic interaction is lively. According to a recent British study (Mellentine et al., 2001) the Scanian ability to incorporate interaction and trust in the competitive dynamics is among the best in the world.

Co-ordination mechanisms. The co-ordination of activities is basically non-hierarchical, based on both single-client and multi-client relations between research institutions, specialized consultants and the industry.

This means that the conditions for innovative dynamics are present in the cluster. The main characteristics of the Öresund food cluster are its breadth and depth. The region's history as the food centre of two nations explains the representation of almost all sectors in the food industry and supporting industries. In some areas, the actors have grown and developed from being the leading companies in Sweden and Denmark to large and/or leading actors in the European and world markets. The depth of the food industry in this region can be explained by the fact that is has proven necessary for the food industry in the Scandinavian countries to develop special areas of competence within agricultural research and the food industry as well as in supply and distribution systems in order to become competitive on international markets.

We have observed an interesting development in the Öresund food cluster. The mobility of highly qualified professionals is increasing. From interviews in small innovative companies we learned that several top-quality managers and researchers have decided to move from large companies to new innovative firms. Quite a few are willing to trade the security and status of the large organization for a position with higher risk in small innovative companies. The reasons behind these moves are related to the opportunity to be an important part of an exciting development, to have more control, less structure and a greater possibility to share the profits.

For these small companies this means that they acquire substantial experience and know-how as well as know-who, represented by the professional networks of their new top-notch managers. This kind of recruitment can be compared with a small football club recruiting star players from the Champions' League. Their ability to succeed increases substantially.

This is one advantage for the individual company provided by the cluster. The cluster also offers advantages in that the close working environment surrounding the company offers a multitude of resources and areas of competence, external to the company but internal to the cluster. In addition, the cluster offers a supporting infrastructure and development visions driven by important entrepreneurs. These resources, which are specific to the cluster, make it a better place for business development than at other locations without a critical mass of resources, competent people and strategic visions. Clusters have at least three important effects on the development and innovation process:

- *The productivity increases.* The individual company can act as if they had scale economies in a number of areas of competence and technology without investing in them. Outsourcing parts of the development process is cost-efficient and maintains flexibility.

- *The development speed and intensity increase.* Simultaneous use of many development arenas and well co-ordinated activities can shorten the time from idea to finished product, service or concept.
- *New companies are created.* The cluster creates opportunities for simultaneous competition and co-operation between a number of large and small companies. From this, the seeds for the creation of new business concepts will grow and create new species of companies, resulting from unique combinations of resources (Porter, 1998c, Nov–Dec).

THE ÖRESUND FOOD CLUSTER IN AN INTERNATIONAL PERSPECTIVE

All clusters are in international competition. In order to make a meaningful analysis of the Öresund food cluster, we must make international comparisons. We will here make short comparisons with other European food clusters and to the food clusters of the USA.

Important European Food Clusters

In order to put the Öresund cluster in perspective, we will refer to other important food clusters in Europe. In earlier benchmarking studies (Denrell, 2000; Mellentine et al., 2002), the following clusters have been identified: the Netherlands, the southeast of England, Emilia-Romagna, Brittany, Languedoc-Rousillon, Catalonia, Aragon and Finland.

The Netherlands, Wageningen
Holland is the largest food cluster considering criteria such as complexity and size of the industry, primary production and R&D. Compared with the Öresund region the Dutch food industry's turnover is twice that of the Öresund region. Furthermore, the Netherlands has access to a larger European market and enjoys a well-developed infrastructure. The Dutch Government has declared food a priority issue.

In the Netherlands, Wageningen is the official centre of the food science cluster. All types of food-related research institutes are located in Wageningen. The Dutch Government and industry have also, together, started the Wageningen Centre of Food Sciences, which is striving to become a centre of excellence.

Italy, Emilia-Romagna

The food cluster in the Emilia-Romagna region in Italy is characterized by a very large number of small and medium-sized companies operating in the food industry as well as in the manufacturing of machinery, particularly packaging machines. The vast majority of the food companies are specialized within a single product category, for instance, Parma ham. The food industry manufactures 15 products, which are protected by the EU 'doc' names, such as Prosciutto di Parma, Parmigiano Reggiano cheese, Borgotaro mushrooms, Brisighella olive oil, Valpadana Provolone cheese and so on.

The combination of the many small and medium-sized companies and rather few large companies makes the Emilia-Romagna region very dynamic. Over the last few years, the regional economy has seen a progressive internationalization of the food production.

France

In France, food has always been in focus. Universities and research institutions are located all over France as are food processing companies. Traditionally, French food policy is decided in Paris, but in some regions we find important regional food clusters. The two most important regions for food production are Brittany and Languedoc-Roussillon.

Brittany Agriculture in Brittany is focused on livestock forming the basis for extensive dairy, meat and feed industries. Brittany is host to 15 per cent of the French food industry. The region has a well-developed infrastructure and a network of research institutions connected with agriculture, fisheries, food technology and safety. There is some production of organic food and the use of biotechnology is expanding.

Languedoc-Roussillon The region produces a wide range of food, wine, seafood and highly processed food products. The region's food industry enjoys the highest growth rate in the French food industry, and the food industry is the most important industry in the region. Combined with the highly developed infrastructure, the region could function as a hub for the Mediterranean region. The region has a wide range of universities and research facilities within agriculture, fisheries and food technology. The food sector in Languedoc-Roussillon is officially supported. The region has a large research capacity with networks of both domestic and foreign institutions

Spain

In Spain, Catalonia and Aragon are the most important regions regarding the food industry and food research facilities.

Catalonia   The food industry in Catalonia produces a wide range of products and the region is the most important in Spain for agriculture. Catalonia accounts for more than 20 per cent of the Spanish food industry's production. The food industry in Catalonia is, to a large extent, focused on the domestic market.

Aragon   This region is characterized by an innovative and dynamic food industry with the highest export rates in Spain. The main export markets are France, Germany and the UK. Aragon accounts for less than 10 per cent of the Spanish food industry and produces mainly meat and fruit. Research facilities are focused on agriculture.

The southeast of England, Reading

The government in the UK has not officially declared any region a food cluster, but most food research is located in Reading in the south-east region of England. Many of the largest European food companies and support industries are also found in the south-east region. The food companies in this region have access to the large European food market. They also have a very competitive home market, where retailers have a very strong position, which has led to a dynamic environment for new small food companies and a high development potential for the region.

Finland

In Finland the agricultural production and the food industry is located in the south-western areas. In the national programme to enhance international competitiveness, Finland's geographic location, clean environment, dramatic seasonal changes and production based on family holdings are identified as the basis for pure, high-quality food and agricultural products. The ambition is to produce quality rather than quantity.[3] The parties in the entire food production chain have together devised a national quality strategy for the production of foodstuffs focusing on safety, reliability and openness. The goal is that by 2006 systematic quality assurance, including certifiable systems, will cover all farms and agricultural production, as well as the food industry, trade and transportation in Finland.

   This national ambition is coupled to considerable R&D investments in leading Finnish food companies. Important innovations have already been launched on the functional foods market and within the areas defined by the national quality programme, some important dynamic interactions indicate a continued and extended role for the Finnish food industry in the quality segment.

USA – Are Regional Research Clusters Dissolving?

In our empirical studies it was also our ambition to compare the innovation dynamics in the Öresund food cluster with the conditions in the food cluster and the related biotechnology cluster in the north-eastern part of the USA. There we find some interesting companies and we had anticipated inter-actions between these companies and the biotech cluster around Boston. We found some industry – academy co-operation and some interaction between food companies and venture capital companies. However, apart from the wine industry in the Napa Valley, the commercial, were, to a large extent, spread out over many parts of the USA.

During the last 20 years, but particularly the last 10 years, the food sector has gone through a massive consolidation process resulting in most food products in each category at retail now being sold by two to five mega companies; over 60 per cent of all grocery products are now sold at retail by 25 companies, with further concentration quite possible. There is a common belief that consumer food product companies with sales under US$ 1 billion per year will not survive in the USA. The mega companies often move their research out of clusters and now network nationwide, and even inter-nationally, and many also have a 'go-it-alone' strategy.

The same consolidation has been going on in both input industries and in retail. Both these sectors have found it more economical to work with fewer big food companies and input suppliers. Financial and advertising activities as well as government relations have migrated out of the cluster area or were never there in the US system. For example, advertising is predominantly located in New York; finance in a few major cities such as New York, Chicago and Washington, while Washington, DC is home to the majority of trade associations, 20 or more.

Even the major governmental food laboratories are now located regionally in four places in the country to serve the crops in that part of the USA. Also the Federal Government has withdrawn from post-harvest research. Land grant schools, that is, State Universities, are still involved in the R&D activities, but the mega companies are decreasing in their inter-actions. Major innovation is increasingly coming from the input industries – processing and ingredients – which interact and service industry on a national basis for profitability and rapid transfer of innovations to the food industry.

There is also a national network of consulting laboratories used by major companies for product development, and so on. Universities are complaining about the lack of contact with major companies. Two research directors informed us that it is management policy to avoid such contacts, as they believe that the university learns more than the company benefits. They prefer the work to be done at consulting laboratories where they own and have control over the results. This should, of course, be seen against the background that the large US food companies have research budgets of US$70–200 million per year and can tap into other international research centres around the world.

Also major companies tend to rely on world famous laboratories nationally and around the world and have no allegiance to a local cluster. There are still some very strong clusters in high-technological arenas and in such commodities as wine in California, but we see few other examples still functioning.

The Florida citrus juice cluster is said to be a thing of the past with regard to innovation. The Florida citrus industry which had a strong cluster through the 1980s has experienced the following: Coca-Cola's Minute Maid moved their laboratory to Houston, Texas from Florida; Ocean Spray, which is the largest grapefruit juice company in the USA, carries out its product development in New England and has very little to do with Florida except scouring fruit, and Pepsi's Tropicana is still in Florida but does not interact with the rest of the citrus industry in Florida. These are the companies involved in innovation in citrus juices, now outside the previous cluster, and they control a large part of the citrus market.[4]

Are the US clusters dissolving or are they expanding geographically due to improved communications through the Internet? Is the tradition concerning co-operation between commercial companies and universities changing? Are the companies so huge that they can carry out all necessary R&D activities within their own organizations? This picture of the USA leads to more questions than answers. It is even more surprising as we know that multinational food companies work actively in European food clusters and that clusters have been discovered by a number of other industries in practically every part of the world. However, we conclude that food research in the USA is more of a bilateral nature between large companies and specific university researchers. We see less co-operation between large and small companies in clusters. Regarding venture capital, we learned from our interviews that state funding for entrepreneurs is much less common. Personal networks are vitally important for small entrepreneurs.

We would like to comment, however, that R&D has, from a historical perspective, not been a very strong part of the food-producing industry in the USA. Larger investments have been made in R&D in grain cultivation and plant breeding as well as at the other end of the value-added chain – retailing and distribution. There is currently rapidly increasing interest in the use of new technology in the food-producing industry. Perhaps companies in the USA and in Europe have chosen different strategies for interaction with government-funded research organizations such as universities.

INTERNATIONAL FUNCTIONAL FOOD CENTRES: BENCHMARKING OF BEST PRACTICES

Another way to put the Öresund food cluster into perspective is to make an international benchmark in one important part of the cluster. Such a benchmarking study has been performed for functional foods and we use it here to illustrate the strengths and weaknesses in one key area of the Öresund food cluster. The functional foods cluster in southern Sweden has been compared with Finland, the Wageningen area in the Netherlands, the Saskatchewan Nutraceutical Network in Canada, Smart Centre Australia, New Zealand, Norwich in the UK, Ireland and Aarhus in Denmark. In this study, carried out for Scottish Enterprise, Julian Mellentine[5] arrives at the conclusion that the functional foods cluster in southern Sweden is the strongest and most dynamic of the nine development areas in the study.

The strengths and weaknesses of the cluster are described in his report in the following way:

Strengths

- Strong science and technology base with strong links between industry and technology/university centres.
- New product development often results from university-led rather than company-led initiatives.
- Highly inventive and innovative individuals in science and technologies.
- Informal but clear and widely shared strategic vision.
- Physical proximity of cluster participants.
- Strong involvement of stakeholders of all types.
- Innovations utilize both agricultural base and wider science base.
- Strong home market to experiment in and many innovations now on the supermarket shelf.
- Significant experience in successfully creating foods with health benefits.
- Health-aware consumers after many years of public health policy on diet and health. (For example, 'healthy eating' foods are defined as those which meet a national standard, and therefore carry the green 'keyhole symbol'. In the UK by contrast, healthy eating symbols vary widely from one retailer to another.)
- Long-term government support and funding of basic research to build up in-depth expertise and to commercialize science.
- Access to private investment capital.
- Very active informal network.

- Many successes.
- Growing international focus.
- Growing focus on competitive environment

Weaknesses

- The emergence of some universities and regions as would-be players in functional foods (see below) threatens to undermine and dilute Lund's leadership. National co-ordination would help optimize functional food activity, but the 'national centre' has been located in Gothenburg, some distance from Lund, which means that some in Lund question its legitimacy and purpose. This issue needs to be resolved.
- Lack of leadership to drive future development. (The National Centre of Excellence is not seen as a leader in Lund.)
- Shortfalls in international marketing and business development have caused some international consumer product launches to fall short of expectation. However it is clear that these issues are being addressed to a greater or lesser extent by many companies.[6]

The international benchmarking results for eight of the clusters that have been compared are summarized in Table 5.1. These results from an independent international observer confirm the results of our own studies. For this book it is not essential to discuss the details. The main conclusion is, however, important. The Öresund cluster contains all the essential qualities needed for an efficient innovation activity inside and between the corporations, between business and research and between public and private actors. This embeddedness for the innovation process is important in order to understand the drivers and key factors behind success or failure in the cases that we have studied. We should also note that this study was carried out with specific focus on functional foods. The fact that the cluster dynamics functions well will also have a positive effect on innovation projects in other areas that can benefit from the interactions between research and industry, between small and large companies and between public and private actors.

Table 5.1 International benchmarking of functional food clusters

Benchmark	Finland	Sweden	Netherlands	Canada	Australia	New Zealand	UK
Strong Science	Yes	Yes	Yes	Yes	Yes	Yes	Yes
SME-friendly	Yes, strong SME involvement	Yes, strong SME involvement	No	Yes, strong SME involvement	Yes	Yes	Not yet
Broad food and health knowledge	Yes	Yes	No	No	Yes	No	No
Clear strategy	?	Yes	Yes	Yes	Yes	No	Yes
Identifiable leadership	No	No	Yes	Yes	Yes	No	Yes
Degree of stakeholder participation	High	High	Small defined group of major companies	High participation from a wide constituency	In development but shows sign of being high	Small group	In development but a small constituency
Near market activity	Yes, very high	Yes, very high	No	Yes, very high	Not yet	Yes	Not yet
Successful commercialization of consumer products	Yes	Yes	No	No	Not yet	Yes	Not yet
Successful commercialization of ingredients	Yes, including one world leader	Yes	No	Yes	Not yet	Not yet	Not yet
International perspective	Yes	Yes	Yes, in science only	Yes	Yes	Some	Yes
Orientation to competitive environment	Yes	Yes	No	Yes	Yes	Limited	Yes
Public health dialogue	Yes	Yes	No	No	Yes	No	No
Availability of finance	Yes from government but major shortage of private finance	Yes, from funding bodies and private sources	Yes, from Dutch government and stake holders	Yes, from funding bodies and private sources	Yes, from funding bodies and private sources	No, links are informal, with no government participation	Yes from government and private sources

Source: The Centre for Food & Health Studies, February 2002.

APPENDIX: THE ÖRESUND FOOD CLUSTER RESOURCE AND COMPETENCE LIST

Swedish Institute for Food and Biotechnology (SIK) is an industrial research institute with the objective of strengthening the competitiveness of the food and biotechnological industries.

The Danish Institute of Agricultural Sciences (Foulum). This research institute is part of the Danish Ministry of Agriculture and Food. Its aims are to pursue research on crop production, livestock production and the use of technology in agriculture.

The Danish Meat Research Institute (DFI). This institute's purpose is to contribute to the enhancement of the competitiveness of the Danish meat industry, particularly for beef and pork.

The Danish Dairy Research Foundation co-ordinates research within dairy technology and joint projects between research institutions and the dairy industry.

The Danish Institute for Biotechnology (BI) carries out research on food, biotechnology and agro industries. The focus is on pure and safe products, hygiene in food production, effective production processes and analysis.

The Danish Institute of Technology (DTI). In one of the departments, research is concentrated on packaging materials and methods as well as logistics technology for food and pharmaceutical products.

The Danish Institute of Agricultural and Fisheries Economics. The aim of the institute is to carry out research, and to give advice on issues concerned with agriculture and fisheries.

The Danish Institute for Fisheries Technology and Aquaculture is a consultancy organization and partner for the fishery and aquaculture sectors and their associated industries.

Statens Serum Institut (SSI) maintains its position as a leading and internationally recognized research institute in its main areas of competence, microbiology and immunology, through basic and applied research in these fields.

Danish Veterinary Laboratory (DVL) aims at preventing and controlling zoonosis in order to enhance the safety and health benefits of food products. Other research areas include developing animal-friendly production methods, for example, providing information on the appropriate use of antibiotics in order to reduce resistance.

The Danish Veterinary and Food Administration is part of the Danish Ministry of Food and consists of two institutes related to food research, the Institute for Food Safety and Toxicology and the Institute of Food Research and Nutrition.

Risö National Laboratory in Denmark carries out research aimed at developing environmentally friendly production methods for agriculture and the food industry, and on the symbiosis between plants and micro-organisms.

On both of the sides of the Öresund there are organizations that work to establish co-operation between industry and academia. The list below provides a short summary of the major organizations in the region, starting with the Danish organizations.

The Danish Research and Development Programme for Food Technology (FÖTEK) dates back to 1990 and is now in its third period. The present programme covers the period 1998–2001 and provides financing from public funds. The budget for the entire period is DKK356 million. The programme is administered by the Ministry of Food and the Ministry of Research. The aim is to promote a total view of food production and to establish a co-ordinated effort for primary produce, health and nutrition, appropriate technology, quality control, the environment and consumer awareness.

Product Development Scheme. The overall aim of the programme is to promote the quality and marketing of Danish food products. The budget for the Product Development Scheme was DKK180 million in 1998.

The Research Centre for Organic Farming (FÖJO) aims at performing holistic research at an international level based on the philosophy of organic farming.

Science Park Symbion is located just outside Copenhagen and is a science park with emphasis on information technology and biotechnology.

Science Park Aarhus houses 50 companies with a total of 400 employees. Among the tenants are companies from the biotechnology, food processing and IT sectors.

The Research Association for Processed Fruit and Vegetables has as its purpose to co-ordinate research and provide funding for research in primary production and product development in relation to fruit and vegetables.

The concept of *Food Centre Lund* is to strengthen the competitiveness of the Swedish food sector through the promotion of technology transfer. Activities include applied research, research and education, conferences and seminars and dissemination of information. The aim is to develop the competitiveness of the Swedish food industry through co-ordination and development of knowledge and technological transfer between the universities and the companies in the food business.

Ideon Agro Food is a network foundation, which establishes and develops contacts between companies and universities. The contact between company and university improves the industry's ability to use research in product development.

Livsmedelskollegiet is a network of departments, which is conducting research and about 10–20 companies that are in the food industry located in the region.

Ideon is a science park whose aim is to provide a platform where innovative ideas, knowledge and collaboration may germinate and grow. Ideon was created with the purpose of facilitating the commercialization of new techniques, developed by academic scientists, innovators and entrepreneurs.

Together, Levnedsmiddlecentret and Food Centre Lund are creating *Öresund Food Network.* The network, which aims to strengthen the competitiveness of the Öresund region in the food sector, is established between industry, the actors in primary production, the food trade organizations and research departments and institutes.

The Swedish Nutrition Foundation has as its aim to support scientific research in nutrition and adjacent fields. The foundation also promotes the implementation of developments within this field of research.

LivsmedelPlus is a joint venture between Teknopol AB, SIK and Lund Food Centre. LivsmedelsPlus is focusing its activities on food and gardening in small and medium-sized companies.

Finally, *The Scanian Food Academy* is a network consisting of private companies, research organizations and government agencies. Its goal is to enhance the competitiveness and the innovativeness of the food industry.

This list includes the organizations that are active and available to the food cluster. This does not mean that they work only within the cluster; quite the contrary, the role of a leading research and networking organization is to have high-class international contacts, thus working as a mediator and a benchmarking organization where regional knowledge and development are compared with internationally available knowledge and development in other clusters around the world.

NOTES

1. www.ideon.se
2. www.oresund.com
3. This part is based on material from the Finnish ministry of agriculture (Mellentine et al., 2002) and interviews.
4. This summary of the situation in the USA has been formulated by our US colleague, Professor James E. Tillotson, Tufts University, Boston.
5. Julian Mellentine is Co-director of the Centre for Food & Health Studies, London.
6. The study can be obtained through the Centre for Food & Health Studies at www.new.nutrition.com. It was first presented in February 2002.

6. Innovation Cases – ProViva, Oatly, Mona Carota

In this chapter we introduce three unique cases on innovation processes. Our approach in the case presentations, and later in the analysis of the cases, is to capture the dynamics of the development process. We do not have a corporate management perspective, because these innovation processes have developed inside the corporations, but also outside and in between corporations. We follow the process to understand the essential features and we will also illustrate important choices that have been made during the journey from idea to product. Instead of a corporate management perspective, we still have a strategic leadership perspective. We will see how the innovation processes are being led through the different phases of development. We will also see that some parts of the process are quite controllable, while other parts are characterized by experimentation with uncertain outcomes – a lot of trials and some errors.

The three cases are different. In the presentations we describe the process according to Utterback's three-phase model, consisting of the fluid phase, the transitional phase and the specific phase. But the development story has different lengths in the three cases. The process that has developed the longest way is ProViva, and we will follow the ProViva story from the beginning of the ProViva history to the turn of the millennium. The Oatly case has not developed as much as ProViva, but has a longer story than Mona Carota. Therefore we will continue with Oatly which is just entering the specific phase, and we end with Mona Carota which is now turning from the fluid phase into the transitional phase.

THE PROVIVA CASE

A research Team in Lund found a New Medical Application for Probiotics (1985–1990)

In the mid-1980s Stig Bengmark, Professor and head of the Department of Surgery at Lund University Hospital, developed an interest in questions related to the nutritional needs of his surgical patients. Antibiotics are given to patients following major surgery, but Stig Bengmark noticed that the patients were often in poor health 3–4 days after their operation.

Organ collapse – nutrient substrate

If the digestive tract lacks bulk (food for it to digest) during a time when the patient is given intravenous fluids and antibiotics, leakage may result, during which bacteria diffuse out into the abdominal cavity, which may cause organ collapse. Stig Bengmark had developed a new type of tube for enteral nutrition. He and his colleague, Professor Bengt Jeppsson, initiated a research project in collaboration with Kåre Larsson, Professor of Food Technology, and Nils Molin, Professor of Applied Microbiology (both from the Lund Institute of Technology). This project was aimed at finding a nutritional solution that could be administered by tube, keeping the intestines functioning and reducing the risk of a leaking gut. The aim was to replace artificial nutrient substrates with something more natural.

A fermented nutrient solution – oatmeal soup

Kåre Larsson suggested that the nutritional solution should have an oatmeal base. Oatmeal has a high protein content, a well-balanced amino-acid profile, high amounts of fatty acids and phospholipids and the advantageous fibre betaglucans. The nutrient solution would not be passing through the stomach and must thus have a low pH. Nils Molin involved his colleagues in microbiology, PhD student Clas Lönner, PhD student Siv Ahrné and Dr Göran Molin. The aim was to find a lactic acid bacteria which could ferment the oats and re-establish the natural balance of intestinal flora, leading to intestinal recuperation. The first issue was to find a suitable bacteria to ferment the oats. One requirement of the bacteria was that it should digest the oats, leaving the nutrient in an appropriate form to be absorbed by the intestines. The trials during the development period of the oatmeal soup were handled by Ingela Marklinder, PhD student at the Department of Applied Microbiology, together with Clas Lönner.

Re-establishing the natural balance in the intestine

Another role of the bacteria was its essential properties for the digestive tract. This objective was additional to the original intention, which was to create a nutritional substrate.

The researchers decided to create an oatmeal 'soup' which would be fermented with lactobacilli, which could survive passage through the intestines and successfully become attached to the intestinal walls and colonize them. They also wanted to use a strain of bacteria that was already naturally present in the intestine.

Where can we find healthy bacteria?

At one of the meetings between the microbiologists and surgeons the idea arose of changing the research procedures from the conventional one. The suggestion was to use biopsies from humans, which means 'in vivo studies' instead of 'in vitro studies in the laboratory'. The microbiologists took 200 biopsy samples from patients with healthy mucosa at the clinic and found that certain lactobacilli occurred more frequently than others:

- *L. rhamnosus*   17%
- *L. acidophilus-like*   15%
- *L. salivarius*   9%
- *L. casei subsp. pseudoplantarum*   5%
- *L. plantarum*   5%
- *L. reuteri*   5%
- *L. fermentum*   4%
- *Leuconostoc mesenteroides*   3%

The next step was to make oatmeal mixtures based on representatives from 19 of the most frequently occurred lactobacilli group. Thirteen colleagues at the clinic volunteered to participate in this part of the study. In the analysis of the study, two bacteria emerged as being particularly promising: *L. plantarum* 299v and *L. plantarum* 299. *L. plantarum* takes its name from its origin – naturally occurring on the surface of a number of plants – including cereals, cucumbers, cabbage and olives and it enters the body from these sources.

Which bacteria should be used and would they improve the patient's health?

The researchers found that *L. plantarum* 299v seemed to have the best ability to ferment the oats and colonize the GI tract. Göran Molin, Siv Ahrné and PhD Student Marie-Louise Johansson gave the oatmeal soup fermented with *L. plantarum* 299v to the colleagues at the clinic that volunteered. Biopsies were taken and examined and the researchers concluded that *L. plantarum* 299v was colonizing the intestines of the volunteering colleagues. Some 'negative' bacteria were decreased in numbers and there was also an improvement in their health.

Patented process

The research project involving this probiotic substrate provided the basis for several doctoral theses at the Lund University. The university provided an environment in which knowledge from different areas could be combined. The research mainly concerned developing the lactic acid fermentation process of an oatmeal soup, isolating and genetically identifying lactic acid bacteria from the human GI tract and studying the healthy effects of the fermented oatmeal soup, containing high numbers of lactobacilli isolated from humans.

Table 6.1   Innovation process in the research team

The problem	Innovation	Applications
Patients suffered from organ collapse due to bacterial leakage from the intestines to the body	Nutritional solution that could be administered by tube (Stig Bengmark, Bengt Jeppsson, Kåre Larsson, Nils Molin)	Medical applications, nutrient solution
Which nutrient profile is best?	Oats as the important component in the nutrient solution (Kåre Larsson)	Oatmeal soup
The nutrient substrate needs to transfer the nutrient to the intestines	Fermenting technology to achieve the right oatmeal mixture (Nils Molin, Clas Lönner, Ingela Marklinder)	Fermented oatmeal soup. Most lactobacilli are used in products based on milk rather than products based on cereals
How can the natural balance of the microflora in the intestines be re-established?	If bacteria colonized the intestines they would offer protection against undesired micro-organisms (Nils Molin, Göran Molin, Siv Ahrné, Marie-Louise Johansson)	Choice of type of beneficial bacteria. Most lactobacilli are used in products based on milk but not in products based on cereals
Which bacteria should be used and would they improve the patients' health?	Identifying and isolating the most common lactobacilli in the intestine (Göran Molin, Siv Ahrné, Marie-Louise Johansson, Stig Bengmark, Bengt Jeppsson)	Fermented oatmeal soup Food ingredient Patented process
Where can we find healthy bacteria?	Biopsies were taken from the healthy individuals that had been given 19 different lactobacilli-strains administrated in fermented oatmeal soup, which showed that *L. plantarum* 299v was best at colonizing the intestine. (Stig Bengmark, Bengt Jeppsson, Clas Lönner, Ingela Marklinder, Göran Molin, Siv Ahrné, Marie-Louise Johansson)	New research procedure using biopsies

It was these technologies that later led to the possibility of filing for patents on the manufacturing process and on the bacteria in the product (*L. plantarum* 299, *L. plantarum* 299v and *L. rhamnosus* 271). The first patent application was submitted in 1987.

Comments

- The researchers involved were senior scientists in their respective fields and contributed to the whole area of knowledge.
- The key to success was combining different research areas and the unique collaboration between surgeons, microbiologists and food technologists.
- The dependence of the researchers on each other encouraged them to collaborate closely.
- The researchers had a genuine interest in the research problem.
- By taking biopsies directly from mucosa of human intestines, a new research procedure was introduced.
- The research on oats started in the 1980s and is described in the Oatly case. The Oatly case is described in another part of this book. The research team was able to include this knowledge about oats in the current ProViva project.

The Researchers' Search for an Industrial Partner Resulted in the Creation of Probi AB (1990–92)

During the first few years of development the researchers were involved in discussions with various potential commercial partners. In the late 1980s Kaj Vareman became involved in the project. Kaj Vareman is a well-known entrepreneur in knowledge-based companies in southern Sweden and is well known both in research circles and in the food industry. Apart from Probi AB, he has started other knowledge-based companies such as Zeol AB, Lundagrion, and Anox AB. Kaj Vareman acted as the spokesman for the researchers and was in charge of the negotiations with potential partners.

First contact between Probi and Skånemejerier

The researchers were depressed after the way they had been treated by some of the largest Swedish food companies. These companies did not even taste the product. Kåre Larsson told his researcher colleagues that they still had the opportunity to approach Skånemejerier (a dairy in the south of Sweden) even if it was a much smaller company. The researchers had practically no contacts at Skånemejerier. However, Kåre Larsson mentioned that he had known Kenneth Andersson, research and development Manager at Skånemejerier, since the 1970s. They had met at conferences when Kenneth was employed by Alfa Laval and SMR (the Swedish Dairy Association).

Kåre Larsson happened to meet Kenneth Andersson at Ideon and told him that he was involved in an interesting research project. Later, Kåre Larsson called Kenneth Andersson and told him about the fermented oat soup project. Kenneth Andersson knew a little about oats thanks to his early involvement in Rickard Öste's oat research project 'Oatly'. (Rickard Öste was a researcher at the Department of Food Chemistry and Nutrition at the Lund Institute of Technology (LTH) in Lund.) Kenneth Andersson knew that Ideon Agro Food was also involved in that project.

Kåre Larsson told Kenneth Andersson that this was something completely different. Kenneth Andersson did not, at this time, know that Probi AB had already presented the fermented oat soup to major food companies. He found out about this a couple of weeks later through Göran Molin. A senior executive at one of the major food companies told Göran:'I believe, Göran that you should not get involved with lactobacilli. We, in the dairy industry know everything about lactobacilli.'

Library meeting autumn 1990

Kenneth Andersson and Kåre Larsson agreed on the phone to meet in the library at the Department of Food Technology at the Lund Institute of Technology (LTH). Göran Molin and Clas Lönner were also present at the meeting. They told Kenneth Andersson that several companies had shown interest in their product. The researchers brought with them the oat soup made in the laboratory. Kenneth Andersson's response was positive and said that it had a 'mild and interesting taste'.

Kåre Larsson asked Kenneth Andersson if Skånemejerier was interested in the oat product. Kenneth Andersson knew that, when Kåre Larsson himself was involved, this was a guarantee of the quality of the project. Kåre Larsson was at that time Professor of Food Technology at LTH. (Kåre Larsson is an internationally well-known lipid researcher and has written a number of internationally acclaimed books.) Kenneth Andersson understood that the research group had discovered something that could become valuable to Skånemejerier. The question was how the matter should be handled. The most interesting thing about this project was not the product itself but the researchers behind it. Kenneth Andersson was thus interested in including these researchers in his network.

Negotiations started and the researchers talked about a contract. Kenneth Andersson realized that this was not a fully developed product although the researchers believed it to be so, and he promised to contact them later. He did not have the funds to cover the down payment of SEK250,000. Kenneth Andersson remembers: 'I went to see our former MD, Ingvar Axelsson, and told him that I needed SEK250,000 to become part of the project with the researchers. He looked at me suspiciously; Do you mean an oat soup without any milk at all?'

Ingvar Axelsson immediately asked for the Marketing Manager, Jan Persson, who was enthusiastic about the idea. Persson's first question was: 'What specific product are we talking about?' Kenneth Andersson answered, 'Yoghurt drinks.'

Kenneth Andersson and Jan Persson argued that the research group consisted of famous surgeons, microbiologists and food technologists. Working with these researchers could lead to new products in the future that were closer to dairy products. Kenneth Andersson emphasized the importance of getting in touch with these researchers. Ingvar Axelsson gave Kenneth Andersson the task of writing a memo about the project. The next time Kenneth Andersson, Jan Persson and Ingvar Axelsson met in the corridor, they all concluded: 'Why not, let's do it!'

The starting point of the collaboration between the researchers and Skånemejerier

The first step was a meeting between Kenneth Andersson, Jan Persson and Ingvar Axelsson from Skånemejerier, and Kaj Vareman, Nils Molin, Kåre Larsson, Göran Molin, Clas Lönner, Siv Ahrné and Ingela Marklinder representing Probi. Kaj Vareman started to describe the project and the researchers filled in the details. At this first meeting Jan Persson and Ingvar Andersson had the opportunity to taste the oat drink for the first time. Ingela Marklinder, who had performed all the laboratory tests, brought with her samples of the oatmeal drink. Jan Persson's reaction was: 'This'll never sell!'

The researchers were somewhat put off and suggested that it may be possible to add flavouring. They also started to discuss the research behind the bacteria. Unfortunately, a sediment settled during the meeting. Kenneth Andersson made note of this and told Kåre Larsson: 'We have to work on the product and process development!'

After a while, Kenneth Andersson declared that Skånemejerier was prepared to become involved in the project. A project group was assembled and a draft contract was drawn up. Kenneth Andersson paid SEK250,000 as the first down payment and arranged a product development group to work on the project hands-on. This group had five members: Kenneth Andersson, Rickard Löfgren (Product Development), Torsten Jönsson (Product Manager) and Clas Lönner participated from Probi. Kåre Larsson joined the meetings when Kenneth Andersson asked him to participate.

At the end of the meeting Kaj Vareman asked: 'When is the launch?'

Probi and Skånemejerier – a good combination of research and industry

The researchers established Probi AB in spring 1991 and in 1992 Skåne-mejerier was invited to become a 25 per cent part owner. Kaj Vareman became the first managing director of Probi AB. When Kaj Vareman looked back on the collaboration he concluded:

> It has been fun to create something completely new in the food industry. Skånemejerier and Probi could serve as a role model for the kind of collaboration researchers and industry should have. In Probi we know everything about biotech and medicine but not much about the market, production or taste quality. Skåne-mejerier is an expert in these areas and also has the advantage of offering direct distribution to the retail store (Wikström, 2000).

It was the perfect combination, in which the two partners could concentrate on what they were best suited for, without thinking of prestige. Skånemejerier gained the advantage of collaborating with a research company and now has the option of becoming involved in any innovations developed at Probi. This collaboration stimulated Skånemejerier's corporate culture and has enriched Probi with Skånemejerier's industrial thinking.

Comments

- The large companies do not appear to have an open mind about new ideas; the 'not invented here syndrome' (Szulanski, 1996).
- Kaj Vareman prepared the ground for the product launch. He created enormous interest before the actual launch.
- Kenneth Andersson understood the importance of building a network of researchers.
- Skånemejerier is an informal organization that encourages people to try new things. Major decisions are often taken in odd places, such as the office corridor.

Consumers Show Interest in Health (1989)

In 1989, *Sydsvenska Dagbladet*, the major newspaper in southern Sweden, published an article and an interview with two of the researchers in Probi, Siv Ahrné and Göran Molin. This provided the basis of the market potential of probiotics.

Jan Persson, Marketing Manager at Skånemejerier, explains that there was fierce competition in the dairy industry towards the end of the 1980s. Norrmejerier (Northern Dairies), based in the north of Sweden, had taken the first stumbling steps with 'Verum', a probiotic Scandinavian sour milk product known as 'fil'. Arla, the largest dairy in Sweden, was experimenting with another Scandinavian sour milk called 'Dofilus'. Skånemejerier, on the other hand, did not have anything to offer this new potential market. Kenneth Andersson was in contact with different research groups.

Skånemejerier had an idea to find other business opportunities than milk-based products. There is a relaxed corporate culture at Skånemejerier which, among other things, encourages people to present new ideas. Skånemejerier has a history of developing new products. For example in 1971 the company was one of the first in the world to launch fruit juices in milk cartons.

Skånemejerier was brave enough to be one of the first dairy companies to try cereals. The first experiment was 'Primaliv' in 1990, which consisted of oat fibre in a Scandinavian sour milk product.

Skånemejerier is becoming involved in probiotic products

'ProViva', described in this case, is an example of the third generation of probiotic products.

- First generation: Ordinary Scandinavian sour milk, 'filmjölk' and yog-hurt
- Second generation: A-fil, Dofilus, with one particular type of lacto-bacillus
- Third generation: 'ProViva,' products with clinical documentation based on the vital bacteria

Comments

- The corporate culture at Skånemejerier encourages innovation. The management has always been prepared to try completely new areas of business.
- Jan Persson had a clear understanding of consumer preferences. Jan Persson initiated together with R&D Manager, Kenneth Andersson, the development of the probiotic products within Skånemejerier.
- Skånemejerier had the courage to become involved in a high-risk project based on the confidence they had in the group of senior researchers.

Skånemejerier uses Unorthodox Product Development Methods (1992–93)

Skånemejerier had previously launched a product called Primaliv in 1990. It was a Scandinavian sour milk product containing oat fibre. The fibre was mixed into Primaliv in a large batch. The product became thick and sticky which resulted in complete failure in the market place. Skånemejerier, therefore, had doubts about becoming involved in another oat project.

Transformation from laboratory to industrial-scale production

When it was clear that Skånemejerier had decided to invest in the researcher's fermented oat soup project, they started to work on major questions, such as: 'What should a good-tasting consumer product look like?' The oat soup used in the clinical trials in hospitals was nowhere near a good-tasting consumer product.

Major issues were:

• Transformation of production in the laboratory to pilot-scale production.
• Transformation from pilot-scale production to industrial-scale production.

Probi had only been producing the oat broth in the laboratory and a couple of batches in pilot scale. Clas Lönner, Product Development Manager at Probi, was involved in the process development at the Lunnarp production plant, which is based in the southern part of Sweden. This was a fruitful process that involved many employees at Skånemejerier and a significant contribution by Probi.

The production plant in Lunnarp had a long tradition of developing new product ideas. This development had the support of the management group, and the R&D Manager, Kenneth Andersson, was at this time, also Plant Manager in Lunnarp. The production staff in Lunnarp showed a great deal of interest and commitment in the development process.

Researchers were frustrated over the slow product development process at Skånemejerier

Other issues were:

• How should the heated oat broth be handled?
• In what way should the oatmeal be mixed with water?
• Was it necessary to homogenize the mixture or not?

During the development process Skånemejerier understood the need for a real 'blender' and started with 400-litre batches. Other important insights were the importance of the rinsing and washing procedures. More problems occurred when the development team started to cook the oat gruel. Kaj Vareman started to feel frustrated and complained that the project was being delayed. The developmental work was completed in the autumn of 1992. The single most important factor for success was Skånemejerier's previous experience with the failure of Primaliv. Skånemejerier was really impressed by the researchers and without their experience the launch would have been too early. Instead, Skånemejerier had the knowledge required for this type of development process and knew that this project would take time to develop.

Important criteria for Kenneth Andersson in product development:

- Taste
- Appearance
- Function

Taste matters to consumers

There is an attitude among some researchers that there is no need for companies like Skånemejerier. However, according to consumer research, there is a gap between what the researcher believes to be the final product and the product preferred by consumers. Researchers often have a product that is not fully developed. This case demonstrates that Skånemejerier had an important role to play as the company contributed the following to the product:

- Good taste
- Good taste as an important element in the development of the concept
- Process development from laboratory production to industrial-scale production

The product development staff, Rickard Löfgren and Tommy Pedersen, were not overenthusiastic about the product. The first step to improve the taste was to add flavour. One experiment involved the fermented oat soup with orange flavour, but the whole batch became too sour after 14 days. Furthermore, Skånemejerier tried to add blackcurrant as a flavour but the benzoic acid killed the lactobacilli. The next step was to try to combine the new product formula with existing products. The product developers found that rose-hip and blueberry 'fruit soups' could hide the oat flavour.

Skånemejerier started to test product formulations with less oat content. The researchers began to worry about the oat message to consumers not being valid. Skånemejerier homogenized the drink to obtain a better consistency and smoother taste. The combination of homogenized products based on a rose hip or blueberry soup gave the best results.

Comments

- The transformation from laboratory production to industrial scale was successful due to the commitment of the R&D manager, Kenneth Andersson, and the production staff of Lunnarp.
- Skånemejerier added a new dimension to product development by introducing 'taste quality'.
- The failures were big enough to learn from, but too small not to get killed (Brown and Eisenhardt, 1998).

ProViva Concept Development (1993–94)

Torsten Jönsson, Product Manager at Skånemejerier, in November 1993 was speaking at the Functional Foods Symposium in Lund. Functional foods were suddenly receiving enormous publicity and the symposium was intended to have 30–40 participants but instead, without prior announcement, 120 people showed up. Skånemejerier brought several products and a tasting session was held after the lectures.

Everybody wanted to talk to Torsten Jönsson afterwards; for example he was interviewed by Swedish national radio, P1, in the programme 'Dialogen'. This programme was about functional foods. Torsten Jönsson talked about ProViva and why there is a need for a special category of foods called functional foods. Also participating in this interview was a representative from the Swedish Food Agency and the R&D Manager from the food company Procordia. Torsten Jönsson was also interviewed on the regional radio station, Radio Malmöhus. They all wanted to know about the product and about functional foods.

Torsten Jönsson said that the communication has to be about the stomach. All this publicity in media created enormous interest in Skånemejerier and ProViva. The launch was successful thanks to the people who tried the product and told their friends about it.

Torsten Jönsson believes that functional foods have to have a relatively fast effect. When consumers try ProViva they immediately have a smooth feeling in their stomachs. It is more difficult to convince consumers about products that lower their cholesterol level. This is something that has to be measured in blood tests by trained medical personnel.

The ProViva health proposition

Torsten Jönsson had previous experience with probiotics and the launch of the first probiotic milk in Sweden, BRA milk. This product was, similar to ProViva, a third generation probiotic product consisting of three types of bacteria: *L. bifidus*, *L. reuteri*, *L. acidophilus*. Jan Persson, Marketing Manager at Skånemejerier, believed that Torsten was capable of handling the new assignment; that is, Probi's new product.

Skånemejerier asked Probi why consumers should be interested in eating or drinking bacteria. Professor Stig Bengmark responded that many of the consumers have IBS (irritable bowel syndrome). Torsten Jönsson initiated a consumer study, which revealed that 40 per cent of all Swedes have intestinal problems and IBS at some time. Lactic acid bacteria can, to a large extent, help these consumers with their problems.

Skånemejerier carried out 3–4 consumer studies and concluded that the new product formulation had the best chance of succeeding when combined with an accepted health drink. Blueberry and rose-hip soup are regarded as healthy foods in Sweden and could, therefore, be used to deliver the probiotic message.

Communication

The message on the package was: 'This is a probiotic drink that tastes of blueberries or rose hips.' Skånemejerier chose not to call it a blueberry drink containing probiotics as they wanted to focus on the bacteria. A symbol resembling a bacterium was created at a meeting between Dr Göran Molin and the Art Director at the McCann advertising agency. Göran Molin told him the story about lactobacilli and explained that there are as large differences between different types of lactobacilli as between a mosquito and an elephant. The Art Director came up with this symbol representing the bacteria.

The package in itself was white, with blue symbols on the blueberry-flavoured product and red symbols on the rose-hip product. The advertising agency drew illustrations of blueberries and rose hips on the package instead of using photographs to direct attention to the bacteria instead of the flavour.

In the consumer tests Skånemejerier also tested the price sensitivity. The Consumers were prepared to pay SEK12 (US$1.30), which was a significant increase compared with ordinary blueberry soup at SEK8. Skånemejerier set the price at SEK15 and created a new product category.

The concept of ProViva had a successful life-style communication in Sweden and Finland: 'A good life-style starts in your stomach' (1994–97). The communication in the UK had a slightly different angle 'A healthy start to a busy day' (1996–2000).

The ProViva name

Jan Persson and Torsten Jönsson were working late and they started to discuss possible names for the product. Jan Persson said that Skånemejerier had the name 'Viva' in mind to be used for a juice product. Torsten Jönsson said that sounded too simple. Together they hit upon the idea of combining Probi with Viva to give ProViva. Later they found out that ProViva means 'For the living'.

Product launch in Skåne

Kaj Vareman, Managing Director of Probi, was preparing for the launch of ProViva. He created enormous interest in the media and in the political establishment before the actual launch. Skånemejerier's Product Manager, Johny Humaloja, created a new type of launch plan based on scientific documentation. He realized that functional foods offered additional health benefit and should consequently imply a premium price point.

The initial sales forecast was 5 tons. During its first week, during spring of 1994, 12 tons of ProViva were sold on the market. The launch of the functional foods product ProViva was thus proven to be successful.

Table 6.2   Innovation process in Skånemejerier

The problem	Innovation	Applications
Giving the product a good taste	95% fruit juice and only 5% fermented oat soup	Fruit juice
Getting a brand new product formulation accepted in the market place	Incorporating the new product into an existing product that is perceived to be healthy	Rose-hip soup and blueberry soup
Getting enough publicity	Choosing a PR strategy to handle the government's rigid rules and regulations (Lotta Törner)	Becoming the voice of consumers who demand healthier food
Gaining consumer acceptance of the ProViva health proposition	Including life-style health arguments in the marketing communication	Life-style advertising campaign

Internationalization

In 1993, as a consequence of Sweden's predicted entry into the European Union, Skånemejerier began to develop a plan to meet new international competition. There was a surplus of milk on the Swedish market and the dairy industry was looking for future export markets. Anders Lareke was recruited as Skånemejerier's first export manager and his first task was to develop an international sales network. This network was initially focused on the export of surplus cheese. However, in 1995–1997, Anders Lareke changed direction and developed a key account strategy based on knowledge transfer regarding value-added products like ProViva.

Export to Finland

The new knowledge transfer strategy was gradually developed in the Finnish market. Anders Lareke realized that knowledge could become Skånemejerier's competitive advantage in the market place. Launching the functional foods product ProViva in Finland in 1995 demanded a new approach to sales and marketing. The traditional launch plan was accompanied by a PR plan based on the research performed by Probi. During the 1990s a number of doctoral theses and clinical studies had demonstrated the positive health effect of *L. plantarum* 299v and ProViva. This documentation served as the basis for information towards medical doctors, dieticians and nutritionists.

ProViva was test-launched in a region of north-western Finland called Österbotten, which was the home market of Skånemejerier's Finnish partner, Milka. Milka supplies the Österbotten region with direct distribution to each store and arranged several tastings in stores. This direct contact with the consumer created genuine confidence in ProViva and its health benefits. The most powerful marketing tool was pleased customers who told their friends about how ProViva had helped them with their stomach problems. Doctors and dieticians bolstered consumer confidence. They all believed in the product and told their patients about ProViva.

Launch press conference

The success of the test launch encouraged Anders Lareke to proceed with a full national launch. A press conference was arranged in Helsingfors on 10 April, 1996. Probi's R&D Manager, Marie-Louise Johansson, presented the scientific documentation behind ProViva and an independent Finnish researcher verified the importance of lactic acid bacteria.

Skånemejerier – expansion in Finland and the UK

Skånemejerier started a sales company in Finland. Anders Lareke employed Kirsi Malinen as the Sales Manager. Kirsi Malinen intended to educate staff in the stores in order to make them aware of the difference between ProViva and ordinary blueberry soup. At the same time it was important, according to Kirsi Malinen, to maintain a dialogue between Skånemejerier and dieticians, medical doctors and nurses.

At the beginning of 1997, Kirsi Malinen and Skånemejerier exhibited ProViva for the first time in Finland at the Finnish national physicians' conference. Moreover, Kirsi Malinen started collaboration in 1997 with the Finnish Association of Dieticians. Skånemejerier subscribed to their database and sent all the updated scientific and product information to the members of the association. In October 1997 Skånemejerier had a stand at the national conference of Finnish dieticians and Probi was engaged to answer scientific questions.

A number of the dieticians, health experts and journalists contacted started to write about ProViva and use it as an example of functional foods. ProViva took on the position of being one of the functional food products together with Valio's yoghurt 'Gefilus' and Raisio's cholesterol-lowering margarine 'Benecol'. The strategy in Finland had been successful, and managed to give SM a competitive edge in a similar way to Sweden.

The launch strategy tested in Finland has also been used for the launch of ProViva in the UK. The relationship between Skånemejerier and the retailer in Finland and the UK has developed into a partnership of mutual interest. Skånemejerier identified the best partner among the retailers and store chains that were of interest. This key account strategy resulted in knowledge transfer. Skånemejerier had knowledge about functional foods and the retailer had knowledge about the interaction with the consumer in the store.

Lotta Törner, Information Manager at Skånemejerier, developed a European PR strategy together with the PR Agent, Jean Garon, based in the UK. This PR campaign was supported by researcher network and clinical trials in a number of countries such as the USA, The UK and Poland. PR activities prepared the market and effectively supported the launches in Finland and The UK. These international experiences have also been helpful in the process of developing the market communication and PR in Sweden.

Comments

- In an international perspective, functional foods such as ProViva require knowledge transfer to selected key account retailers.
- Medical doctors and dieticians bolstered consumer confidence.
- ProViva became one of the examples of functional foods in Finland and has thereby contributed to developing Skånemejerier's corporate profile.
- An international PR strategy managed by Information Manager, Lotta Törner, supported the launches in Finland and The UK.

Probi Develops a Probiotic Recovery Drink (1998–2000)

In August 2000, ProViva Active, a further development of ProViva, was introduced onto the Swedish market. ProViva Active is a recovery drink aimed at sportsmen and others who take regular exercise or anyone who puts their body under physical strain. The product contains the vital ingredient *L. plantarum* 299v, fast and slow carbohydrates, whey proteins and anti-oxidants in the form of vitamins and minerals. During physical exercise, free oxygen radicals are formed in the body and antioxidants provide protection against them. Probi has carried out a number of studies to document the health benefit and a large number of sportspeople have been involved in testing the product to find the best product composition. A number of national Swedish sports teams, such as skiing, handball and table tennis, as well as individual athletes in tennis and athletics, have also been involved in the testing of the product. These athletes are, to a large extent, now using the product regularly.

The idea behind the project came from Dr Jörgen Wiklander specializing in orthopaedics, who is a former professional athlete, and who had developed an anti-oxidant tablet suitable for athletes. Jörgen Wiklander approached Probi as the research company behind ProViva and asked if it was possible to combine his tablet with the ProViva drink. Jörgen Wiklander was aware that many athletes had stomach problems. Such a drink may provide a solution to these problems and at the same time give them anti-oxidants.

Through this project, Probi has demonstrated that the fermented oat base with *L. plantarum* 299v has other applications than the ProViva fruit drink. In this case the bacteria were combined with antioxidants, probably giving a synergistic effect, to produce a product concept for a specific group. Involving the end-users, that is, well-known athletes, was a way of creating publicity and goodwill, but also to really test the effects of the product on extremely hard-working people also having a stressful situation.

ProViva Active partnership between Probi and Skånemejerier

Initially there was some misunderstanding between Probi and Skånemejerier concerning the organization of the ProViva Active project. Probi was more involved in the product development process than in previous projects and had their own PR activities. This new situation caused some concern at Skånemejerier. However, Torsten Jönsson, who was managing the project at Skånemejerier, never had any doubts. He claims that he was unsure about ProViva to begin with, but never hesitated about ProViva Active. Torsten Jönsson managed to interest Skånemejerier's Marketing Manager, Gunilla Törner Nylén, and Product Manager, Mats Lönne, in the project.

The product was successfully launched on the Swedish market in August 2000. The launch was supported by PR activities involving the Swedish national skiing team and the national handball team. Probi and Jörgen Wiklander supported the launch by initiating PR activities in close collaboration with the athletes.

The financial strategy of Probi

According to Kaj Vareman, Managing Director of Probi (1992–2000), money is always the problem in knowledge-based companies like Probi, despite the fact that it has become easier during recent years to obtain external capital through the Swedish Stock Exchange. Probi was floated on the Stockholm Stock Exchange in May 1998. Kaj has always been part owner of his companies and made sure that the companies had sufficient liquid assets. Personal commitment is a good strategy in avoiding unnecessary risk. The researchers in Probi never needed to invest any money. The activities in a small knowledge-based company cannot solely depend on external capital. The companies must be able to rely on its own capital base.

A good strategy for small research-based companies such as Probi is probably a combination of personal long-term commitment by a small group of owners, venture capital and the Swedish Stock Exchange.

Probi is a biotechnology company in the area of probiotics

According to the new Managing Director of Probi, Monica Wallter, from 2000 the company now has a leading position in the world in the area of probiotics. Monica has a background in the pharmaceutical industry and has identified the potential of Probi's probiotic knowledge in different market applications. Probi is actively looking for appropriate partners in different applications of the probiotics knowledge base. The selected areas of interest are:

- Functional foods
- Health and recovery drinks
- Pharma-nutraceuticals/dietary supplements
- Animal feed

Probi develops and produces bacterial cultures and oatmeal soup with a high content of probiotic bacteria for their partners. The selected partner develops the Probi product concept into value-added products that match identified consumer needs.

Table 6.3   Innovation process at Probi

The problem	Innovation	Applications
Connection of probiotic science to industrial applications	Entrepreneurship in the interface between academia and the food industry	Foundation of Probi AB
Finding a suitable long-term partner	A medium-sized regional dairy company with immediate access to a test market of 1 million consumers	Skånemejerier and ProViva
Reassurance of health claim in Sweden	Doctoral theses, clinical studies and lobbying of the research community and government	PR plan
Reassurance of Swedish health claims in other countries	Reference researchers and clinical studies conducted at reputable universities and research centres	PR plan
How to find new applications for the oat base	Through further development, where a combination of the probiotic bacteria, a nutritious additive and antioxidants, resulted in a new product formulation (Kaj Vareman, Jörgen Wiklander, Clas Lönner)	ProViva Active

Skånemejerier – A Knowledge-Driven Food and Health Company (2000–)

Rolf Bjerndell, Managing Director of Skånemejerier, has a clear idea about the company's strategic focus. He has been involved with Skånemejerier since the late 1980s, initially as a Management Consultant. One of his first realizations was the need to transform Skånemejerier from a regional dairy to a modern niche food company in Europe. According to Rolf Bjerndell, this process was possible through knowledge alliances with researchers and strategic partners, and a constant focus on product development and innovation. Skånemejerier has a tradition of experimenting and is always interested in trying the new concepts and technologies. Skånemejerier has achieved this transformation successfully and is now reckoned to be an innovative food company.

During the past 12 months, Skånemejerier has started to redirect its focus from functional foods to the more general area of food and health. Skånemejerier wants to take a leading position in the food industry with regard to the development of positive health concepts. The health trend illustrates a fundamental change in society, where health is no longer an issue concerning those past the age of 40. According to Rolf Bjerndell, the modern life-style is not in balance with our bodies:

> We are sitting in offices not moving around enough and at the same time we have food available 24 hours a day.

The new message concerning food and health is difficult to communicate to retailers, while at the same time consumers are asking for more information on these issues. Skånemejerier has a great opportunity to deliver not only products, but also the health aspect about their products. This is a proactive position where Skånemejerier is actively trying to seek business opportunities with concepts that can help consumers achieve better health.

Final Comments

- Professors Stig Bengmark, Kåre Larsson and Nils Molin represented the kind of research looking for multidisciplinary collaboration.
- Professor Bengt Jeppsson, Dr Göran Molin, Siv Ahrné and Clas Lönner executed this multidisciplinary research and collaborated with other researchers and external contacts such as Skånemejerier.
- Kaj Vareman, Managing director of Probi, was the 'strategist' and entrepreneur who was able to mobilize the knowledge within the university and build bridges to the food industry.
- Rolf Bjerndell, Managing Director of Skånemejerier, as the 'synthesizer', had an important role as a visionary, understanding, and positive top manager.
- Jan Persson, Marketing Manager at Skånemejerier, as 'patcher', has long and thorough experience of the dairy industry and an optimistic pragmatic approach. Jan Persson usually says 'Let's test it, and see if it works.'
- Torsten Jönsson, Product Manager at Skånemejerier, as 'patcher', was the practical 'doer' and realist in the innovation process.

- Lotta Törner, Information Manager, as 'patcher' managed the PR and communication process regarding Skånemejerier's profile in functional foods and food & health.
- Kenneth Andersson, R&D Manager at Skånemejerier, as 'strategist' had the double role of R&D Manager and Plant Manager in Lunnarp during the first critical years until 1997. In this position he was an important figure concerning access to vital internal small-scale resources such as the laboratory and a production line to test new products.

THE OATLY CASE

This is the story of how the Oatly brand developed out of nutritional and engineering research in the environmental of industrial know-how.

Case Background (1985–89)

Boom in US interest in oats

The starting point of the massive consumer interest in oats in the USA was in 1987 with the book *The 8-week Cholesterol Cure* (Kowalski, 1987). The sales of oats doubled in a very short time. This newborn interest in oats could also be seen in the increasing number of proposals and number of oat projects within the Skånska Lantmännen Research foundation in the late1980s.

At that time Rickard Öste was a researcher at the Department of Food Chemistry and Nutrition at Lund Institute of Technology (LTH) in Lund. The head of the department up to 1984, Professor Arne Dahlquist had discovered human lactose intolerance in 1963, and much of the research at the department was focused on various aspects of milk intolerance and low lactose milk. Rickard had in his research been studying the chemical reactions that follow the production of low lactose cow's milk. Such milk was produced by the injection of the enzyme lactase into sterilized milk. This was a development project initiated by Professor Arne Dahlquist, head of the department, in collaboration with TetraPak and Alfa Laval. Alfa Laval had also in the 1980s been developing and selling equipment for soymilk production. Rickard had also experienced working with soymilk, and had seen the successful marketing of soymilk in Tetra packages in chilled containers on the streets of Tokyo in 1985.

In the research world the interest in oats started with an article in the magazine *New England, Journal of Medicine* (New Medicine) which reported on a study on oats and cholesterol. In 1989, at an Ideon Agro Food meeting Rickard Öste met Sigurd Andersson of Swedish Grain Trade. Sigvard Andersson had observed the increased sales of bran in the USA. At the same time as the bran export increase there was an interest from Sigvard Andersson to find new business based on the oat kernel. Various different food products were discussed as potential end products from oat kernels at this meeting, and at a later lunch meeting, between Rickard Öste and Sigvard Andersson in Stockholm. Due to the interesting nutritional profile of oats, they found non-dairy milk products to be the most interesting candidate for a development project. However, Sigvard Andersson, although supportive of this concept, had no means to fund a research project.

Rickard Öste engaged Inger Ahlden, one of his former students, to make an overview of the potential of oats as a raw material for the production of a 'non-dairy milk' suitable for milk-intolerant people. In her diploma work, Inger Ahlden had been investigating by-products from soya milk production, and at the time was supervised by Rickard and Dr Ingegerd Sjöholm, a food engineering scientist. Inger's literature review clearly indicated the potential of oats as a raw material for a 'milk'.

The next task for Rickard Öste and his colleagues was to find finance for the project. At this stage, Rickard invited a friend of his, Dr Lennart Lindahl, to the emerging project. Rickard Öste realized that development of an oat milk needed expertise of different types, and Lennart Lindahl would contribute with his knowledge in physical chemistry of foods. A research group was thus formed, with top knowledge in enzymes and food chemistry (Rickard Öste), physical chemistry of foods (Lennart Lindahl), foodprocessing technologies (Ingegerd Sjöholm) combined with the practical skills of Inger Ahlden.

It would take time and a lot of meetings to get the money needed for the practical development project to start.

Cereal farmers in southern Sweden invest in research

The cereal farmers in Sweden invested in research through their own foundations such as the Skånska Lantmännen Research Foundation and the Cerealia Foundation. The cereal farmers in Skåne, the southernmost province of Sweden, created the Skånska Lantmännen Research Foundation. Sweden has also been a world leader in cereal breeding since the 1920s through the plant breeding companies Svalöf and Weibulls, later Svalöf – Weibull. These foundations and Svalöf – Weibull have had a long-term interest in supporting cereal research, and have played an important factor in the process of building up a Swedish cereal know-how.

Skånska Lantmännen started their Research Foundation in 1985 and allocated SEK24 million to the Foundation. The Foundation focused on raw materials and production. In 1990, about 20 projects were in progress in bioenergy, grains and prairie wheat (high protein). Lennart Wikström was employed by Skånska Lantmännen in 1989 as R&D Manager and, at the same time, appointed Secretary of the Skånska Lantmännen Foundation.

Lennart Wikström had ideas about how Swedish agriculture could be transformed from traditional bulk production to high-value products. The goal was no longer production volume but the development of grains for the future, healthy grains and new ways of doing business. At this time Lennart Wikström had several ideas in the back of his mind, and one was a 'cereal drink'. Lennart believed that one way of succeeding would be through a more proactive and co-operative approach with researchers in Lund.

Cereals know-how in the research environment

The scope of extent cereal basis know-how in Sweden around 1990 covered:

- Starch technology: Professor in Cereals Technology, Ann-Charlotte Eliasson, at the Department of Food Technology at LTH in Lund, where Lennart Lindahl received his PhD.
- Fibre: Department of Food Chemistry and Applied Nutrition at LTH in Lund, under the supervision of Professor Nils-Georg Asp, Dr Margareta Nyman and Dr Rickard Öste.
- Glycaemic index: Dr Inger Björk, Department of Food Chemistry and Applied Nutrition at LTH in Lund.
- Svalöf Weibulls AB and the Swedish Agricultural University in Alnarp and Svalöf were in front line of cereal plant breeding
- Small-scale production: Department of Food Engineering at LTH in Lund, Dr Ingegerd Sjöholm.

Examples of the application of new cereals know-how

Bionova was the first company to attempt wet processing of wheat. Their project resulted in a brand new technological idea of making fluid products out of cereal flour. This was of great interest to Swedish farmers who produced large amounts of wheat and sugar. They would achieve better profitability if their raw materials were further processed. Bionova's business idea was based on the fractionations of cereal flours. This process made it possible to extract protein and other high-value raw components. Bionova built a factory and had great plans for the future. This all created a great deal of publicity. However, Bionova failed and the company went bankrupt in 1991.

Comments

- A driving force behind this development was the transformation of the Swedish food production. A protected home-market-oriented food industry facing international competition was looking for market opportunities in health-oriented niche products.
- Swedish research in cereals had attained a high level internationally and collaboration between research and industry was increasing.
- The first ideas were based on product development with oat as a base.
- There were signs of consumer interest in the USA.
- There was unique knowledge on soya milk and lactose intolerance in the research and industrial cluster in Lund.
- The Skånska Lantmännen Research Foundation through Lennart Wikström was a key actor to identify development opportunities for cereal production in southern Sweden.

Oatly as an Example of Entrepreneurship in Research (1989–93)

Ideon Agro Food – connecting research and industry

Rickard Öste, a university researcher, was also a project manager at Ideon Agro Food during 1989–1990. Ideon Agro Food is a network connecting research and industry. At one meeting, the industrial member Skånska Lantmännen, represented by Lennart Wikström, R&D Manager, expressed an interest in oats and Rickard was given the assignment in June 1990 on behalf of Ideon Agro Foods to arrange an 'Oats Seminar'.

The oat milk project

At this seminar in June 1990 about future 'Oat Products' Rickard Öste and Inger Ahlden presented the concept of oat milk. Lennart Wikström and Rickard Öste then started discussions about the possibilities of financing by the Skånska Lantmännen Research Foundation. Rickard was in charge of the project based on his researcher role. At an early state Skånemejerier and Tetrapak were invited to support the project but left the arena.

The aim of the project was to develop a milky type of drink, that is low viscosity, with an oat or cereal base with native, unprocessed, untouched betaglucans. Three basic aims of the project were expressed:

- To produce lactose-free milk and similar products.
- To perform the groundwork for a functional food product that should have the ability to lower the blood cholesterol level.
- To produce a product with good taste.

Regular working meetings were held every four to six weeks with very open and focused discussions in order to develop a product in a scientific way without creating the traditional academic explanation and excuse of how it could be. Only reality and scientific knowledge were on the road. Every step in the process was carefully studied. To convince all four researchers in the group a lot of wild and humorous discussions were held on the different steps and knowledge.

Skånska Lantmännen Foundation sole financier

The project was started in the spring, and in June 1991, after some months, Kenneth Andersson announced that Skånemejerier would not be taking part in the project. As a result of Skånemejerier's decision, TetraPak decided not to join the project either. The Skånska Lantmännen was suddenly the only financial partner. Lennart Wikström decided to handle the situation by extending the project from two to three years. As a consequence, the project was reformulated and the ambition was no longer to develop a full-scale commercial product.

Lundagrion founded

Four partners founded the company Lundagrion: Rickard Öste, Kåre Larsson, Lennart Lindahl and Kaj Vareman. Kaj Vareman and Kåre Larsson were experienced entrepreneurs who were encouraging the inventors to pursue the exploitation of the invention. The company was created to own various patents.

Later Lundagrion was reorganized to fit the oat concept. The new owners were Rickard Öste, Lennart Lindahl, Ingegerd Sjöholm and Inger Aldén. The rights of the oat milk patent (application at the time) was then given to the company.

Comments

- Ideon Agro Food, an early cluster of researchers and industry, initiates the development of oat milk.
- The Skånska Lantmännen Research Foundation makes a significant contribution as a strategic financial partner.
- Entrepreneurship in research is about getting along well with each other and having fun.
- Two industrial partners, Skånemejerier and TetraPak, backed out of the project.

- Experienced innovators Kaj Vareman and Kåre Larsson inspired the inventors to create an innovative company. Kaj and Kåre served as role models.
- Parallel research project was going on, for example, Hydrothermal-treated oat kernels. The project was presented at the Oat Seminar arranged by Rickard Öste in June 1990. The project-holder was Kerstin Fredlund from Kalmar University College. Kerstin Fredlund came to the seminar with products made of hydrothremally treated (Kowalski, 1987) flour:[1] pancakes, bread, soap and porridge. Everyone at the seminar was enthusiastic. Ingegerd Sjöholm was very interested in Kerstin Fredlund's idea and some weeks later the project was connected to the Department of Food Engineering. Kerstin Fredlund, raised on a farm, believes in antroposophical ideology and is a medical doctor. Kerstin tries to develop natural products with minimal processing. Most Swedish children are raised on infant formula/gruel which, according to Kerstin, is an 'industrial' unnatural product with low levels of B vitamins and iron. She wanted to develop food for children, which made better use of the bioavailability of nutrients in cereals. One way of doing this is through breaking down the phytic acid in the oats and creating hydrothermally treated flour. Kerstin Fredlund, in addition to being a medical doctor, was a passionate antroposophist and ran the hydro-thermal research project part time in Lund in parallel with normal duties at the hospital in Kalmar 250 km. north of Lund University. Kerstin Fredlund encouraged Ingegerd Sjöholm to recognize the importance of the combination of simple practical trials, medical hypothesis and food engineering studies. This research project later resulted in a patented food process owned by the participant companies including Semper, part of Arla Foods. Semper is one of the major infant formula and gruel manufacturers in Sweden.

The First Industrial Application Turns Out to be a Slimming Drink (1992–94)

To be able to work with the oat concept the inventors and Skånska Lant-männen decided to form a company based on the commercial exploitation of the oat milk patent. The partners in Ceba started to look around for different industrial projects that were related to their oat concept.

Industrial partners

During the project Rickard Öste and Lennart Lindahl made the initial contact with industrial partners who might be able to exploit the 'oat base.' A number of potential partners were approached. A director at Arla came to Skåne in March 1993 and met the project group. He tasted the oat drink and spat it out, saying: 'This is not milk, this will never become a product. Don't call us we'll call you.'

During the spring of 1993, Lennart Lindahl contacted Gustav Lindewald at Procordia Health Foods that was at the time a company consisting of Anjo (herbal pills, health pills) and Friggs. The product development department personnel at Friggs were interested in the idea of making a diet formula based on the oat base. This product could be a competitor to Nutrilet, made by the Norwegian company Nutripharma. The company planned to launch a synthetic diet formula but this product never reached the market place.

The inventors in Lundagrion also tried to sell the idea to Unilever, Nestlé/Findus, Felix and Skånemejerier. All of them answered that it was an interesting project; however, they were not really interested in participating.

Foundation of Ceba

Ceba was founded on 17 February, 1994. The Skånska Lantmännen Foundation had supported the project with money and the researchers contributed with their knowledge and innovation. Ceba became a company owned equally by Skånska Lantmännen and the researchers. The Skånska Lantmännen Foundation provided additional money to set up the limited company and the researchers Rickard Öste, Ingegerd Sjöholm, Inger Ahlden and Lennart Lindahl financed the patent rights through their mutual company Lundagrion. Lennart Wikström was appointed the first Managing Director of Ceba.

Agreement with Friggs regarding the slimming drink 'Complätt'

Lennart Wikström's first assignment as Ceba's Managing Director was to negotiate a contract with Friggs, owned by Procordia Health Foods. Friggs presented a marketing plan for the brand 'Complätt' (complete in English). Ceba and Friggs decided to carry out a clinical study on the slimming product. This took place during the autumn of 1993. It was a 24-week study that ended in April 1994.

The agreement stated that both parties should invest in the product. Development and production of the product was to be subcontracted and Ceba had the right to evaluate the subcontractors before accepting them. The agreement was limited to the slimming drink based on oats. The product appeared on the market in May 1994 with the flavours tomato and asparagus. Later on, the flavours mushroom and apple were added.

The Trensum apple juice factory became the subcontractor. Friggs already used Trensum for subcontracted production. This is one of the few companies in southern Sweden with aseptic packaging lines. Trensum was already involved in a similar product, that is, the soymilk 'Tufoline', Carlshamn Mejeri. Ingegerd Sjöholm and Lennart Lindahl also had previous contact with Marc Ljungström, Managing Director and part owner of Trensum. Suitable equipment was chosen based on the long-term industrial experience of Marc Ljungström and the theoretical knowledge from the entrepreneurs from LTH. As soon as the equipment was in place the inventors started new process development and fine-tuning. Trensum was not used to this type of sensitive production process. Lennart Lindahl, Inger Ahlden and Ingegerd Sjöholm had to be present of all times to monitor the process.

'Complätt' lost its 'home base' when Procordia Health Food sold Friggs to Semper. The product lived on thanks to the Product Manager, who believed in the product. When the Product Manager left Semper and started at ICA in 1998–99 Semper decided to remove the product from the market.

Comments

- The innovative oat base had at this stage proven itself to be an interesting ingredient. The first application happened to be a slimming product.
- Rickard Öste was the entrepreneurial scientist who enthusiastically told everybody about this new great idea. Ingegerd Sjöholm was responsible for choosing the equipment. Lennart Lindahl contributed through his knowledge of processing cereals and other protein products. He was familiar with this type of development from his previous work on egg whites. Inger Ahldén had practical experience from the laboratory tests and developed expert knowledge on the taste and quality of oat flakes.
- Almost all of the food companies that were approached turned the idea down. The only exception was Procordia Health Food/Friggs. According to Utterback, large companies in the 'specific phase' have problems developing new products.
- The choice of a slimming product as the first application was due to the fact that it was for this product that the researchers could get financial support. It was not the most interesting application from the researchers' point of view.

Oat Milk to the Market (1994–96)

The inventors were never really satisfied with the slimming drink. The slimming drink was an idea that came from Friggs. The inventor had set out to make a milk alternative, oat milk.

So far, however, nobody was interested in marketing such an idea, until autumn 1994, when Rickard had a meeting with Friggs and Gunnar Levander, Gustav Lindewald, Peter Thesleff (marketing man from the UK, agent for Arla/Scan), Sven Sahlin (trader), Jan-Olof Bengtsson (Food From Sweden).[2] Rickard Öste was about to present the process of oat milk as the base for the slimming formula, when Peter Thesleff and Jan-Olof Bengtsson expressed: 'Oat milk, really good! Why not sell the oat milk as pure milk? That's something that I (Peter Thesslef) would be able to sell in England.'

Ceba initiated an important meeting, in May 1995, between Food From Sweden and their representative, Jan-Olof Bengtsson, and Peter Thesleff. At this time, they were discussing a project totally different from the slimming drink project.

Peter Sahlin, Sven Sahlin, and Jan-Olof Bengtsson reported that the interest in soya milk in England was increasing but nobody seemed to like the taste. Jan-Olof Bengtsson said that he would be able to arrange some type of financial support from Food From Sweden. Rickard Öste talked to Christer Quist, Business Area Manager at Skånska Lantmännen. Skånska Lantmännen would be interested in supporting the project, but wanted someone with sales experience to be involved. Skånska Lantmännen chose Bengt Anker Kofoed, who was the Managing Director of the SL-owned company Scanian Farmers.[3] Bengt Anker Kofoed engaged Peter Thesleff in the project. From this moment on it was agreed that the sales of oat milk should be channelled through Scanian Farmers, and the profit should be transformed to Ceba. The arrangement was later changed into a royalty agreement between the companies. In 2001, when Ceba expanded its activities, Scanian Farmers was bought by Ceba.

Bengt Anker Kofoed, with 15 years of experiences from the food sector, was in charge of the marketing of oat milk from 1995. He is currently (2002) active in Ceba as a manager of exports.

The agreement with Friggs applied to Complätt only. When Lennart Wikström was Managing Director of Ceba it was a principle that Ceba was not allowed to invest money in internal development work. Development projects should always be conducted in partnerships where the partners shared the financial responsibility.

In 1996 Ceba appointed Rickard Öste as the new Managing Director of Ceba. They gave him a consultancy contract that resulted in the presentation of a new business plan, which led Skånska Lantmännen to become interested in investing more money in Ceba. Later, equal amounts were invested in the company by the group of scientists, thereby keeping the ownership structure (50/50) of the company. Rickard now had the opportunity to work on other industrial applications.

Oat milk, the second application of the oat base

Ceba was already collaborating with Trensum concerning Complätt. It was thus natural to subcontract the oat milk to the same company.

Everything was working well: Inger Ahldén and Lennart Lindahl were performing all the laboratory tests. The transformation of the production process to industrial scale at Trensum had to be supervised constantly and some parts of the researchers always had to be present at Trensum due to the complexity of the product and the demand for quality control.

Inger Ahlden was on maternity leave with her first child in 1996. At the same time, Lennart Lindahl spent a year in Australia. Inger Ahlden and Lennart Lindahl could then view the oat milk from a new perspective. Angie Öste, who has a PhD in enzyme technology and is Rickard's wife, came into the project in 1995. Angie's assignment was to identify better enzymes that were quality assured and GMO-assured. These projects were also financed by The Skånska Lantmännen Foundation.

Comments

- The innovation process has proceeded to the next phase. Oat milk technology has found new applications.
- Oat milk becomes a tasty alternative to soya milk.
- Peter Thesleff formulates a new product concept in the innovation landscape. His idea transfers the project to the mountain top. The product concept matures with impulses from the market.
- Rickard Öste formulated a new strategy for Ceba as an ingredient company.
- The new product concept corresponds well with the concepts of the research team.

Oat Milk – an Alternative for Lactose-intolerant Consumers (1995–96)

Product launch in the UK

Food From Sweden partially financed a market study in the UK. This study confirmed that there was interest in another lactose-free milk beside soya milk. Bengt Anker Kofoed engaged Peter Thesleff as a sales agent for oat milk in the UK.

Peter Thesleff, the marketing representative, and his sales manager, Brian Bath, had a full understanding about the mechanism of the UK retail market and drew up the plan for the UK market launch. They were looking for maximum publicity at low cost. The presentation of the product was supported by a general health presentation by an independent UK reference researcher. One of the most fashionable places in London was chosen to host this PR exercise. An Indian chef had been hired to create a large number of dishes from the oat base, such as drinks, soups, lunches and desserts. The timing was perfect and many journalists, purchasers and other contacts participated.

Peter Thesleff believes in the beauty of PR and, together with Scanian Farmers and Ceba, arranged a PR launch in November 1995 at the Café Royal at Piccadilly Circus, London. The arrangement attracted around 60 journalists, Kellogg's research director, purchasers and so on. An independent researcher from Nottingham gave a lecture about breakfast habits in the UK. The health food trade was, according to Brian Bath, thrilled by the product and the oat drink was listed at most of the health food trade wholesalers. Sales through the health food trade by 1996 were 200,000 litres. An article about the oat drink in the *Daily Mail* on 27 August, 1996 meant a breakthrough in awareness among consumers. Peter Thesleff wanted to get the oat drink listed at a 'mainstream retailers' (for example Tesco, Sainsbury, Asda, Safeway) to ensure big sales volumes. This was, however, not achieved until 2001, when the product was listed in Tesco and Waitrose, when more marketing money was invested.

Oat milk became an oat drink in the Swedish market

On 29 May 1996 Bengt Anker Kofoed managed to get Christian Wiechel, head of ICA's Own Label, interested in the product. Christian Wiechel had two children who were lactose-intolerant and did not like soya milk. Sales through ICA reached 300–400,000 litres during the first year. Early in 1997, the Swedish dairy industry was not very keen on the idea of calling a cereal drink cereal milk. They met with Scanian Farmers and referred to European regulations. Bengt Anker Kofoed had to accept this and changed the product description from oat milk to oat drink.

Introduction to the US market

Through Peter Thesleff's contacts the oat drink was launched by Scanian Farmers in March 1996, in the USA, at the Natural Food Expo in Anaheim, California. This was the starting point of the sales boom in the US market. The sales had an incredible development at the US health food market but more or less collapsed after a while. The explanation to this was that Ceba/Scanian Farmers were not able to supply the demand and when the supply started to work properly, US competitors, such as Pacific Food, had started to sell me-too products at a lower price.

The new management of Skånska Lantmännen, Chairman of the Board, Per Sorte and Managing Director, Jan Persson, were alarmed by the investments in the US market. The new management changed the focus from distant markets to markets closer to Sweden.

Market introduction in the wrong order

Bengt Anker Kofoed admits that Scanian Farmers delayed the advance on the European market due to the fact that the focus during the years 1997 and 1998 was on the US market. Scanian Farmers did not have enough knowledge about the European health food market initially. They did things a little backwards and in the year 2000, Ceba/Scanian Farmers started to look to the Nordic market.

Experiences from Finland and Denmark show that to accomplish high-volume sales of functional food products like oat drink you need to be part of mainstream retailing. The health food trade is a minimal market in the Scandinavian countries. Finland is of particular interest since the Finns' ethnical background makes them genetically lacto-intolerant. The climate also makes it impossible to cultivate wheat, and as a consequence the Finns have a long tradition of using oats and rye.

Comments

- Peter Thesleff was an entrepreneur with marketing skills and was part of an international cluster.
- Peter Thesleff understood the potential of the health food market in the UK and the USA. The health food trade also served as a showcase to attract interest from mainstream retailers.
- It is important to have first-hand experience like in the ICA case. The purchaser's children were lacto-intolerant which led to his interest in the product.
- Market launches internationally must be accompanied by upscaling and fine-tuning of production volumes and distribution efficiency.

Oat Milk in Safe Hands at Skånemejerier (1996–98)

At this time Skånemejerier showed a growing interest in working together with Ceba on a regional level. The Managing Directors, Jan Persson of Skånska Lantmännen and Rolf Bjärndell of Skånemejerier, presented their idea of greater collaboration between the two companies. This would provide a good combination of Skånemejerier's flexible production and concept thinking, with Skånska Lantmännens' know-how. However, Skånska Lant-männen was not the natural choice of partner for the group of scientists.

Collaboration with Skånemejerier

On 30 August 1996, Jan Persson, the new Managing Director at Skånska Lantmännen, and Rolf Bjerndell, Managing Director at Skånemejerier, were interviewed in Sweden's top business newspaper, *Dagens Industri*: 'New food in a hungry market – Swedish companies export food that is close to medicine.' This article surprised the staff at both companies because they were not told in advance. This PR boom describing new, extensive collaboration between Skånska Lantmännen and Skånemejerier resulted in a number of changes. The major consequence was that Skånska Lantmännen wanted to move production from Trensum to Skånemejerier's dairy in Lunnarp.

Closer collaboration between Skånska Lantmännen and Skånemejerier happened through:

- Production collaboration
- The new Managing Directors viewed regional collaboration as a strength
- Collaboration in export had started between the companies regarding the oat drink
- R&D collaboration concerning carrots

Trensum was, rightfully one may say, furious about the article in *Dagens Industri* and refused to collaborate. Finally, Marc Ljungström Managing Director of Trensum, agreed to a step-by-step closure contract valid until the end of 1999, when Lunnarp was finally to take over all production. Trensum was allowed to continue to produce Complätt for Friggs. A new industrial process was successfully developed and implemented at Lunnarp by the plant manager at Skånemejerier.

Lennart Wikström, in his role as R&D Director at Skånska Lantmännen, and Christer Quist both wanted to take part in development projects with Skånemejerier and not only the oat drink. They were invited to a presentation and discussion with Skånemejerier's management group where they presented the idea 'AB Skånska Bär' (in English, Scania Berry Company) based on working with new raw materials, for example, fruit and vegetables from the province of Skåne. The 'carrot' project 'Mona Carota' is such a project.

Export collaboration between Skånemejerier and Skånska Lantmännen

Skånemejerier's export department and the Skånska Lantmännen-owned Scanian Farmers were merged in 1997. Scanian Farmers' Managing Director, Bengt Anker Kofoed, became Key Account Manager for a number of export markets such as Denmark and Norway. Skånemejerier's Export Manager,

Anders Lareke, focused on the two major export markets; the United Kingdom and Finland.

Anders Lareke wanted to launch the oat drink concept in Finland. There is a preference for oats, since there has been a tradition in cultivating oats in Finland for centuries. Skånemejerier has experience of working with health products since 1995, when the functional food fruit drink, ProViva[4] was launched in Finland. Contacts with the media, researchers and dieticians were believed to be ways of promoting claims of the product.

Politics in the 'inventors'

The closer collaboration between Skånska Lantmännen and Scanian Farmers caused problems between the inventors. Rickard Öste and Ingegerd Sjöholm started to plan the production process in Lunnarp and Lennart Lindahl and Inger Ahldén preferred the Trensum alternative.

Ingegerd Sjöholm planned the second version of the process line based on experience from laboratory tests and earlier production together with new knowledge about the process. Then, during the autumn of 1998, Rickard Öste started to work for Ceba full time. Rickard Öste increased his commitment to Ceba and the production was moved to Skånemejerier. At this point Lennart Lindahl and Inger Ahlden decided to no longer remain partners in Ceba. Rickard's brother Björn Öste bought their shares in Lundagrion, and later on invested money in Ceba through Lundagrion.

Comments

- Two of the researchers, Rickard Öste and Ingegerd Sjöholm, were more deeply involved during this period than the other two, Lennart Lindahl and Inger Ahlden.
- The Managing Directors of Skånska Lantmännen and Skånemejerier did not understand the importance of informing their employees about the strategic alliance. In this respect they acted like old-fashioned managers.
- The timing of the health issue was perfect and the article in *Dagens Industri* had an enormous PR effect.
- 'The concept carrier' in this phase, Ingegerd Sjöholm, chose Lunnarp from a technological perspective. This change was necessary to continue the process innovation. She was now able to apply all her know-how and previous experience to the production process in Lunnarp. This enabled a production process to be designed from scratch, without too many compromises.

Oat Base as an Ingredient on the Market (1997–2000)

The initial sales success made the partners of the oat milk interested in exploiting the oat base. To be able to expand the oat base into other areas Ceba needed more financial backing. Ceba got new financial support through the Business Angel, Björn Öste, who also became engaged in the business development of Ceba. Björn Öste and Rickard Öste executed Ceba's new strategy to become a food ingredient company.

Danone – the first industrial partner

At this time the large companies started to show interest in the oat base technology. Danone had seen the oat drink at a health food exhibition in Blackpool in the UK, and Danone brought the product home to France to test before they contacted Ceba. Representatives from Danone and Ceba met for the first time in April 1996; Danone and Ceba signed a contract in 1998. Danone wanted to launch a vegetarian alternative to dairy yoghurt with a nice taste. A product based on oat base and soya was launched in France, but was taken off the market after a time because Danone was disappointed with the sales results.

Comments

- Björn Öste came into Ceba at exactly the right time. He brought with him two essential assets, capital and professional business know-how. Björn made it possible for Ceba to become an ingredient company.
- The people around the oat drink seem to be successful without partnership with big companies.
- We are now in the borderland between the transition phase and the specific phase. Consumer responses were very important in the guiding of the development.

Ceba has Become 'The Green Dairy' in the Swedish Market (2001)

Ceba has then changed its mission from being a food ingredient company to being a food company with branded products in the market for alternatives to milk products in Sweden. The new Managing Director, Mats-Ola Kindstedt, is launching the idea of 'The Green Dairy'. New financial partners started to show interest in Ceba, and in the spring of 2001 a large mutual fund managed by Carnegie became involved as leading investor.

Ceba is expanding

In May 2000, under the chairman Jan Persson,[5] a new Managing Director, Mats-Ola Kindstedt, was employed. Mats-Ola Kindstedt previously worked for Nestlé, Solanum (a potato company) and ICA (a retailer). The Board was eager to employ a new Managing Director with good business experience. This gave Rickard Öste the opportunity to focus on research again.

Sales of oat drink had increased to 3 million in 2001, of which 1 million was sold in Sweden. The sales increase has been 30–40 per cent every year. During 2001 Ceba and Scanian Farmers merged into one company, Ceba.

New products

According to Mats-Ola Kindstedt, Ceba is a company that will only work with a wider focus than functional foods. Ceba develops products that people really need. Ceba wants to develop products with its own brand rather than focusing on developing ingredients. The pancake batter and ice cream were launched during the summer of 2001, followed by vanilla custard and cooking cream. New products are in the pipeline for 2003. Production and sales collaboration are with Skånemejerier and SIA – Glass.

Ceba's oats contain 100 per cent pure Swedish oats, guaranteed not to contain any other cereal. This makes it possible for even gluten-intolerant consumers to eat Oatly products.

Focus on research

With the new financial situation, Ceba increased its research efforts in five defined areas. In collaboration with different scientific partners, European and Swedish (VINNOVA) research projects started, that utilize Ceba's technologies and new patent applications in the health and functional food areas. Notably, the EU Commission has decided to contribute with SEK17 million to a research project regarding cereals that was initiated by Ceba and the unit of biomedical nutrition at Lund University. The purpose of the project is to achieve betaglucans products with a high degree of purity and to be able to evaluate their sensoric, nutritional and chemical properties.

Comments

- Ceba changes mission and establishes 'Oatly' as the green dairy brand.
- It is very important to develop clusters and maintain a continuous dialogue in the cluster.
- The appointment of Mats-Ola Kindstedt as Managing Director was important. One reason for engaging a new Managing Director was to

organize Ceba as a professional company, and the other was to allow Rickard Öste to concentrate his time on R&D issues.
• Rickard has been successful in building a cluster of researchers and companies on a European level.

Final comments

• All the early corporate customers of the oat drink had personal involvement in the product. They have themselves or within their families food-related problems such as lactose intolerance.
• An ingredient branding strategy has been changed to a product branding strategy during the last two years.
• This case demonstrates that it is more important to be active and to do things rather than do things right.
• Ceba managed throughout the fluid phase and the transition phase in the innovation process without major external financial support.
• The oat drink case is now in between the transition phase and the specific phase, according to Utterback's model.

Bibliography

Books and articles

Heasman, M. and Mellentin, J. (2001), *The Functional Food Revolution*, London: Earthscan Publications Ltd.

Heasman, M. and Mellentin, J. (1999), *Swedish Oats for Heart Health*, The newsletter for functional foods, nutraceuticals and healthy eating, October, p. 23–24, London.

Hellbom, O. (1996) *Ny Mat på hungrig marknad – Svenska företag exporterar livsmedel som gränsar till medicin*, Dagens Industri, 30 August, p. 17, Stockholm.

Internet

Skånemejerier.se
Adavena.com

Table 6.4   Personal communication in the Oatly case

Person	Function/company	Time/place of personal interview
Lennart Wikström	MD of the Sl-foundation	1999-06-09 Malmö 2000-02-29 Klågerup
Bengt Anker Kofoed	MD Scanian Farmers	2000-02-02 Malmö
Mats Ola Kindstedt	MD Ceba (2000-)	2000-05-30 Lund
Thomas Wennerholm	Project Manager Ceba	2000-05-30 Lund
Rickard Öste	R&D Manager Ceba	2000-05-24 Lund
Kirsi Malinen	Head of Skånemejerier sales in Finland	2000-03-08 Malmö
Ingegerd Sjöholm	PhD Food engineering Lund Institute of Technology	2000-04-08 Lund
Jan-Olof Bengtsson	Project Director Food from Sweden	2000-01-25 Malmö
Anna Persson	Product Manager Scanian Farmers	1999-03-29
Sven Sahlin	Chairman First Food	2002-04-10
Brian Bath	Organic Food Consultant	2002-04-07
Kenneth Andersson	R&D Manager Skånemejerier	1999-03-29

THE MONA CAROTA CASE

Background

In December 1993 Gert Göransson, Ideon Agro Food (IDAF), organized a brainstorming meeting on the 'cool chain' of vegetables. Representatives from different categories from farmers to consumers were invited. This meeting resulted in the formation of a joint project between the companies ICA Frukt och Grönt AB, Frigoscandia AB, Sydgrönts Försäljnings AB, Perstorp AB, Grönsaksodlarnas Riksförbund and SLU Trädgårdsvetenskap Alnarp together with a project leader from IDAF. The companies invested SEK5000 each and Ingegerd Sjöholm, a researcher at the Department of Food Engineering, Lund University, became the Project Manager. A pilot study focused on cooling and cooling techniques, and the quality of chilled products and packing materials was presented a year later in December 1994. The study carried out applied to tomatoes, lettuce, cucumbers and carrots. Apart from the cool chain aspects it induced a simple economical analysis of possibilities and potential of exporting and importing vegetables to and from Sweden. The analysis clearly showed the possibilities and advantages of growing carrots in the south of Sweden. The climate is very favourable, the farmers have well-developed and controlled harvesting technology and good knowledge in post-harvest treatment. Also the price level of fresh carrots is competitive with those in, for example, Denmark and Finland.

Intensive cultivation, post-harvest technology and winter storage of carrots were well implemented through an association called 'the carrot growers' organization' initiated by the farmer Marianne Härning Nilsson, Marianne's Morötter AB, Strövelstorp.

> This learning and development of knowledge was later identified to be a part of a broad knowledge investment in vegetables taking place in the early 1960s when Findus developed the concept of frozen green peas from Sweden. Marianne's father and grandfather grew carrots before the Second World War to be sold, for example, in Stockholm, 600 km north of the farm. During certain periods Marianne's farm was co-operated in different ways with Findus, later owned by Nestlé.
>
> Ingegerd Sjöholm, from Lund University, teacher and researcher, specialized in applied industrial food engineering, became the project leader. Ingegerd, who obtained her PhD at Lund University in 1986, had just started to look for deeper and more long-term research projects in which PhD students could perform work for their theses and not only Master's students, which had been the procedure for quite some time.
>
> The development of basic and key knowledge in the area of fruit and vegetable technology has long been one of Ingegerd's visions, based both on childhood experience and collaboration at the cell level with a colleague, Vassilis Gekas. In 1997 Vassilis Gekas accepted a full professorship in Environmental Technology in Crete, in Greece. Their collaboration has strengthened with time and includes a number of projects.

In February 1995, Ingegerd approached Lennart Wickström, the co-ordinator of the Skånska Lantmännen Research Foundation to ask whether farmers in Skåne might be interested in growing carrots. The response was very positive but with one clear proviso: 'The person launching the product must sponsor the project from the beginning.'

> Wickström's response was the result from earlier experience in a joint project between a group of researchers, including Sjöholm, and the companies TetraPak and Skånemejerier, in which funding failed, perhaps because of the delay between the idea and the development of a consumer product. The project was eventually successful and the company Ceba AB is described in another chapter. Skånemejerier is now one of the owners of Ceba AB, but Tetra Pak is not.

The first company identified that might be interested in developing carrot juice was the dairy, Skånemejerier, and the response to the question delivered by R&D Manager, Kenneth Andersson, was without hesitation, 'Yes'.

Carrots can provide the raw material for several different consumer products but juice was chosen as a result of the poor availability in the existing market for fresh carrot juice with a good taste and a reasonably long shelf life. Fresh carrot juice was only available at that time as a kind of 'home made' juice, packed in a small plastic cup wrapped in plastic film. The typical consumer was an impassioned vegetarian. In the food market as a whole, however, there was also the beginning of a trend towards non-alcoholic beverages and on nutritional drinks.

Starting up Period and Literature Study

As a project leader at Ideon Agro Food, Ingegerd Sjöholm submitted a proposal for funding by the Skånska Lantmännen Research Foundation and Skånemejerier to finance a short literature review on carrot juice production. Two months' funding of SEK60,000 were received. Charlotte Alklint was employed to perform the study in spring 1995. Charlotte Alklint had just completed her MSc on 'Drying of Rose Hips' at the Department of Food Engineering, Lund University, and had also carried out three other industrial literature commissions one concerning alternative cooling methods, the second on peas and finally the use of meats in sausage production. These different projects made Charlotte eligible as the PhD student to take on the carrot juice project.

A preliminary review was presented orally on 4 May 1995, and the stakeholders decided to continue the project. The project was called 'Mona Carota' after the name Monica which is the name of 4 May in the Swedish calendar and the Latin name for carrots. The literature review was completed and the written report was presented on 14 June 1995.

Initiation and Aims of the Project

Skånska Lantmännen and Skånemejerier found the literature review very valuable and were eager to find a way to initiate the project. On their request Ingegerd Sjöholm wrote a full two-year proposal and submitted it to the companies. The proposal was accepted and it was decided that it should be an Ideon Agro Food project with a steering group consisting of Lennart Wikström, Skånska Lantmännen and Kenneth Andersson, Skånemejerier. Charlotte Alklint was to carry out the work with Ingegerd Sjöholm as the project leader. The work was to be carried out at the Department of Food Engineering, at Lund University, as a postgraduate project. The steering group was to meet frequently and everything was to be documented in written protocols.

The objective of the Mona Carota project was as follows: *to determine how to produce a stable carrot juice with good flavour and appearance and long shelf life without using additives.*

Product Testing

At the first meeting of the steering group on 4 June 1995 different juices available on the market were sensorially evaluated. The tested juices were fresh and frozen 'Morotsjos' (carrot juice) from Brämhult, organically farmed fresh and frozen juice from Änglamark, Friggs 'Megakaroten' and Friggs 'Morot Fruktjuice'. The Brämhult carrot juice was awarded the highest grade, sweet, good taste and only a slight bitter off-taste. Änglamark received the lowest grade; it had an off-flavour and tasted of soil. Kenneth Andersson did not even taste it as he claimed the juice was full of undesirable microorganisms. Friggs' 'Morot Fruktjuice' was good but had a slight taste of metal and was too thick. Friggs' 'Megakaroten' just tasted wrong; synthetic, somewhat too acid and was too thick. In the general discussion after the sensorial evaluation all agreed on the meaning of the keyword: 'clean taste', by means of no bitterness, a smooth viscosity, no metallic taste and a fresh taste.

One more juice was found on the market later, Granini carrot nectar. This juice was also sensorially evaluated and found to be more acceptable than the other heat-treated juices.

At this first steering group meeting, which became the kick-off meeting, strategic activities for the coming years were planned. The working areas identified were:

- Soil, cultivation and species
- Hygiene
- Pre-treatment
- Sensorial evaluation

Project Plan

The following timetable was presented in the written proposal in spring 1995.

Milestone 1　　　15 April – 15 June 1995
　　　　　　　　Inventory and formation of the collaboration teams
　　　　　　　　Product strategy

Milestone 2   June1995 –December 1996
                Practical trials focused on critical control points
                Methodology and continuous evaluation
                Work by the various collaboration teams
                Shelf life studies.

Milestone 3   January 1996 – June 1997
                Consumer tests
                Process optimization
                Quality assurance of process and product

In close collaboration with Skånska Lantmännen two sub-projects involving the cultivation of different species and carrots with different levels of fertilization were planned.

According to the wide and creative discussions and brainstorming meeting different areas of competence were identified. Key persons were identified and contacted.

Collaboration Between the Departments of Food Engineering and Plant Biochemistry

The Department of Plant Biochemistry, Lund University was contacted in order to establish expertise in common technologies when analysing cellular components. Ingegerd Sjöholm was simultaneously looking for contacts that could be useful in two other new PhD projects, 'Osmotic Treatment of Apple Pieces and Processing of Frozen Berries (Strawberries).' A meeting with senior researchers from the Department of Plant Biochemistry took place in September 1995. This meeting proved to be a meeting between two cultures. Researchers working with plant cells on a microscopic level examine what happens inside the mitochondria and in the cell membrane. They often extract the component they want to study from a large amount of cells and then perform the analysis. The need in the project was to identify sensitive analyses, suitable for following changes in the juice along the production line. In the laboratory-scale production line the aim was to have at least a few hundred litres per hour. The meeting progressed in an atmosphere where Ingegerd tried to inspire the plant biochemists to think in terms of how to utilize their broad knowledge in the engineering world. Unfortunately, attempts failed, and the meeting ended with the following words from our colleagues at Plant Biochemistry: 'This is of interest but we don't think and work in the way you do.'

This meeting was somewhat unusual and the Food Engineering group did not feel comfortable with their discussion partners. However this contact was the beginning of co-operation between the Departments of Plant Biochemistry and Food Engineering. Five years later there was intense collaboration concerning components of the cell walls of carrots and the activity of ATPs in plasma membranes of potato cells.

Plant Breeding – Carrot Juice

The plant breeding company Svalöf Weibull/Hammenhög was contacted with the aim of inducing them to grow different cultivars fertilized in different ways. We met researchers at Hammenhög, their test farming place and discussed the role of 'cadmium' and the general bioviability of carrots, with regard to the effects of storage conditions and storage time on sensorial changes in carrots, whether these could be detected in the juice. They informed us about their ongoing research projects focused on carrot breeding. In their breeding experiments financed by governmental funding they study, for example, yield after harvest and storage in different climates. No parameters are measured or optimized with regard to the taste of processed carrots or the yield of fresh carrot juice. However, we learned that some carrots are called 'juice carrots', and other are called carrots for the fresh consumer market. The nitrate content varies in different species. Different hypotheses regarding where the carotenes are located were also discussed. The conclusion of this meeting was that they offered us a number of species from the 1995 harvest to be tested in our laboratory juice production equipment.

Discussions were held with 'Potatisspecialisten', a local SME specializing in potatoes, on the pre-treatment of carrots. At this time the company ran some trials in order to try to develop carrot products in parallel with their concept for potatoes. Some carrot samples were tested for juice production but these pre-treated carrots tasted bad and were too old.

Contacts were made to obtain carrots from a farm called 'Stockholmsgården'.

The breeding company, Svalöf Weibull, was asked to perform some analyses.

Ingegerd Sjöholm discussed with Kåre Larsson, Professor of Food Technology, Lund University, the difference in bioviability of beta-carotene in fresh carrots when consumed as shredded carrots and when eating a whole carrot as a snack.

Tetra Pack was contacted in order to plan heat treatment and aseptic packaging of fresh juice.

Lennart Wikström, Skånska Lantmännen, contacted Agrolab, a company selling analysis and competence around the analysis to be performed during the cultivation and harvest of carrots in 1996. The analyses were related to understanding the levels of cadmium and beta-carotene.

The Project is Divided into Subprojects

At a meeting in January 1996, Lennart Wikstöm decided to divide the Mona Carota project into the following areas:

1. Species and growing location
2. Pre-treatment
3. Processing
4. Juice extraction
5. Reducing level of microorganism
6. Packaging and distribution
7. By-products

Parameters to be optimized were taste and aroma, microorganism level and nutrients. Lennart Wikström took on the responsibility for the first area dealing with species and growing location and conditions. Charlotte Alklint was given responsibility for pre-treatment, processing, juice extraction, reducing the level of microorganisms and aseptic packaging.

Kenneth Andersson, Skånemejerier, has previous experience of cloud formation in juice. The decision was made to investigate this phenomenon in an effort to understand when it occurs.

Lennart Wikström presented the results of the analysis of cadmium content in different species received from Svalöf Weibull, Hammenhög.

Skånemejerier handed over the signed contracts for the two-year project. Skånska Lantmännen had done this earlier.

At a meeting in February in 1996 juices were tested from the different species received from the breeding company Svalöf Weibull. All the juices were sensorially evaluated. The taste and the aroma differed considerably and it was quite easy to decide which species were suitable to grow in the next season.

Juice extraction was discussed and the decision was made to run trials in a decanter.

Later, in March and April, Charlotte Alklint participated in a PhD course on antioxidants at Uppsala University. She wrote a summary of all the lectures and presented the contents at a meeting. Subsequently, the book *Plant Vitamins, Agronomic, Physiological and Nutritional Aspects,* based on the course, was published.

Lennart Wikström and Charlotte Alklint set up the strategy and plans for experiments after the next growing and harvest season. Controlled cultivation of a number of carrots was planned and a larger amount of one-carrot species was to be used for be ordered for pilot-plant trials.

Skånemejerier's Previous Carrot Project

During spring 1997 it became more and more clear that Skånemejerier had earlier had run an almost full-scale carrot project. Kenneth Andersson informed us from the beginning that they had already tried to start up a juice project together with Alfa Laval in collaboration with a company handling cut vegetables, but this project was never realized. During the spring of 1997 Kenneth Andersson provided us with more information involving these earlier trials of carrot juice production. In one meeting Kenneth provided the names and companies involved in the project, together with the drawings of the process line. It was clear that Salico, a Medium Sized Enterprise in Helsingborg specialized in cut fresh vegetables, was one of the participants. No information was given regarding how far the project had progressed, the financial situation, or whether it had been abandoned.

Charlotte Alklint telephoned Salico and asked about the equipment that was used in the former project and was informed that it was rented at the time from Tetra Laval. In other meetings it became clear that Tetra Laval actually owned it and that it was hired by Skånemejerier who later bought it. Nobody seemed to know its whereabouts. To proceed with the Mona Carota project the possibility of hiring various mills was discussed in order to test them before the start of the next carrot season in September.

We also had a meeting with the professor of Crop Production Science at the Agricultural University, SLU, in Alnarp. The meeting received information about the difference in content of beta-carotene, soluble fibres, and the increase in sucrose after 150-days' storage. Growing carrots does not require much extra nitrogen. Carrots take up potassium and nitrate when available in the soil. The length of the carrots is a function of the density of planting. It is possible to grow around 8 kg carrots/m^2. The dry substance of the carrots is relatively constant in relation to their size. Carrots should be grown in fields with a low cadmium content, high topsoil content, a high content of sand and the depth of cultivated soil.

At another meeting the Mona Carota project was discussed with some other senior researchers from the Agricultural University and the breeding company, Svalöf Weibull. They expressed an interest in joining the project and were interested in writing a proposal together with us. However, we have to define more precisely what we want to focus on. To produce a juice that can be described as 'a stable carrot juice with good flavour and appearance and long shelf life without using additives' was a too weak concept for them. Neither could they understand why we were concerned with discussions on how the juice could be produced when the first, as yet unsolved, part is how to grow the carrots.

The trials involving growing carrots with different fertilization levels were evaluated and continued by Lennart Wikström and Charlotte Alklint. Collaboration with other organizations is not always easy. When Charlotte Alklint came to Hammenhög to harvest the extra carrots they were providing for our project, she found that they had sprayed insecticide to prevent carrot fly. Instead, we had to use the Dutch species Nandrin acquired from Stockholmsgården.

In Quest of a Proper Mill

In order to test different mills Charlotte Alklint and Ingegerd Sjöholm went to southern Germany and Switzerland in September to visit two mill companies. The boot of Ingegerd's car was loaded with test carrots. They drove the car to Hamburg in Germany and travelled on by car-train almost to the Swiss border. This ensured that the carrots were kept at a low temperature and the cool chain was not broken. Trials were run at a large well-established company and at a smaller, specialized company. In total, 13 different milling trials were run at the two companies and samples collected for later analysis, all with the ambition of finding out how to produce a stable juice with good taste and appearance and a reasonably long shelf life without using additives.

> Both companies offered exceptionally good test equipment on which to run the trials. At the smaller company we were allowed to do whatever we suggested. They were very flexible in trying both the conventional and not so conventional set-ups. At the other company we were almost not allowed to touch the equipment. They had special employees to set up and run the trials and everything had to be planned in detail before each run. The company did not seem to be used to female researchers working under the same premises as male colleagues. After a couple of hours one of them asked Charlotte Alklint if Ingegerd Sjöholm really was her supervisor and boss, and asked if this method of working really was normal procedure in Sweden. However, after some time we managed to investigate what was of interest to us. Later, we also found out that they were perhaps being protective about different procedures because a new Swiss carrot juice had just been launched on to the market. We tried the product and we found it to be far from satisfying our objectives for the Mona Carota juice.

In autumn 1997 Charlotte Alklint presented the Mona Carota project on a poster at a General Meeting arranged for the National Swedish Food Researchers. The poster was focused on how to process carrots when the raw material is well defined and controlled. Later, the carrots grown by Svalöf Weibull were harvested and stored in a cooling room at the farm in Hammenhög.

The results of the expedition to Germany and Switzerland to look for mills were not as successful as the reserchers and entrepreneurs had hoped. It was decided to rent the best mill and use it in the pilot-plant hall at the Centre for Chemistry and Chemical Engineering, Lund University.

The Question of Patenting

At this point a discussion on how to protect the juice-making process from competitors started. Is there a need to take out a patent, is it possible, or is it better to keep everything secret?

The discussion on quality and methods of characterizing the juice continued. The most important parameter was defined and called 'mouth feeling'. This property will be difficult to measure in an objective way. One way of obtaining some objective data is to use rheology measurements. It was decided that tests should be done with the new Bohlin rheometer at Food Engineering called Rheo Cue. (These measurements were unfortunately unsuccessful.)

A new method of sterilizing the surface of peeled carrots was discussed. Skånemejerier started to show an interest in the possibility of fermenting the fibres in the carrot waste.

Kenneth Andersson nominated a contact person at Skånemejerier to be our working partner in the final development before launching. Later on, in another project, it was found that this person had never heard about the Mona Carota project.

Pilot-plant Production

In February 1997 all the juices from the carrots grown at Hammenhög were evaluated. The stored carrots were peeled and the juice was sensorially evaluated. The taste was a catastrophe compared with the previous year. Nematode worms in the soil had attacked the carrots and destroyed the quality.

Lennart Wickström planned new test cultivation at Hammenhög for the coming season. Three repetitions include three varieties. For some reason this plan was never carried out.

A set of juice production trials in the pilot-scale was performed and the results reported. The results were not clear and sometimes contradictory. Different kinds of handling and pre-treatment milling were discussed and it was even suggested that a local consultant might be able to help. There are problems associated with working on the pilot-plant at the Centre for Chemistry and Chemical Engineering, Lund University, as the locality is built for research and not for production of consumer products, and it is difficult to maintain good process control through out the tests.

In our geographical area there are small, highly specialized consultants and family engineering companies that provide back-up or a kind of buffer for the larger engineering companies, pharmaceutical companies, Lund University and also the Ideon Science Park. These entrepreneurs are often very skilled and interested in working with new concepts. The ideal place to run these experiments is at Tetra Laval in Lund, in their pilot-plant, but this costs around SEK25,000 per day.

The work on milling the carrots to produce juice and flesh continued. The small laboratory mill we ordered did not arrive as promised in the contract. After some discussions it was agreed that we should only pay for the transport cost. The manufacturer stated that the mill met high hygienic standards, but in fact it was found to contain some components made of corrosive material. As a result we decided to hire a second-hand mill from the company Maseko. Repairs were to be made at the workshop of the Centre for Chemistry and Chemical Engineering, Lund University. The mill was repaired but found not to be useful for our purpose.

Despite all our work and the problems encountered in pilot-scale experiments at the University, Charlotte Alklint found the equipment necessary to set up the line using what was available at the University. To be honest, nothing was working reliably. Nevertheless, at one steering group meeting Charlotte Alklint was able to demonstrate the different steps, the pieces of equipment required and the logistics of a future production process. At a later meeting it was decided that Charlotte Alklint and Ingegerd Sjöholm should continue to look for more professional equipment.

Potential Partner or 'Research Espionage'

The progress of the carrot project was presented on various accessions. This information also came to the notice of TetraPak and Ingegerd Sjöholm was invited to a lunch meeting to meet the process salesperson for TetraPak in Germany. This salesperson was interested in meeting Ingegerd and discussing the processing of carrots. He informed her of the normal procedure in Germany and also what he knew from the rest of Europe. They all seemed to use pre-cooked carrots as a raw material for juice production. The representative was then later invited to the University and was very interested in the project, but behaved very collegially about our secrecy. The information about carrot juice production in Europe was helpful for the Mona Carota project.

It is also worth mentioning that a former PhD student, now working at one of the internationally owned companies, entered Charlotte Alklint's room to see what kind of research was taking place. The University is of course an open facility but visitors are normally preannounced and a planned meeting takes place. Charlotte Alklint was naturally puzzled as to why this project could be of interest, and why it was the only project of interest?

During May 1997 the German mill producer came to Lund and visited Charlotte Alklint and Ingegerd Sjöholm. The company was represented by one of their R&D employees in Germany and their salesperson in Sweden. They were curious to know how our project was progressing and noticed directly that we were testing equipment from the Swiss mill company, their competitors. We explained once again the aim of our milling unit operation and repeated the advantages and disadvantages of their milling system and their competitors. We demonstrated our small-scale mill and they understood the concept. After a pleasant lunch they left and promised to try to solve our problem. *Unfortunately, no response was received in the first five-year period.*

Preparations continued for the next season's carrot juice. The decision was made to use commercially grown carrots and the discussion on pre-treatment continued. We wanted to achieve 'food quality' in the carrots to be used for juice production, without introducing soil bacteria into the production area. We looked at other similar products such as cucumbers; how they are cleaned, and also potato product lines. We also wondered why the potato company 'Potatisspecialisten' had not responded. The company later explained that they had decided not to work with carrots in parallel to their core product, potatoes.

Lack of Mutual Understanding Between Researchers and Skånemejerier

A recurrent question from the researchers at the steering group meetings was: Where is the equipment and especially the mill that was used in the previous carrot project at Skånemejerier? The reason was that a complete inventory did not exist at Skånemejerier as a result of reorganizations, and the selling and purchasing of premises and equipment.

During the autumn of 1997 a student from ETH, Switzerland enquired about a Master's project in Lund at the Department of Engineering. The student was invited to work with Charlotte Alklint. This Master's project was to be concerned with the shelf life of carrot juice. A Swedish student also asked for a Master's project focused on pre-treatment of carrots.

At one meeting Kenneth Andersson and Lennart Wickström informed us of a new person, employed by Cerelact, who would be working in the Mona Carota Project. Cerelact was a new developing company, 100 per cent owned by Skånemejerier and Skånska Lantmännen. The mission of the new company was to deal with ideas and newly started projects to allow them to grow and implement them later in the mother companies. Cerelact could thus provide help for the Mona Carota project in planning trials, organizing meetings, contacting people, finding the right raw material and also one extra resource when running pilot-scale experiments.

The next carrot season was approaching and at a meeting in June 1997 the effects of cultivation conditions were discussed, as we had decided not to run any of these trials in the project. The result was that carrots from Stockholmsgården and Marianne's Vegefarm were to be compared and evaluated. At this meeting Charlotte Alklint and Ingegerd Sjöholm also reported the results of Kenneth Andersson's suggestion of contacting a nearby food company that might have some equipment suitable for the milling and separation of carrots. Testing this set-up was then given the highest priority.

On the initiative of Skånska Lantmännen and Skånemejerier contact was made with the quality laboratory Agrolab in order to study the microbiology of the juice. Contacts were also made with TetraPak and the research institute SIK in order to run some final tests on the juice in high-pressure equipment. The technique was Pulsed Electrical Field (PEF). To run one experiment required 50 kg of juice, which is a considerable amount compared with small-scale tests. The plan was to try to run this experiment in collaboration with another project at the Department of Food Engineering. Unfortunately, this new PEF project was on a more basic level and the collaboration never materialized.

A scientific meeting in connection with a PhD course at Lund University took place at which carrot juice was discussed. Ingegerd Sjöholm, Charlotte Alklint and two professors, one from Crete and the other from Bahia Blanca University, Argentina, discussed the possibility of using an osmometer to study degrees of cell fission, to measure the potassium level and analyse whether the starch influences the Brix number of the juice.

In the autumn of 1997 Lennart Wikström took the decision to leave Skånska Lantmännen and set up a private business by establishing the company CultiMedia Information. Lennart relinquished all his duties at Skånska Lantmännen, apart from the Research Foundation.

Different Student Projects Support the Project

The preparation and practical trials at the Department of Food Engineering continued. Work was done to mend the decanter belonging to the University. Hopes and ideas were developed to run some experiments at TetraPak. The alternative equipment obtained from a nearby industry was tested and found to be excellent. This equipment was superior to everything we had tried before.

In the summer of 1997 a summer student worked on the correlation between milling carrots and processing parameters such as temperature and time. The Swedish student started to do her Master's project on pre-treatment methods of whole carrots predestined for carrot juice. The work was focused on different kinds of mechanical treatments, microbiological infection and water quality. The Swiss student from ETH arrived in September. Her work was focused on storage studies on the final juice.

In January 1998 one of the international Master's students at the Centre for Chemistry and Chemical Engineering, Lund University requested a project in the area of vegetables. The project started with 50 per cent in the Mona Carota project and 50 per cent in a project on frozen carrots at Nestlé and concerned how to cut carrots. The possibility of using the concept of an electronic nose for sensory tests was discussed.

In the first few days of September Charlotte Alklint had become a mother and had to take a break from the project. During the following months the students were supervised by Charlotte from home and by Ingegerd Sjöholm at the Chemical Centre.

Getting to Know 'Marianne's Morötter'

Lennart Wikström organized an industrial visit to Marianne's Morötter in Strövelstorp one hour north of the University by car. This meeting was the starting point of a very sincere relationship with the owner, Marianne Härning Nilsson. This has been very important for the whole Mona Carota project. For Charlotte Alklint and Ingegerd Sjöholm the meeting was proof that the concept was still working. Marianne told us about her quality programme for fresh purchased carrots. Marianne was open and very willing to discuss the different problems associated with stored carrots, their post-harvest period and how fresh carrots could be used for new consumer products. The discussion also dealt with what we can do at the University regarding carrots and the knowledge available at the research institutes such as SIK in Gothenburg. One result of the visit was that we decided to get into touch with another company in the neighbourhood working with cut fresh vegetables. This company was the partner that Skånemejerier and TetraLaval had had in their previous juice project.

During the autumn, the Master's project continued. The suggestion of Kenneth Andersson to use lactic acid as part of pre-treatment was discussed. Towards the end of October the carrots from Hammenhög, the plant breeding farm, arrived. The juice from six different varieties was evaluated. None of the juices was in the same class as the previous year, because all carrots had been attacked by nematodes. At the end of November, Ingegerd Sjöholm attended a meeting in Belgium dealing with minimal processing where some

Dutch researchers presented a model of heat treatment and their PME activities.

The Continuation of the Project During the Next Three Years

The three Master's project diploma works were completed and presented in the spring and autumn of 1998. One of them indicated the possibility of using a colorimeter to follow the growth of microorganisms. The other MSc projects penetrated the critical points of cutting carrots and the necessary pre-treatment of the raw material.

In March the representative for Cerelact and Charlotte Alklint drew up a plan for the Mona Carota project from week 15, 1998 to week 14, 1999. This plan was executed totally.

In the spring of 1998 it became obvious to Ingegerd Sjöholm that it was impossible to continue to run this project as a combined development project and a PhD project, especially as Skånemejerier appeared not to have the motivation to construct a pilot-plant production line based on the concept developed. The intention was also to repeat the very promising test production of carrot juice achieved at the Centre for Chemistry and Chemical Engineering, Lund University under very primitive conditions and to transport the juice in sterile tanks to TetraPak for aseptic packaging. These preliminary products were very popular with the managers at Skånemejerier but have to be tested in broader consumer studies.

A Future Vision was to Set Up a New Pilot-plant Production Line

During the spring of 1998 Ingegerd Sjöholm was engaged in searching for process equipment on a pilot-scale to set up in the process hall at the Centre for Chemistry and Chemical Engineering, Lund University since there seemed to be a delay in the test equipment planned by Skånemejerier. By chance Ingegerd found some old equipment in a school in Malmö. It consisted of a mini-pasteurization line developed for teaching high-school students but not used during recent years. All the equipment was moved and installed in the experimental hall at Lund University.

During the autumn of 1998 a complete small-scale carrot juice processing line was assembled from the old pasteurization line and the formerly tested equipment. All the processing steps were optimized and in January and February 1999, there were two large pilot-scale trials using one ton of carrots each run. The first run failed in some aspects because of mill problems but some Tetra Brik packages of carrot juice were produced. During the second trial, which went well, more valuable results for large-scale production were obtained, and carrot juice in 200ml Tetra Briks was handed over to Skånemejerier for their planned sensorial evaluation.

Different species of carrot were used and possible future production sites were discussed. Charlotte Alklint, together with the Cerelact representative, went on trips to find suitable equipment for the future plant. Plans for CIP (cleaning in place) installation were also discussed.

In the latter part of 1999 Charlotte Alklint started to concentrate on the more theoretical aspects of yield and the nutritional properties of the juice.

As part of the activities of Ideon Agro Food and the University, Ingegerd Sjöholm and Magnus Lagnevik, Department of Business Administration started to run smaller projects where economics and technology were combined. Grants were obtained to finance this interdisciplinary research and Federico Gomez was able to start on his PhD in the Mona Carota project in November 1998. Federico was one of the Master's students who worked on the Mona Carota project. During his first two years, Federico Gomez dealt with the basic information of post-harvest conditions and later concentrated on shelf life and aspects of heat treatment.

> Financing multidisciplinary research can be challenging. The main financier had approved the application because the combination of economics and technological research strengthen the project. Later in the project, when funding was due to the final phase of the project, Federico's support was withdrawn due to administrative and managemental changes at the main financier. After this change in management and administration they argued that 'we can obviously not pay for technological research', something that they had done for the last three years.
>
> In April 1999 Kenneth Andersson surprised us by telling us that the mill from the previous carrot juice project had been found and that we could use it. Charlotte Alklint and Ingegerd Sjöholm pointed out that this kind of mill would not work in our process. Later in June 1999 Kenneth informed us that he had bought a decanter and if we could not use it, it would be easy to sell again. The mill was tested in August 1999 and worked in a mediocre way. In February 2000 Charlotte had her second child. In September 2001 Charlotte returned to write scientific papers for her thesis.

Epilogue

Between 1998 and 2002 Marianne's Farm invested in approved buildings and production lines for fresh carrots. Thus, Marianne's Farm may be a possible future producer of a *stable carrot juice with good flavour and appearance and long shelf life without using additives.*

APPENDIX: NOTES ON THE METHODOLOGY

In this book our ambition was to write primarily about innovation processes in food clusters and to minimize the methodological discussion. However, there are some methodological choices and problems that we believe should be mentioned briefly. They are the nature of the case studies, the information gathering and the special features of multidisciplinary research.

The Focus of the Case Studies

Our ambition in the case studies was to capture the unique development aspects of innovation processes. Thus we followed the processes in longitudinal studies in order to describe and analyse the dynamic processes over time. Since the focus is on the innovation process itself, the cases may seem unusual to the reader. We agree; they are unusual. We do not follow the traditional paradigm, using the corporate management perspective and following the new product from decision to success in the store. Rather, we want to show how innovative ideas are born and how they develop into more and more concrete concepts and products. We want to illustrate cluster activities, meaning that the focus in the cases is sometimes – actually quite often – outside the companies that develop and sell the final product. The reader is given the opportunity to follow activities in research laboratories, at business meetings and in informal discussions. All the strategically important decisions are reflected in the cases, but they are not always portrayed from a top management perspective. It should be mentioned that the processes that we describe here are top management issues and that the organizations involved have devoted a great deal of time and serious attention to the top management in order to make the innovation processes successful. Since the outcome of innovations cannot be fully predicted or controlled, the reader can see that other persons than the top management make decisions, which has wide strategic importance.

We describe the cases openly with real names. This is possibly due to the generosity of the people and organizations that we have studied. In processes of this kind, mistakes, dead ends and false expectations are part of everyday life. Although we have described the setbacks of these innovation processes, we would like to point out very clearly that we are analysing three successful cases. The actors involved managed to create innovation as intended, which is something to take pride in. The reader who enjoys summarizing mistakes has missed the central point of our book — that hard work and long-term commitment are necessary for the innovation process to succeed.

Information Gathering

Innovation is a research subject that has appealed to researchers from many theoretical disciplines. We have thus found many theoretical approaches, and the same phenomena described with different labels and concepts. Our ambition is not to give a complete presentation of all the theory on innovation or to analyse how these models and concepts are related. Rather, our ambition was to find and apply theory that is relevant to the understanding of our research topic – innovations in food clusters. We combined some theories, but we also used complementary theoretical approaches in order to analyse important aspects of the innovation processes from different perspectives.

Our survey was carried out with 25 very experienced executives in top management positions who had experience of innovation. In this way we were able to quantify attitudes to innovation and the indications were so clear that we abstained from further questionnaires. In the top management interviews we also collected information about successful innovations, as well as failures. We learned of the importance of the embeddedness of the innovation, about cluster management and market forecasting. The same kind of interviews were also carried out with a large number of other executives during the project, which has lasted for four years. In our roles as advisors or actors[6] in innovation projects, we have gathered information that is often hard to find, and the fact that we have studied or been active in many companies and organizations has helped us to compare innovation patterns.

In order to relate the characteristics of the Öresund food cluster with the characteristics of other clusters we have conducted interviews in the USA and have carried out or participated in benchmarking studies. We have also made study visits to successful innovation companies in order to learn not only how they describe and analyse the situation, but also to learn how they work and think. We believe that our professional and personal relations with key actors have helped us to gain access to vital information. We also believe that the fact that one of us is a successful entrepreneur with personal experience of many development projects has helped us considerably in understanding the nature of the innovation process. Another researcher in the group has many years' experience in international marketing of the very products that we have investigated. This also helps our understanding. Last but not least, three of us have experience of multidisciplinary innovation projects in joint projects between academic departments and business organizations. That experience, together with the opportunity to gather reflections and advice from our colleagues in Ideon Agro Food, is a key factor in the success of our project. It was also the basis on which the project was founded.

A Multidisciplinary Approach

When we applied for research grants, it was considered an advantage that we had a multidisciplinary approach. In retrospect we agree wholeheartedly. The approach of combining strategy and marketing with engineering, and with sociological and ethnographical theory and methodology has given us an insight into the processes we have studied, which we believe could not have been obtained with a single-disciplinary approach. We found it extremely important to understand the content of the process in order to understand the process. Likewise it has been important to us to problematize the context of the process since we have followed high-technology food products from the laboratory to their position in the consumers' social meaning of everyday life. If you do not understand the nature of biotechnical or food engineering problems, it is not easy to understand the meaning of these problems in the innovation process. But there are limits to our own knowledge. Fortunately, we have had the advantage of working in an organization made up of top researchers from several disciplines. There has always been someone to ask.

What we did not foresee from the beginning was how differently we conceptualized 'research'. The meaning of 'research' is very different in business administration and food engineering. For a doctoral student, every-day life is very different in the two disciplines. Expressed simply, in food engineering you spend your normal day in a laboratory, you meet the same people and build up social contact with a small group. The quality of your work is dependent on how well you understand your equipment, how courageously you investigate new parameters and how precisely and consist-ently you present your results. In principle, you dislike writing and want to make it as short as possible. If you have to read something, you do it in the evening – 'after work'.

In business administration you work alone. If you want to meet people you have to go to seminars or visit companies for fieldwork. Reading is very important and you prove your skill in writing. Well-written texts, good refer-ences, creative interpretations and language development are marks of high quality.

It took us more than a year to realize these differences existed and to understand them, since the concept of 'research' was taken for granted by us all. The best means of establishing a common research platform was joint trips to study companies and clusters, trips where we had the opportunity to discuss internally what we had actually seen and what our observations meant. Later on, we made attempts to lecture at each other's departments. Our colleagues were polite, but marginalized these 'foreign' contributions, because they had not created the same common platform that we had. One of our closest fiends in food science still makes a point of expressing publicly that marketing and strategy is just a lot of fuzzy unscientific talk, very closely related to politics or witchcraft. Our personal experiences of combining knowledge that is different helped us considerably in the interpretation of the innovation processes that we studied.

A practical conclusion from our side was that although our PhD students are involved in the whole project and have made great contributions, it would be harmful to their careers to publish under any other paradigm than those used at their own research departments. Thus, apart from contributions to this book they publish articles that are better understood in the specific research cultures. The senior researchers in this project handle the complexity of multidisciplinary approaches.

NOTES

1. Hydrothermally treated oats are something you can get by pouring boiling water over oat kernels and leaving them for half an hour. This is what the bakers did in older days. This procedure inactivates the lipases, which would have oxidized the lipids after the milling of kernels from oat to flour. The treated oat kernels were dried in the extreme heat of the baking oven. Afterwards the oats were ground and the flour did not get rancid. This process makes it possible for the flour to pass over the iron and the minerals to the human body. This flour does not have to be fortified by iron.
2. Food From Sweden, is a government-supported organization, which at this time was able to support individual companies in specific export projects.
3. Scanian Farmers was Ceba's marketing company for the oat drink between 1995 and 2001.
4. The ProViva case is dealt with as another case in this book.
5. Jan Persson, Managing Director of Skånska Lantmännen (until 2000) and Chairman of Ceba.
6. One of us has experience as an innovator-entrepreneur and has been the advisor for more than 100 industrially based MSc/PhD thesis projects. One of us has managerial experience as export and development director in a food company and 15 years experience as a consultant. One of us has 20 years' experience as a strategy consultant and of top executive development and education. We all have practical experience of innovation project management.

7. The Nature of Innovation Processes – Results

We have found that innovation processes in clusters can be well understood with the help of the general innovation theory. In principle, our findings support those of Utterback (1994). However, some of the special features of cluster innovation processes need to be elaborated further.

From Utterback's research we have learned that there are three phases in the innovation process – fluid, transitional and specific (see Figure 7.1). In the fluid phase of the innovation process, several product ideas, several actors and several technical solutions form a dynamic competitive landscape. In the second, transitional phase, the process development takes off, and there is a close connection between product and process innovation. In the final, specific phase, products are targeted for specific users or segments, and the process is focused on maximizing value and cost efficiency for users in the segments.

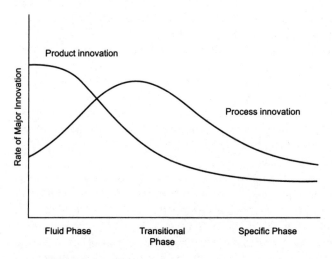

Source: Reprinted by permission from Harvard Business School Press from *Mastering the Dynamics of Innovation* by James M. Utterback, Boston, MA, 1994, p. 91.

Figure 7.1   Product and process innovation

THE FLUID PHASE

Innovations are born in the fluid phase. Many technologies compete, many actors are active in the innovation game and many different applications of the technologies are tested. Eneroth and Malm (2001) have described this as continuous dynamics forming the competitive landscape. In this foggy landscape it is important for the innovators to find the technology with the highest peak. In the long run and in the establishment process for a dominant design, only those innovations based on the premium technology will survive the competition.

When it comes to orienting in the competitive landscape, we remember Eneroth and Malm's illustration in which telecom companies invested large amounts in different technologies. The choice of investment area was very difficult since the outcome of the technological race was difficult to predict.

In the Mona Carota case one can observe that the positioning of the project idea in a cluster but outside a commercial organization will create advantages that are difficult to obtain when the project is driven within a company. In this case we can see how the entrepreneur – Ingegerd Sjöholm – together with her doctoral students scanned the scientific and commercial environment in search of efficient technologies that would produce superior carrot-based products.

The testing of the different technological peaks in the landscape is done on a small scale, with very little investment using internationally acclaimed specialists for the trials. Of course we realize the difference in size between this project and the Bluetooth project (see Eneroth and Malm, 2001, p. 176), but the working method is still interesting. International conferences are used with the specific purpose of trying out suitable approaches to solve the problems that need to be solved in order to create an innovative food product. Colleagues in several countries are encouraged to present views on the new product idea and how it can be produced. Ingegerd Sjöholm and Charlotte Alklint loaded a car full of carrots and went south through Germany to find the best machinery producers and to test their equipment on the specific products that they were intended for.

If we compare this working method in the cluster, bearing in mind that doctoral students are high-quality low-cost resources with the situation in which the company hires people, buys equipment and 'goes it alone'. we believe that the point is made – that *handling innovation projects in the fluid phase in a cluster context offers cost advantages as well as opportunities to make quick changes from one technology to another*. With no employees tied to specific technological knowledge, and the freedom to choose among a wide range of professionals, the 'switching' cost becomes lower. The entrepreneur has a freedom of action and the number of world-class check points is directly related to the entrepreneur's professional and social networks.

It is important to realize that openness to new ideas and impressions helps the innovator to find new resources and opportunities. In an earlier section we highlighted the importance of exploring new technologies, experimenting with emerging and pioneering technologies (see Chapter 3, Table 3.3). Here the advantages of cluster innovations become very clear. For many food companies, the cost of maintaining knowledge on relevant technologies is simply too high. In principle, we can see large multinational companies that can afford almost anything, but as we have already indicated, and will continue to show, the really large organizations risk falling into development traps. They usually make copies, line extensions and 'me-too' products.

Shared Visions Across Organizational Borders

According to Eneroth and Malm (2001), shared visions across organizational borders are essential when guiding the innovation process on its way from idea to product. The ability to create these visions and make the participants in the innovation process share a common vision is a great leadership challenge.

This cluster management task involves choosing the right partners, because if the partners have complementary knowledge and benefit from the same vision, the task will be substantially easier. It is also important to realize that the task must be understood in the same way, and that the working methods and practices are accepted and understood by all partners.

In the Methodological Appendix (Chapter 6, p. 157) we made reference to our own experience from the research project, that is that our understandings of the concept of 'research' were not the same. This was revealed when we progressed to actually doing things that needed to be done, in order to proceed in the research. In the Mona Carota case we can see the same thing happening when researchers from the Department of Food Engineering met colleagues from the Department of Plant Biochemistry. After several attempts by the entrepreneur Ingegerd Sjöholm to inspire the plant biologists to apply their knowledge to the engineering world, their colleagues say outright: ' We don't think and work in the way you do'.

From this episode in the *Mona Carota* case we also learned that co-operation is possible. Five years later, there is intense collaboration between the departments regarding components in the cell walls of carrots as well as other projects. In order to get there, the two departments formulated a joint vision and started long-term collaboration. Knowledge integration takes time[1] and shared visions across organizational borders help the process considerably.

We can also see in the *Oatly* case how Richard Öste co-ordinated actors from different branches of knowledge, from academia and commercial actors in a very efficient way, thus creating a common vision about what was to be achieved.

THE TRANSITIONAL PHASE – CHANGING FOCUS

When the project has reached the transitional phase, quite a few important changes will have occurred. The choice of product technology will have been made and the key technological features of the innovation been decided. The wide range of partners and competitors will have been narrowed down to a few, and the contributions to the product from all the actors will have been clarified.

It is in the borderland between the fluid phase and the transitional phase that the Mona Carota case ends. The basic technological production problems have been solved, and the key qualities of the innovation have been identified. However, a major shortcoming in the project is that the product is produced with rather primitive laboratory equipment, bought second-hand from a secondary school. It is obvious that developing efficient process equipment on a commercial scale will require a great deal of work.

To advance from the basic concept and the second-hand secondary school process equipment requires process knowledge, investments and a knowledgeable 'product champion' who understands both the product and the process technology. It is in this new phase that large companies often enter the innovation process. They have the experience, the financial resources and often sound process knowledge. If large corporations do not enter the project at this stage, process competence and financial capital must be obtained from elsewhere. Venture capitalists, business angels or financing through national or international research funds are options. We can learn something about equity sources from a study of small high- technology firms at the Mjärdevi and Berzelius science parks (Zachrisson and Sjögren, 2002). There we find the distribution of sources shown in per cent, as shown in Table 7.1.

Table 7.1   Sources (in per cent) of equity in small, innovative companies in two Swedish science parks

Founders	Venture Capital	Private Investors	Employees	Corporate Venture Capital	Public Sector Financiers
57	15	2	8	6	6

The relatively high proportion of financing from employees is due mainly to consultancies where the partners own the company. The only public sector financier is Teknikbrostiftelsen – a regional development support organization. The venture capital has mostly found its way to the telecom sector.

In some cases, future customers are willing to step in and provide capital. The downside of financing by customers is that the price is often loss of independence. Another possibility is to fix delivery prices for a long period, so that most of the profit goes to the customer. We leave the Mona Carota case wondering about the next phase. Who will promise what in exchange for what?

In the Oatly case, the process has developed further. *There we can see that the actors have spent quite some time in the transitional phase.* The location of production has caused major discussion within the project. Some actors leave the stage or take a more peripheral role. Others take strong positions based on specific knowledge in the areas needed in this stage. We also note that one specific reason for locating production in Lunnarp was the possibility of designing the process equipment consistently, from the beginning to the end of the process. Of course, the ability to design a full-scale production plant without too many compromises on process efficiency and quality is a necessary condition for production of a competitive product.

Apart from pure cost and efficiency considerations, it is at this stage that all the requirements that need to be fulfilled in order to sell the product to retail chains and consumers become highlighted. *Questions of hygiene, traceability, safety and others are raised.* When this chapter was written, the debate was focused on the British Retail Consortium (BRC) guidelines and their demands for traceability. The demands on future food products will be precise and high, and BRC guidelines also contain the demands of Hazard Analysis Critical Control Point (HACCP), Good Agricultural Practice (GAP), Good Manufacturing Practice (GMP) and Good Distribution Practice. But *these are demands that must be fulfilled in order to participate in the competition not to succeed.*

Retailers must present products that are associated with defined quality standards, safe products, sustainable products and products which, through traceability, can guarantee high-quality input. But the innovation partners must produce innovations that consumers buy voluntarily and repeatedly, because they fulfil a specific need, taste good, are convenient, well branded, properly distributed and exposed. The product should also have a trustworthy brand, good sales activities and even a good story about the product that makes it interesting. These are matters that are dealt with in the *specific phase*.

THE SPECIFIC PHASE: FINE-TUNING AND TARGETING

When the innovation process enters the *specific phase*, the concepts of the basic product are well defined. The production process is specified. Investments have been made and continuing engineering keeps the production cost down and safeguards the competitiveness. The issue in this phase is, among other things, to create margins. For a period the innovating firm or cluster will have a temporary monopoly because they are producing a unique product. After a while, copycats will stray into the alley, cutting profits through competitive pricing and in some cases lowering the quality so that the reputation of the original product is threatened.

At this stage it is time to be more specific. The innovating firm must find target customer groups and fine-tune the products and the marketing concept to the needs of these groups. Now is the time to strengthen the brand, to show excellence in understanding consumer needs, and to exercise skill in the choice of market partners and distribution channels. Convenience and availability are other important factors in this phase.

The target customer groups may be in the same market or in different markets. An example from the non-food area is the business sphere around the innovator Christer Fåhraeus.[2] The same kind of technological knowledge is used in C-Pen, a pen that can read text digitally and translate it, and in Anoto, a company producing pens that can digitalize information directly from the paper. We find the same technology in security equipment developed by Precise Biometrics, and we will no doubt see the technology used in various kinds of add-on services in mobile telephones.

Turning to our own cases, we find that the *ProViva* bio-active ingredient is available both in a product that aids digestion and in a product that promises recovery of the body after strenuous activities. We also find that *L. plantarum* has found its way into horse feed. Racehorses often have poor digestion, which makes horseracing an interesting place for ProViva, but under a different name.

For each of these applications the product, its distribution and the message associated with it must be fine-tuned to gain the full attention of the consumers. The company will thus invest increasing amounts in specific products and specific markets.

In the *Oatly case we find the innovation just leaving the transitional phase and entering the specific phase as the study ends*. A major strategic decision has been taken by Ceba. The company redefines itself from being an *ingredient producer* to becoming a *producer of branded products*. This also means that the Ceba company has decided to enter the specific phase with full force. A number of different consumer products are put on the market: oat drink, ice cream, 'cream,' vanilla sauce and pancake batter. They must all be sold by specific arguments directed towards specific consumer groups through well-chosen channels with a supporting marketing strategy.

In the transition to a brand-producing company, we also notice that the specific character of the products, 'lactose-free', is not accentuated any more. Rather, some of the new products are marketed as good and tasty products. Health claims are not found on the package. Instead the brand 'Oatly' is intended to remind the consumer of the oat base. However, the transition from a product for lacto-intolerant consumers to a number of interesting and tasty products is very conscious and well implemented by the company. The Managing Director also backs the product concept with a new identity for Ceba – 'the green dairy' thus creating expectations of more products in the pipeline.

Innovation Traps in the Specific Phase

As the innovation concepts are specified more precisely in the specific phase, investments are made in areas of key importance. The organization of the companies involved is adapted so that the specific offerings to the market and to the end-consumer receive full support and an efficient production and distribution structure. This is necessary and important in order to make an attractive offering to the market at a competitive price.

There is, however, a consequence of the fine-tuning that must be addressed. *When a company is focused on production and sales of specific offerings, organized in well-structured business areas, the organization will encounter difficulties in addressing the development of new innovations.* Since many food producers are working on food production in the specific phase and want to infuse innovation into their organizations, conditions limiting possibility for new innovation processes may be present in many companies. The specific innovation traps that we have found in companies in the specific phase must be addressed.

In this section, we will therefore describe and analyse some of the most important innovation traps. We will use some examples from our empirical studies to illustrate how the traps work and how destructive they can be for the organization. We have found three important reasons why innovation processes may be stopped, why good thinking and hard work are not implemented in successful innovations.

- Earlier investments
- Dominating patterns of thinking
- Organization, management and reward systems

Earlier Investments

Making investments in products, production and marketing is necessary in order to reach the market and achieve sales volumes that make the investments profitable. For a company that has managed to produce a product in a cost-efficient way, that has invested in marketing activities and has built a strong brand, it is very important to defend the investment. Competitors should be discouraged from trying to capture market shares in the same customer segments and consumers should be educated so that they are loyal to the brand. Managers and employees should be highly motivated to produce and sell the products. Management control and incentive systems should thus be designed so that performance in the day-to-day operations is measured, evaluated and improved.

In the *specific phase*, the market is mature. The successful corporation has gained substantial experience in procurement, production and marketing in this phase. This situation can be found in large, highly successful multinational food companies.

An organization that is well designed and fine-tuned with the purpose of producing and selling established products is so focused on this task that the *rules and procedures that defend earlier investments often limit the opportunities for new – especially radically new – products and services.*

The *defence of market position* can have a direct impact on product development in the sense that new products can be designed to be unsuccessful.

> We noticed that one of our competitors on the German market was launching a product that was closer to the key customer segment for our leading branded product than we desired. Then we developed a product that was very similar to that of our competitors, we added some extra gadgets and sold the product at such a low price that the consumers preferred our new product to the competitors' product. Our competitor terminated their project with losses. We accepted losses for two years, and then we took our new product off the market. We had lost some money on that specific product, but it was worth it, since we kept the segment for our leading branded product free from competition.[3]

What we see in this statement is that in some cases the intention of launching a new product is neither to present an interesting new product to the market, nor to earn money from that specific product. The intention was defensive. The new product was launched in order to defend the position of an existing product. In the next quotation we find that protection for existing products in another form. The company refrains from launching a new product because they fear that a new product may harm the reputation and sales of their established product portfolio.

One important reason why the big corporations have been unsuccessful in new product development, e.g. functional foods, is that they do not want to risk the degrading of their strong brands. Another reason is that innovation demands that the company redefines its borders, limits and key activities. The big ones don't want to do that.[4]

Another finding of our qualitative interviews is that the corporate top management is often under pressure to produce short-term results. They play it safe and harvest short-term profits as far as possible, rather than risking their careers on 'extravagant costly new ventures'.

Wall Street expects so much. They're not happy about our profit levels. As a result we have a huge consolidation of the whole industry. We try to produce the old products at lower cost with higher margins. This won't help innovation. Another problem is that even if we wanted to make innovations it's very hard to attract capital. It's invested in other sectors than food.[5] The United States is a model for innovation – but not in food![6]

A result of the defence of earlier investments is that the focus in many large food companies is on restructuring and consolidation rather than innovation. Thus, it is difficult for innovative ideas to enter the decision arena and retain the attention, despite the fact that it is known that successful innovation can increase margins and profitability. This can be illustrated by a number of quotations concerning the same company.

We are in such a competitive situation with our present products that innovation is the only thing that drives our growth.[7]

Those who have the muscles use their power and resources in internal battles. They forget the customer.[8]

I tried to present our new product idea to them. There were four guys from different departments. They tried to synchronise their calendars. They failed so we could not have any meeting. In my mind they are four times too slow.[9]

The product that was referred to in the above quotation was later put on the market by another company. It is making a profit and the small entrepreneurial company has continued to develop new products. This lack of interest in new ideas is by no means unusual. In the interviews that we have carried out at small innovative companies, we learned that they had all presented their product ideas for large corporations at an early stage. *The ideas were all turned down, with the exception of one*, a medium-sized Swedish food producer who declared an interest in the new product directly. This company was not focused on defending their present product portfolio. The were actively searching for new products; a rather uncommon attitude.

Dominating Ideas

Established production and day-to-day running create a view of the company, its mission and vision, and also focuses attention on specific parts of the working environment. A set of dominating ideas is institutionalized in the corporation. If innovation and development issues are not deliberately included in the agenda by the top management, the business logic of the day-to-day operations will form the dominating ideas.

> In the food industry there's something very wrong. The R&D departments have too low a status while the status of the marketing people is too high.[10]

The statement above illustrates that the marketing of existing products has become the dominating idea in several companies, nurturing these products while leaving the innovation process no support.

We also note a tendency in large corporations to take a pride in their own knowledge and their own resources. In some cases, the strategy seems to be not to let new thinking into the organization. Accepting ideas from others is considered a loss of prestige in some companies. We have an example from a world-class scientist who described his experience of sitting on a scientific committee in a major food-producing company. He had accepted the position since he thought that the committee's task was to contribute to the development of the company.

> I sat on the committee for a couple of years. I noticed that they didn't ask us any sensible questions. If we had ideas, they were not picked up by the company people. I discovered that they were using the committee for cosmetic purposes. They used us to create an atmosphere of legitimacy around the company. The Vice President of R&D later found the committee to be too expensive, so he disbanded it.[11]

The scientist in the example above learned that the scientific committee had been appointed to create an image of legitimacy around the company. It was not intended to contribute to the corporate innovation and development process, at least not among the research and development (R&D) people.

> The scientific committee is necessary. If something goes wrong we have somebody to blame.[12]

At this point we must point out the fact that the behaviour described above is common, but not the only behaviour we have seen in the food industry. As we show in this book, there are companies in which the development of innovations works well, and where there is meaningful interaction with other companies and with universities, but this is not the most common picture.

Now, we would like to focus on the fact that behind dominating ideas there is a knowledge base and a bundle of resources that are unique for the company. This is of great importance when analysing innovations and new thinking. We shall address the issue of the *Not Invented Here* syndrome.

The *Not Invented Here (NIH)* syndrome is well known in most organizations. The core of the syndrome is resistance to change. The meaning behind the syndrome is that everything that is *NIH* is inferior and must be rejected for reasons of power and status. There are also references back to Donald Schön's (1983) classical writing about how social systems seek stability. When faced with change, social systems resist by:

- pretending that the need for change – the threat to the organization – does not exist,
- trying to actively resist change,
- actively limiting the effects of change.

In the process analysed by Schön, the end effect is that social systems tend to accept only a minimal amount of change. In this field of organizational inertia an interesting contribution was made by Gabriel Szulanski (Szulanski, 1996, p. 37ff). He carried out an in-depth empirical study in which he investigated why good ideas are not accepted and why good projects fail. His main result is that the NIH syndrome is rejected as the main cause of organizational inertia. According to Szulanski, it is not hostile attitudes towards the thinking of others, or protection of one's own territory, or general resistance to change which stops good projects. Instead, the most common reason is that the employees of the *company do not understand what to do with the idea.* They can also be uncertain about the context in which the idea should be developed (ibid.). This finding provides quite another context and calls for another agenda when we want to understand failures of innovation. If we accept that those who resist change do not do so mainly because they are envious, self-protective or seeking stability, then the arguments for change and the methods of change will be different. Ways of overcoming resistance due to power or status defence may be relocating people, enforcing decisions on parts of the organization or imposing economic sanctions.

However, if the situation is that people do not know what to do with the idea, power and money do not help. We must understand how deep the knowledge gap is. If our staff simply do not understand how to use the new knowledge and the new ideas, it helps to explain, show success stories or to provide assurance and security. It pays to guide and lead a knowledge formation process in the company.

In this context it is an important managerial issue to keep the innovation dynamics vibrant in the organization and to guide the process skilfully to

innovative results. This also demands a thorough and many-faceted understanding. The process managers must have a broad insight into several kinds
of knowledge bases and understand well how the unique resources of the
company can be utilized and combined. This can be illustrated by the
following quotation in which a Chief Executive Officer describes his product
development manager:

> He has been with the company for a long time. He has a solid background in
> several marketing assignments. Then he made his career in product group man-
> agement and continued to be sales director. That was all very fine, but then we
> promoted him to business area manager for new products. I wonder why. He
> understands only meat and he cannot think across borders and areas of com-
> petence.[13]

The knowledge gap can, however, be more fundamental. Perhaps our innovation ideas are founded on new specific technological knowledge? In that
case, personnel with the wrong technological background must be kept away
from the development of the new product. New people with relevant
technological education and experience must be hired, and this competence
must be integrated with other competence bases in the company that are
important for the innovation. In the same way, a radical change of customers,
for example, moving from consumer products to food ingredients and
components for other food producers, or changing from component sales to
systems sales, calls for new marketing knowledge in the company. The
existing sales organizations are no longer the experts when such changes
occur in an innovation process. It is very difficult to explain to experts in a
particular area that they are no longer the experts, since the conditions have
changed. In fact, it is so difficult that some organizations would rather
stick to established thinking and are outcompeted by others, as shown by
Utterback (1994). In other cases the innovation is so radical that it is sepa-
rated from the company and developed in an organization of its own.

There are several important implications of this insight. Let us return to
the need for innovation strategies to be an important and well-integrated part
of the top management general strategy for the corporation. But what if the
corporate top management does not understand? We tend to assume that top
management has all the necessary knowledge and sufficient insights to make
strategic decisions. Below is a statement from the empirical material, by the
Vice-President of a large US food-producing company.

> You have to understand that marketers and accountants dominate our executive
> offices. They do not understand how to use technology.[14]

In the continued discussion with the Vice-President he explained that the lack of technological insight in the executive echelons has had the effect that new ventures in product development and innovation are not part of the agenda. In his position, being responsible for strategy and R&D, the Vice-President had quite a few contacts with smaller research-based companies in which he found 'remarkable achievements'. However, *none* of his suggestions for new technologically-based developments had been accepted – in spite of his being a board member. The company spent 'well below' 1 per cent of its turnover on R&D, and that was mainly aimed at rationalization in production.

In an example from a Swedish company we find success in terms of money spent on R&D but no major changes being achieved since efforts are carefully guided within the accepted ideas and using existing knowledge base.

> We spend quite a lot on R&D, but we play it safe – mainly line extensions and me-too products. I think it's a management issue. Our problem is not to develop new things – it's to get them through the whole process all the way to the market.[15]

Product modifications and long-term engineering efforts to improve efficiency are of course important for the corporation and should not be neglected. But in this book we raise the question of how innovation and radical changes can be achieved in the organization. From what we have learned from the empirical material, innovation is in demand, the attitude towards it is positive, but we see little of it. In the language of Ahuja and Lampert (2001, see Chapter 3: Innovation Strategies and Development Traps) we can find examples above that illustrate the *Familiarity Trap* as well as *the Maturity Trap,* and *the Propinquity Trap.* The remedy could be to *explore technologies new to the organization, to experiment with technologies not yet known to their competitors and to search for fundamentally new solutions* that solve the basic problems and their root causes.

The first step in this direction is to explore technologies new to the organization. As we have mentioned earlier, this can be done in a simple and cost-efficient way, by using the resources in the cluster, specifically contacts with academic research institutions and their professional networks. In our cases, we saw examples of this several times, for example, in the Mona Carota case. If these explorations are to succeed, however, knowledge management skills are required. Heads of research units in large organizations must allow for input to their organizations that mean exploration of areas where others are the champions.

Organization, Management and Reward Systems

New product ideas should be scrutinized thoroughly. The question is in what context the analysis should be performed. As described above, many food companies are fine-tuned to produce and market existing products. This can lead to a new product being evaluated by people who do not have the requisite knowledge about new technologies or new markets. It can also have the effect that innovations are judged a priori by people who are organized and rewarded by promoting the ongoing activities with the present product line. We find this both in food production and in food retailing.

It's a good product, but it does not fit into any of our product groups.[16]

It looks very interesting, but we have no category manager who can sell this kind of a product.[17]

Another large company in the food machinery business has a very thorough project management system for new product development with innovation and idea management as an integrated part. Since the projects are very costly, the process is implemented stepwise. Evaluation takes place after each step to ensure that the project meets the objectives and that the milestones set up have been reached. The problem in this company is that after several steps when concepts and prototypes have been developed and tested in the field, quite a few projects are stopped, despite heavy investments.

The final decision to launch the project is taken by a committee headed by the company's president. The other participants are the presidents of the marketing companies. The committee is formed such that the tasks of the majority of the executives are to sell the existing products. They also receive a bonus for good short-term sales results. The organizational and reward systems are constructed so as to analyse whether the new product will 'steal' market shares from existing products. After long development processes and after spending vast amounts, the great majority of innovations are stopped at this point.

From what we know about the incentives for the decision makers we are not surprised. What is more surprising is that the multinational company that we studied continues this practice of scrapping projects late in the process, resulting in wasted development costs. Another effect is that the innovation project managers are demotivated and may not put all their energy into the next innovation project. We have full understanding of the importance of maintaining market positions for well-known and successful products, but from an innovation point of view, this is an innovation trap, and a costly one. From what we know about innovations already, it is clear that if they are innovative enough, the competitive map will be changed. The question is whether 'our' company should initiate the change or leave it to their competitors. We quote the two last sentences in Utterback's book.

> Even the strongest product or business strategy will eventually be overturned by technological change. The central issue is not when or how, but that it will happen for sure. In the final analysis only that understanding will allow a firm to bridge a discontinuity, because only a total commitment will win the day (Utterback, 1994, p. 231).

Finally, in this section on innovation traps, we would like to refer to an experience of one of the authors as a consultant in a large programme of change at a major food company. 'Innovations and new products' was one of the topics on the programme.

> A group of senior managers in the company was assigned the task of coming up with new products. Intense activity ensued and after a couple of weeks the group presented 37 new product ideas to the Vice-President. He was impressed, but said that the company could not invest in so many new things at the same time. The managers were told to prioritise and identify the best dozen new ideas. They did so. At the next meeting they were told to choose six premium product ideas and at the meeting after that they were to pick three. In the end, the group was told to pick the best idea and present it professionally. This they did. The suggestion then went to the Line Manager of the product group that the new product would belong to. He looked at the suggestion and replied that the idea had been presented 'years ago' and that 'thorough calculations had shown that there was no market for such a product.' Besides the product used so little raw material that the effect in volume – measured in tonnes – would be marginal.

What went wrong? Did so many experienced managers produce product ideas without checking how realistic they were? That was not the case, they were all experienced and successful managers. They developed a new, interesting product which they thought would be interesting to the consumers and give a reasonable margin. They had not expected, however, that the innovation would be evaluated against the criterion 'volume of raw material used in the product'. This story demonstrates the importance of a well-orchestrated dynamic process involving the whole golden triangle of production, product development and market intelligence. We also learned that if we want to stop a new product, it is almost always possible to make a calculation that shows that it will not pay off. Anybody with insight into economic calculations knows that the opportunity of making conservative assumptions for projects not yet tried is considerable.

The Road to Possibilities

This ends the presentation of key activities in the three phases of the innovation process. We concluded this presentation with some of the innovation traps in the specific phase. We would like to remind the reader that we have also presented the actions that made the innovations 'tick' through the three stages in our case studies.

Later in this book we will return to the possibility of infusing creativity into innovation processes in large organizations and compare this with the possibilities offered by innovation clusters when used in an efficient way. We will also address leadership issues. But first we should spend some time on the dynamics of innovation in an analysis of the key forces at work in the innovation process.

THE DYNAMICS OF THE INNOVATION PROCESS

In this section we will focus on the nature of the dynamic innovation process. In order to identify the essential aspects of the process, we will use a model based on a biological metaphor, not a technological one. The model springs from chaos theory. We will start the analysis with an illustration.[18]

The reader is now asked to imagine a new landscape. O'Hare Airport in Chicago should immediately be restored to what it was 200 years ago – a prairie. What should be done in order to accomplish the task? We cannot interact directly with the reader in this matter, but we can relate what other people have done when given the same task. The suggested solutions for remodelling the landscape usually follow the following lines:

- Buy a plot of land at O'Hare.
- Search libraries. Make a complete list of plants and animals present at that time.
- Collect seeds, plants, and male and female animals.
- Clear the plot of land.
- Plant the seeds and a few trees.
- Release the animals into the plot of land.
- Watch and wait.

The method seems reasonable. The ownership issues are solved. Previous knowledge about prairies is utilized. Everything needed is put in the right place – but *the project will fail.* In fact there is empirical knowledge about these things, since prairie recreation projects have been implemented at several locations. The results of early projects of this kind were as follows:

- The prairie grass was taken over by urban weeds.
- The prairie vegetation never took hold.
- No functioning eco-system was created.
- A number of 'foreign' plants emerged.
- The result was a mess of animals and plants.

In later projects the experience from these failures were analysed and the knowledge gained was applied to successful prairie recreation projects. What was wrong with the early approaches and what was learned? Briefly, the following knowledge was gained:

- A prairie cannot be assembled – it must grow.
- The starting point is important.
- Order matters – the results differ depending on what comes first.
- Missing links are important. All the essential ingredients are not visible at the end of the process.

If we have an image of a garden or a landscape that we want to realize with specific plants and animals, living together within a functioning ecosystem, it can be fairly well understood that *order matters*. If some plants or animal species are dependent on other species, these must be planted first. Likewise, the starting point is important. We do *not* start remodelling the landscape from a *tabula rasa* – a clean sheet of paper or a laboratory bench. Instead we start from a situation where something was there before – the landscape has a fauna and a flora to start with. History matters. This is different from a controlled experiment or a laboratory pilot test where the input parameters can be set as the researcher pleases. Another feature of the process is that it cannot be fully controlled, and that *uncontrolled events will influence* the outcome. When we analyse the prairie, the prairie fire is such an uncontrollable event, which will form the landscape. Even if it is not controllable, it is an essential ingredient in the creation of the prairie, since the fire burns some plants and kills some animals, while others survive. Some seeds thrive in the ashes from the fire and the evolution creates a landscape that is dependent on prairie fires, even if they cannot be detected in retrospect by simply looking at the beautiful landscape and its vegetation and animal life.

In our own field of investigation, we claim that we can capture the essentials of the process if we realize that *innovations grow – they are not assembled*. This can be seen from our three cases.

Starting Point Matters

In an innovation process it is efficient to start the development by utilizing the existing knowledge in the organization and that of the cluster partners. Starting from a totally new position with entirely new partners means investing an appreciable amount of time and money in constructing competence bases and building a common understanding about how they should be used. Taking advantage of what has been done and the sources of excellence available in day-to-day operations creates a much more cost-efficient and effective starting point for the innovation. In both the ProViva case and the Oatly case there is reason to believe that history and past investments were extremely important for the development that took place.

During the 1970s considerable investments had been made at the Lund Institute of Technology in cereals research. The cereal farmers in Sweden invested in research through their organizations such as the Skånska Lantmännen Foundation and the Cerealia Foundation. The Skånska Lantmännen Foundation was created and managed by cereal farmers in Skåne, the southernmost province of Sweden. At the same time, Sweden has been a world leader in cereal breeding since the 1920s through Svalöv–Weibull. These foundations and Svalöf–Weibull had a long-term interest in supporting cereal research. They have been important in the process of building up a Swedish cereal know-how.

This long-term investment in research was the corner stone of a vital cereals research programme. The programme was not customer adapted, or guided in specific directions. It was the researcher's task to develop the research field. A number of very interesting scientific publications resulted from the programme. The Lund Institute of Technology established competence in the subject. The research programme also resulted in a number of PhD projects. These postgraduates have been very useful in research and in industry. And, which is important for our cases, they are also the key players in the innovation activities that we find in the cluster some 10–12 years later. History matters.

It is also interesting to note the connections between basic research and goal-oriented research. The investment made by the Cerealia Foundation was intended to strengthen the platform for cereals research in Sweden. This was also the effect. The response to the question of whether it would have been better to target a company-specific area for the research programme is no. At the time the money was invested, nobody could foresee the kind of projects and the kind of products that would result from the process. It could of course be argued that other companies than Cerealia gained from the innovations. On the other hand, the innovations that have been developed offer high-value-added product applications for cereals from Sweden – which is in the interest of the owners – the farmers.

In the Mona Carota case we have a project in which the aim was to produce high-quality products from carrots. Again, this is an example of a cost- and time-efficient starting point. Carrots are grown with great success in the Öresund region. The climatic and soil conditions are excellent for carrots, which can therefore be produced, with high quality, at a competitive price. Again, the benefit of developing products grown in the region becomes apparent. In principle, this also means that there are better opportunities to experiment with various types of carrots. As we have seen from the case, not just any carrot suits the product, it must be a specific kind. Another part of the history is that the entrepreneur herself grew up on the farm and had early experience of skilful farming. The third part of the story is that Skånemejerier had tried to make carrot juice unsuccessfully, so when they were approached they knew exactly what could be gained. Their learning from historical experience qualified them for the special attention that we as researchers give to companies that say 'yes' to an innovation project as soon as they are approached.

In the ProViva case, the enquiry from the hospital about how newly operated colon patients could be helped to digest their food received a quick and knowledgeable reply from the researchers since they had so much competence in the cereals area. At another hospital located in another food cluster there may have been competence available about the positive effects of other food products. Probably there are other solutions available, but that is irrelevant for us now. The point is that all three cases started from something well known and that previous investments mattered. This is one reason why it takes time for a cluster to evolve. It is a fact of life that many try to find novelty and fortune in faraway places although it may be more profitable to take a creative look at your own backyard.

Order Matters

In the innovation process, competence and insight are developed in the learning process where previous knowledge is tested in new situations, and experience from new ventures is incorporated into the learning process.[19] Some of the order issues are evident in all three cases. For example a knowledge base must be created before product and market can be developed. In all three cases the product idea was born before the process equipment was designed. This is in line with the three-phase model from Utterback.

We can see the possibility of a product development process in which the ownership of a process line is the starting point for product development.

Somebody asks the question 'What else could we make with this equipment?' However, this is more common in the development of variants of existing products. In radical innovations and architectural innovations the starting point is not existing equipment, but rather existing scientific knowledge or insight into consumer needs.

In the Oatly case we see that one of the important innovation managers, Lennart Wikström, asked himself at the beginning of the case what kind of high value-added products could strengthen the competitiveness of Swedish grain production. He was influenced by a medical journal in the UK and a consumer study in the USA. At the same time, he was aware of the areas of research competence in Lund, since he was managing the Skånska Lantmännen Research Foundation. Market needs and scientific possibilities met for the first time very early in the process.

In the ProViva case the same meeting between market needs and scientific possibilities is explicit. The knowledge-need meeting occurred when the surgeon Professor Stig Bengmark asked Kåre Larsson, Professor of Food Technology, if he could suggest a form of a treatment for patients after abdominal surgery. Bengmark was looking for a product that would help recovery of the function of the digestive tract, so that the patients can digest their food – thus reducing the number of deaths after surgery. Here we have a very clear early meeting between a consumer need and relevant scientific knowledge.

In the Mona Carota case, the entrepreneur Ingegerd Sjöholm was dissatisfied with the quality of carrot juice and searched the market for the best product available. To her mind there was no satisfactory product, but one could be made with the right kind of carrots, with existing process equipment if enough was learned about carrots on the cellular level and how they react to temperature.

We can see that order matters in the Oatly case when so much is sold on the US market that production volume becomes a limitation. This problem shows the delicacy of the balance between market activities and efficient, safe and sustainable production of volumes well adapted for the markets.

Missing Links Matter

Missing links are important parts of the process that are not visible in retrospect. They occur in our cases and are of great importance for the development of the processes analysed in the cases. The actors involved are essential at a particular time and suddenly disappear.

One such missing link in the Oatly case is Kerstin Fredlund. We recall the story about Kerstin from the Oatly case.

Kerstin Fredlund has new ideas about how oats could be developed. Kerstin is a very practical woman who believes that research is a tool for accomplishing more advanced product development. Kerstin was raised on a farm, believes in 'antroposophical' ideology and is a medical doctor. She is dedicated to the task of solving the problem of gluten intolerance in Sweden.

Kerstin made her entrance into the project with 'hydrothermic' products at the oat seminar in June 1990. She came to the workshop with products made of 'hydrothermic flour', pancakes, bread, soup and porridge. Everyone at the meeting was enthusiastic.

This seminar became the starting point for the research project in which Kerstin Fredlund was performing the laboratory work and proved the new process for hydrothermic oats. The research project resulted in several patents.

Like a prairie fire, Kerstin appeared without warning, in a way that absolutely could control. She made significant contributions to the thinking and the generation of ideas in the Oatly case and she performed some of the important research herself. Then she left the arena to concentrate on other, similar projects, hydrothermal cereals with a medical focus.

In the Mona Carota Case we were able to identify another type of missing link. The financial resources were expended and there was very little hope of finding new venture capital within a reasonable time. The researcher Magnus Lagnevik entered the scene with the ambition of developing a theory for innovation processes. Financing was thereby obtained for the entrepreneur Ingegerd Sjöholm; in the project, this source of money was precisely what was needed to carry the project into another phase. Ingegerd Sjöholm realized that something could be learned of use in future projects, but the main motivating factor was that the new project provided resources that would keep the original project floating. Part of the money was designated for her own research, but she refrained from using this to finance her own research. Instead, the Mona Carota project was placed at the top of her list of priorities. The money was taken to finance the doctoral students, Charlotte Alklint and Federico Gomez. During this time a revolutionary breakthrough occurred in the research project; the breakthrough that made it possible to complete the Mona Carota product.

Since we conclude that missing links are also important in other innovation cases, we expect to find that the history of innovation is filled with missing links. This means that we have a large number of unknown heroes who have made contributions to innovations and then disappeared. We pay tribute to those contributors who are often missing in the official history of innovations, not because they were neglected or outmanoeuvred, but simply because their contribution is not visible in retrospect.

Summing up the innovation cases, we indeed find that *the innovation grows*, *starting point matters*, *order matters*, and *missing links play a vital role*. However, we would like to add three more characteristics of the innovation process that we have identified in our cases. These factors are not included by Brown and Eisenhardt but can be found in other studies. They are *role models* and the *ability to reinterpret*. The third factor is *timing*.

Role Models

From the cases studied we learned that role models are of great importance to help entrepreneurs see opportunities and to allow themselves to behave differently from the work culture that they experience in their everyday lives.

In the Oatly case, the Gang of Four found good role models in Kaj Vareman and Kåre Larsson. These two entrepreneurs contributed to the Oatly case at a time when they had already been successful with ProViva. It was also important that Rickard Öste had previous experience of a successful innovation project, a grain scanning device developed by the company Agrovision under the product name GrainCheck.[20]

From them the Gang of Four learned the spirit of the innovation process, but also the practicalities of everyday life and the tricks of the trade. They could, in practical terms, learn about applying for patents, setting up companies and negotiating and defending immaterial rights. This knowledge, or rather skill, is difficult to obtain by reading or from consultants. Learning from somebody who has already succeeded is easier. Details and judgement are the key to mastery here, and learning from someone else hands on, is very efficient. Besides, earlier success creates credibility, hope and inspiration for the new entrepreneur.

In interviews the entrepreneur Ingegerd Sjöholm tells us that she was very inspired by Kerstin Fredlund. The way in which she progressed to a new stage without any fear at all, moving faster than most other actors, and mixing advanced science with a practical approach, were impressive. It gave Ingegerd Sjöholm the courage to find her own way, fear nobody and disregard some of the codes on 'proper behaviour' in a scientific environment. It is important to stress here that only some of the codes of behaviour were set aside. As a scientist, the respect for the profession cannot be lost and credibility is of the utmost importance for the scientific entrepreneur. An example of the spirit of going straight for the target is the trip to Germany; the German mill producers finding two extremely competent women with a carload of carrots outside the factory entrance. They are probably still wondering.

Role models thus serve two purposes for entrepreneurs; they provide skills and hope. The hope they instil is, to a large extent, the hope that it is possible to make an innovation successful. Most qualified people in scientific laboratories have difficulties appreciating the value of what they produce. They have even greater difficulties in realizing that the substances in their tests can actually be transformed into high-quality food products sold to consumers who buy the products voluntarily and pay prices that make the production profitable.

Reinterpretation – the Ability to See Something as Something

To make an innovation is to see possibilities that others have not seen. The cases we have studied illustrate a number of situations where actors reinterpret the situation and find new possibilities. For example it is not at all self-evident to see oat grains as a fluid product. The concept of oat milk was actually born twice in the Oatly case.

> At a meeting in 1989, at Ideon Agro Food, Rickard Öste met Sigurd Andersson who represented the grain producers. Sigurd asked Rickard: *'Why not make milk out of oats? Yes, why not, was Richard's reaction!'*

The project had to become more practical, tests were made on pills and a slimming formula. The reason was that the slimming formula was the kind of product that the distributor could accept. Later in the process, the same idea was reborn from the marketing side.

> During the autumn of 1994 Rickard Öste had a meeting with a representative from Friggs, Peter Thesleff (from the staff marketing in England, agent for Arla/Scan), Sven Sahlin (Trader), Jan-Olof Bengtsson (Food From Sweden). Rickard Öste was about to present the process for the production of the slimming formula when Peter Thesleff expressed: 'Oat milk, really good! Why don't we make milk, an oat milk? That's something I would be able to sell in England.'

Naturally Rickard recalled his comment from 1989: 'Yes, why not?' But now the situation was different; there were actors who were willing to sell the product to consumers. This reminds us of another key feature of the innovation process: timing matters.

Another example of reinterpreting and seeing something as something is when one of the members of the Gang of Four visits a colleague in his office. Kerstin Fredlund had left a bagful of hydrothermic oat flour with him in the hope that he would be interested. The professor had put it on the shelf during the summer and when the member of the Gang of Four visited him in the autumn, he showed her the bag of flour. She asked about it and found it very interesting. Furthermore, she took the bag and conducted some interesting laboratory tests on its content.

The same bag of flour was understood completely differently by the two researchers. The professor saw it as something he could not just throw away since it had been given to him. He left it on the shelf. The Gang of Four member saw it as an exciting opportunity for a new product.

Our cases also include other important reinterpretations. On of these is the changed product definition in the ProViva case. The product was intended as a medical product to cure illness, when first invented. Later in the case the product was redefined and became a probiotic health drink to be sold on the consumer market. A similar redefinition appears in the Oatly case when the product is redefined from being a food ingredient to being a series of branded consumer products. Both these redefinitions were vital to market success.

In some innovation presentations this is referred to as *luck* or *serendipity*. *It is not. Only those who work intensively in an area and have their mind set on development within that area can reinterpret everyday situations* – that is, can understand the possibilities arising from apparently trivial findings or objects. Attributing a new, specific meaning to an object is not done randomly. It takes years of hard work and trials to develop the mindset necessary to capture the butterfly of opportunity when it comes your way. We will return to this topic later when we analyse creativity in innovations. For now, we will summarize the analysis of the innovation dynamics, where we have found the following:

- An innovation cannot be assembled – it must grow.
- The starting point is important.
- Order matters – the results of the process differ depending on what comes first.
- Missing links are important – not all essential ingredients and actors are visible at the end of the process.
- Timing matters – what is not usable at one time may be invaluable at another.
- Role models are important.
- Reinterpretation is important. Only those who work intensively in an area and have their mind set on development within this area can reinterpret everyday situations and capture the butterfly of opportunity when it comes their way.

CLUSTER LEADERSHIP

A fair degree of insight is necessary in order to manage innovation processes in clusters in an efficient way. The conditions for strategic management are different, firstly because the innovation process has specific characteristics, and secondly because when working in several organizations in a cluster there is no single chain of command.

Companies that work with innovation processes are balancing on the edge of chaos, where uncertainty is ever present and where the process is only controllable in part. The innovation grows. Starting point matters, order matters, there should be a balance between structure and chaos, between the old and the new. Timing and pace are important, results can often not be anticipated. Experiments with unforeseen outcomes must be made, and still the process can be, and should be, governed.

As a result, corporate top managers do not have enough insight into the process to develop and implement a complete strategy. The strategies must be developed at business level, while the role of the corporate management is to create joint visions and generative themes. Only the people working close to the development and experimentation can learn from the experimentation and adapt the structure of the business to develop promising business ventures. They have the role of *strategists*.

In our cases we find the strategists very close to the innovation process. We can illustrate this with the Oatly case, where we find three strategists at work. In the *fluid phase* Rickard Öste plays that role, using his skills to find interfaces between the unique areas of competence and the unique actors that together can develop the Oatly concept. It appears that this ability was of key strategic importance, since information about similar oat development projects tells us that these projects failed because one or several of the areas of competence needed for success were just not present.

In the *transitional phase* Ingegerd Sjöholm takes the strategic leadership. In this phase a key success factor is creating an efficient, safe and sustainable production line with high hygiene standards. The dominant design had been established and the problem in this phase was to adapt the process to the product and to produce large quantities of the right quality and at a reasonable cost. We note in this case that the change from the fluid to the transitional phase was a painful process, interpreted here as a strategic focus change and a change of strategic leadership

In the *specific phase* a new strategic manager enters the scene. Mats-Ola Kindstedt becomes the Managing Director of Ceba at a time when the strategic focus changes to developing specific products for specific markets. The product is redefined from being an ingredient to being a series of branded consumer products. Brands must be built up. Supporting concepts, such as the green dairy, are developed and issues concerning communication of immaterial qualities of the product are included in the agenda in a professional way. The organization is tightened. New professionals are recruited and marketing and sales become top priority.

This leads us to an important conclusion; *the strategic leadership changed in the three phases of the innovation project*. The strategic leader was the person with the competence that was most needed during that particular development phase. We have only three cases so we must be careful not to make general statements based on this conclusion, but there is an under-standable logic behind this development. It should also be pointed out that these changes were not planned by an executive on a higher level; they were the result of learning from the daily operations. In one sense we could describe these changes *as the innovation process seeking and appointing a leader, rather than a leader managing the innovation process.*

From all three cases we also know that there was a certain instability among the investment capital providers over time, so precise guidance could not be obtained from the owners at all times. From our interviews with venture capitalists we also learned that they often enter the process at one stage and leave at another, so they do not follow the whole innovation process from beginning to the end.

> For our company, the development time in the food sector – and in biotech – is too long. We try to define promising offers. Then we buy into them and estimate what value can be created during a two-to-three-year period. After that period we find a buyer that is interested in running the next phase while we collect our returns.[21]

So the owners do not always have the ambition of completing the process. We find another version of this behaviour in large companies that acquire small innovative firms when development has progressed so far that the innovation seems reliable and is regarded as a reasonably safe bet.

In the Oatly case discussed here we also have two large companies working together as owners and the division of leadership between the two cannot have been self-evident. We see an important guiding signal, however, in the joint declaration made by the two presidents when the innovations left the fluid phase into the transitional phase. This was of great importance for the strategic refocusing.

But we must search elsewhere for the leadership of the whole process on a higher level. We are looking for *the patcher*, who reviews the patterns of businesses, markets and technologies and makes new patterns. The patcher searches for relevant partners and suitable projects to help the innovation process grow. We are also looking for *the synthesizer*, who, in the original meaning, hires and fires top management. In the context of cluster manage-ment that cannot be done explicitly since many organizations are involved. However, the synthesizer can influence the choice of people working in the innovation project. The synthesizer also articulates common visions and values, which should inspire people to work in the right direction. The syn-thesizer also encourages and cheerleads.

In the Oatly case we find the roles of *patcher* and *synthesizer* are borne by one person – the journalist, the research foundation managing director and the consultant Lennart Wikström. He was the first person to define the field of opportunity and to see a possible outcome of the process. In his position in the research foundation, he had contacts with all the relevant researchers as well as top managers in the organizations involved. Being simultaneously in a position in the top echelon of the organizations involved and in the borderland between the organizations, he has the areas of competence and the position of a *borderrider*.[22] A borderrider can see phenomena from several perspectives, has the ability to communicate across borders and is seen as a trustworthy person. If such a borderrider is successful in the creation of common visions and values, the cluster leadership will be efficient. From Jonnergård's studies we learn that there is a downside to being a borderrider. Part of leadership is to give credit to other people when things go well. Borderriders rarely become heroes. But the effects of their leadership can be traced in retrospect as we have done in this study.

In the *ProViva case* we can identify *two strategists*. One is Kaj Vareman in the company Probi and in the group of researchers. He searches for and finds a way to transform the researcher's ideas into successful innovations. One very important reason for the success of this project is that at Skånemejerier, there is another strategist, Kenneth Andersson, who is willing to venture into new partnerships in order to create new innovative products with high added value. He manages to lead the process inside and outside the company in very good co-operation with Kaj Vareman and many other people.

The *patcher* in the process is Skånemejerier's Marketing Director, Jan Persson, who works hard on matching market opportunities and technological possibilities. The patching includes both resource allocation and market evaluation. Another important part of the patching work is to set the scene and to position the product in the political and regulatory arena. When ProViva was launched it was by no means clear what a 'functional food product' was. This part of the patching work is conducted by Skånemejerier's Information Director, Lotta Törner. In the *ProViva case*, the *synthesizer* is the Chief Executive Officer of Skånemejerier, Rolf Bjerndell, who supports the experiments with the new products, evaluates and develops the innovation cluster, identifies the possibilities quickly when the first signs of success occur and then gives clear signals about the new strategy of Skånemejerier. This strategy is based on growth in high-value-added products, it is articulated through clear statements, 'sound bites', and models that explain the situation. Furthermore, the new strategy is made possible through heavy investments in production facilities that can simultaneously – but in different places – cater for the need to produce small batches of new non-dairy products as well as efficient, full-scale dairy production. It is through the joint work of the strategists, the Patcher and the synthesizer that direct links are created and maintained between market intelligence, production and product development.

Thus we have learned six things about cluster leadership:

- Cluster leaders are not always formally set up.
- The strategic leadership seems to change in the three innovation phases.
- The strategic leadership is closely related to the key competence needed in each innovation phase.
- It is not self-evident or even common that an innovation project in a cluster has the same owners during the whole process.
- Patcher and synthesizer roles are helped by an ability of the role bearer to see the innovation from several perspectives, to live and work on the edge and to lead others towards common visions and values.
- Cluster leadership is heavily dependent on the leader's capacity to allow experimentation, absorb and interpret the results and to re-allocate resources as the innovation grows.

INNOVATION AND PRODUCT DEVELOPMENT PROCESSES ARE DIFFERENT

Innovation processes are difficult to plan in advance. However they still require a strategy, commitment and conscious resource allocation. The leader of an innovation process is constantly balancing on a tightrope. He or she can fall off the tightrope in two ways. On one side there is the risk of rigidity in planning. On the other side there is the risk of uncontrollable chaos.

We also know that innovation processes are much more demanding than product development processes. In radical innovations, the key resource bases of the company will change and areas of competence, consumers and structures will have to be reviewed in the light of the new innovation. *Our main contribution in this book is perhaps to identify and highlight the differences between innovation and product development.*

In our empirical work we have seen many innovation processes that were stopped because they were managed like traditional product development processes. Several companies have spent large amounts of money on manuals and handbooks for development. These handbooks often depart from 'good project management practice' and have given very direct guidelines and evaluation methods for a project. However, they disregard the specific character of the innovation process that we have identified in this book. Thus, a steering instrument for one situation – product development – has been used in another situation – innovation. The results can be disastrous. However, since the failures occur in products and services that are not produced or delivered, they are easier to hide or forget about. It is accepted that innovation processes have a high failure rate. But if the management tools were adapted to the conditions, the result would be more and better innovations at a lower cost.

WHAT DOES HIGH-VALUE-ADDED MEAN TO THE CONSUMER?

The concept of high-value-added products is problematic in that it mirrors a managerial, often cost-based, view of the value of a certain product. A starting point for understanding consumers' perceptions of high-value-added products is *that consumers buy and use certain products for the benefits they hope they will bring to their lives.* The cost, time, effort, and so on, that a company has put into developing the products are usually not of any interest to consumers. They care about the final products and assess what benefits these products can bring to their lives relative to other products on the market that they perceive to be alternative ways of gaining the same benefits. What this boils down to, from a managerial standpoint, is that *it really does not matter how brilliantly engineered a certain product might be if consumers do not perceive that product to be the best way of achieving a certain goal.*

An illustrative example that is frequently used in basic marketing textbooks is that a consumer does not buy an electric drill because he or she desires to own one *per se* but because he or she wants to drill a hole. The machine is not important – the hole is. It is thus a certain product's ability to create value, 'to move a consumer from point A to point B', that is the reason for a consumer to buy the product.

This method of reasoning has a number of implications for managers contemplating developing and marketing a certain high-value-added food product. One approach is to envisage a potential consumer asking the following questions:

- Where is point A and where is point B?
In other words, one has to be able *to explain what problem the product is promising to solve.* If this cannot be explained to consumers in a relatively clear and easy way there is a considerable risk that it will be difficult to motivate consumers to buy the product. We see this problem very clearly in the food industry, when functional food producers work hard to give the consumers information that is correct, but at the same time understandable.

•   Why do I want to go from point A to point B?

Consumers must perceive the problem to which the product provides a solution to be relevant. It is not necessary that consumers are aware of the problem and are looking for a solution. However, *the company must be able to explain to consumers what benefits they would get from solving the problem.* The consumer might understand that the product lowers the level of cholesterol in his/her blood, but is it important for me as a consumer to engage in such activities? When is it important?

•   In what way does this product move me from point A to point B?

This is a tricky question as the answer is usually too complicated for a layperson to understand. Consumers must be given the illusion of understanding the (often) complicated mechanisms behind the solution. With a product like ProViva this is complicated. However, evidence from the interviews discussed in Chapter 4 shows that a very rudimentary understanding seems to be sufficient for some consumers. In one of the interviews a consumer explained that he was using ProViva rose-hip soup as a remedy for his sometimes upset stomach. When asked what ProViva did to his stomach he just shrugged his shoulders and explained: *Well, you know, it's those bacteria.* When asked to explain in more detail what the bacteria did he said that he really did not know too much about it but that the bacteria 'was good stuff.'

•   In what way does this product move me from point A to point B in a better way than other products?

It is important that the relative merits of the particular product are stressed. If similar products are available, the distinguishing features must be highlighted. *Should the product be a radical innovation so that no similar products are likely to be available on the market.* Nevertheless, it should be kept in mind that consumers have no other way of making sense of a new product than to relate it to their categorization of presently available products. *A (perhaps false) comparison with some product known to the consumers is therefore likely to occur.*

•   How can I trust that this product really will move me from point A to point B?

Consumers are used to being bombarded with large amounts of more or less outrageous claims about products. Especially concerning food products' potential health qualities, companies seem to be very innovative in stretching the limits of what can lawfully be claimed. It is therefore important to make clear to potential consumers why the claim made about a particular product should be assessed as more trustworthy than other claims.

As high-value-added food products are usually based on thorough scientific investigations, there is ample opportunity for making reliable claims. This is an extremely beneficial marketing standpoint as consumers seem to be reluctant to believe what is written on packages. The logic of *not believing in any short cuts* plays out strongly in the interviews. As many high-value-added products are just that – short cuts to better health – the claims are only believed if it is communicated to the consumers that there is a reason to believe that what is being said in the marketing information is backed up by scientific research. Other related questions are whether the particular product will move me from A to B in a safe and controlled way, if there are any potential disadvantages with moving from A to B in this particular way, and if I really want to go to point B or is there a potential point C somewhere that I would rather go to.

The above-mentioned consumers' questions regarding a potential high-value-added food product *give a rather instrumental view* of why consumers use products, that is, to solve a certain problem. In a way, this might be a fair description, although it has to be stressed that it is far from certain that consumers are looking to solve *the same* problem as the company had envisaged. We learn from the *Oatly case* that the products were designed to help consumers with gluten intolerance. However, we have met consumers who buy the pancake batter just because it is convenient or the icecream just because it tastes good.

A similar example can be drawn from the interview material where one of the interviewed consumers told us about an ice-cream brand he really liked – Godhälsa. This is a product containing the same active ingredients as the ProViva drinks. When asked more about the ice cream he confessed that he loved the taste but bought it mostly for its low calorie content. He was unaware of the fact that it contained *L. plantarum 299v* and the potential beneficial consequences of this.

Unique Marketing Aspects of High-value-added Food Products

When it comes to marketing high-value-added food products a number of things must be considered in addition to those mentioned above regarding high-value-added products. As health and healthy food products are topics gaining much attention in contemporary society, consumers are becoming more aware and more interested in these issues. *The role of food both as a potential risk and a potential means to healthiness* is stressed in all sorts of ways. Consumers are fed with these messages to the extent that a 'risk society' is created in which everything becomes measured in terms of its potential of avoiding or tackling risks. With both media focusing on these issues and companies launching and relaunching products that cater to the health-aware, markets consumers have plenty of information to try to make sense of. Considering the vast amounts of information *available it should come as no surprise that consumers often adopt ambivalent positions towards what they consider to be value added from a health perspective.*

To further complicate things, *there are many connections between consumers' food consumption and their identity.* Consumption of food is an important part in consumers' construction of a coherent narrative of the self. *Therefore, food consumption habits cannot be easily changed if consumers feel that the changes do not mesh with their overall lifestyle.* It should be acknowledged, however, that it has become increasingly important over the past few years to actively care for one's body. To be physically fit is stressed as an important part of being successful in most contemporary lifestyles.

In addition to the more overreaching pointers regarding marketing of high-value-added products given above, companies marketing food products with various health claims must take into account the *ambivalent attitudes consumers have to the concepts of healthy and unhealthy foods.* In the interviews it was found that the categories of healthy and unhealthy foods were used as ideal types of what should or should not be eaten. Rather than referring to these ideal categories, consumers talked about the food they ate on a daily basis as being 'not unhealthy'. They thus exhibited the kind of risk avoidance logic suggested by Beck (1992). Furthermore, *food that normally belonged to one of the categories healthy foods or not unhealthy foods could be moved to the category not healthy foods if eaten at the wrong time or in the wrong quantity.* This illustrates the ephemeral character of the system. One more thing requiring consideration is that an *implicit norm of what should be eaten seemed to be in effect.* Consumers exhibited *a need to justify their deviation from this norm.* They did so by explaining that the reason for consuming foods that they considered less than optimal was beyond their control. Finally, the interviews provided evidence that *there are strong syntactical patterns that govern how a meal is composed* – it appears that these patterns are not easily changed. The issue of *consumers feeling that they had no control* seems to be a key issue in producing desirable solutions for the consumer market. *Giving consumers a sense of regaining control over their own lives* would thus be an attractive position to hold in a healthy food market.

CREATIVENESS IN CLUSTERS AND LARGE ORGANIZATIONS

Cluster innovation projects differ from those created in large organizations. In this section we will discuss the flow and components of innovations in clusters. We will use the framework crated by Robinson and Stern (see Chapter 3). In our work we have not only studied in-company processes but also innovations in clusters. Therefore, we can further develop the analysis and compare the innovation process in companies and in clusters. We will also comment on how creativity is enhanced in universities. Cluster innovation projects have a stimulating effect. The key concepts when analysing creativity in innovation processes are:

- alignment
- self-initiated activity
- unofficial activity
- serendipity
- diverse stimuli
- within-company communication

Most food companies developed during the twentieth century. There are two types of companies: those that were built sufficiently large from the beginning because of the need of energy, such as sugar factories and dairies, and those that started as small production units in someone's kitchen or cellar. Many of these family businesses established from 1940 to 1980 were later incorporated into larger companies and are today owned by multinational companies such as Unilever, Nestlé or Succard. This development has been the result of the world economy, prices of raw materials, labour costs, energy costs, transportation costs, customs, technical improvement and is sometimes simply described as the general phenomena *rationalization*.

As a result of these enormous production lines and demand for high productivity and leading to the necessity to run the production lines almost 24 hours per day, there has been little opportunity to try new varieties and new concepts employing alternative raw materials or providing some other added value. As a result, smaller enterprises have been able to produce unique products with an added value, such as functional foods, from a special raw material, such as organically grown crops, or by using high technology in a unique way. These small enterprises can also be very flexible and provide a high level of traceability. We will investigate if and how the keywords above are applicable to the three cases and the cluster environment presented in this book.

Alignment

In small enterprises, the participants, employees and owners work closely together and it is very easy to follow the main intention of the development or production. There is no need for formal information about the latest news or next strategic step. The energy tanks of the company are replenished during coffee breaks.

In Europe much effort has been devoted to small and medium-sized enterprises (SME:s) since the middle of the 1980s in order to help and advise traditional small production units in the implementation of new technologies to strengthen their competitiveness. Many university cities have set up science parks or 'greenhouses' where entrepreneurs from the university and industry can meet and work together to create and develop innovative projects. In this book we have focused on the SME companies close to the 'greenhouse' Ideon in Lund in the very south of Sweden. The fact is that the buildings and the organization that together define Ideon is the prerequisite for *alignment* in the three cases described in this book. The platform around Ideon has then provided a means for the academic researchers and the industry to find new ways to collaborate.

The traditional alignment in business has been to stick to the business concept and one starts to talk about the success when a line or a product generates money. University-based projects also deal with researchers' inner scientific conviction of what the product should be. It is not self-evident for researchers and industry to align with the same goals and values. In the *ProViva case* the researchers more or less dictated that the product could not contain any milk. Of course this was not self-evident in Skånemejerier, as milk used to be, and still is, their main product. However, on a strategic level, production of high-value-added products could be combined also with non-dairy products. This meant a strategic reorientation for Skånemejerier.

Another alignment factor, a common motivating idea in the cases, is that the products have to have a good taste. All the researchers involved in the practical development steps used the problems that arose as a challenge. They used all knowledge available inside and outside the university to solve these problems in order to achieve a product with good taste and appearance.

In the *Oatly* case the Gang of Four accepted a deviation from the agreed common vision when the opportunity arose to transfer the laboratory-scale process to industrial production. Of course, there was enthusiasm over the challenge of the slimming product project, but it was not the kind of product they had envisaged from the beginning. The product was mixed with soy protein which, in a way, was a competitor to the originally planned oat-based product and then fortified with many minerals and vitamins. The healthiness of oats was pushed to the background, although a nutritional study was performed later which strengthened the product concept. Then when the oat drink or oat milk was born, everyone in the Gang of Four felt that this was the main product. Even if a tactical departure had been made from the agreed common vision, there was no doubt in the minds of the researchers what the goal was.

In the *Mona Carota case* the goals were set during one of the first meetings between Charlotte Alklint, Ingegerd Sjöholm, Lennart Wikström and Kenneth Andersson by the definition of the juice as 'stable, good tasting, with a good-looking appearance and a reasonably long shelf life without using additives'. This goal has been understood and followed by everybody involved. Thus everybody in the project has felt alignment to this goal through the whole project.

Researchers are very willing to take risks by investing working time; they don't even call it work but just research. Research is evaluated by the number of scientific papers published but this does not reveal anything about how long it took to produce the results and write the paper, which can vary from a couple of weeks to more than a year. In contrast, a consultant controls his or her time minute by minute and has to report and deliver results on time. The new clusters at Ideon served to establish how researchers and industrial partners can collaborate step by step and how objectives should be identified.

The driving force of the clusters must include both a speaker and a listener from the industry and from academia. In the *ProViva case* Kenneth Andersson from Skånemejerier and Kåre Larsson and Kaj Vareman were the visionaries. The Gang of Four together with Lennart Wikström is the same as in the *Oatly case*.

University regulations in Sweden allow academic staff to work extra hours after their normal 40 hrs per week for someone else, as long as this does not compete with their university work. *Research results also belong to the researcher and not to the university.* Help is then offered to patent interesting results and to find partners for collaboration. Both the academic freedom and the fact that researchers can exploit their results through patents are important for the new high-technology companies being established in or attached to the clusters in the Öresund region. Gert Göransson, the President of the Ideon Agro Food Foundation has always emphasized the importance of encouragement in motivation. Both academics and company staff should be inspired to work towards a common vision.

Self-initiated Activity

A small enterprise is a result of an initiative and it owns the concept or knowledge that will grow and ripen into a business idea. Of interest in this book is the way in which large companies arrange platforms and arenas for affiliated companies. This happened both in the *ProViva* and the *Oatly cases* through the establishment of the Probi and Ceba companies. The reason for setting up small, partially independent companies is to let the new company make its own decisions and not be involved in other ongoing strategies. Perstorp AB, a petroleum-based company in southern of Sweden established some years ago a company called Pernovo to nurture innovative ideas. Ideas were developed into businesses are thereafter incorporated in the Perstorp business, sold to someone else or launched on the stock market. When an idea appeared in the Pernovo company for production of nutritional substrate, the mother company made the decision to establish a new company called Perbio in another place where it was closer to natural clusters. The new business idea was so different from the traditional business. In order to give the new business self control, it was located at some distance from Perstorp. The ability to create platforms that nurture innovation is important. It is important, however to review the value of the new businesses for the mother company. Currently new owners have decided that the Pernovo company did not contribute enough and closed it down.

The initiative may also take the form of a request to purchase a special brand or license from a larger company. In Massachusetts, USA, the Ocean Spray company made the decision to stop production of their tropical beverages. Mauna La'i Tropicals Ltd, a start-up company, took over and have been very successful in expanding the market for tropical fruit drinks. There is a similar case in Malmö, Sweden where the Finnish company, Fazer, moved from Malmö to Ljugsbro, 250 km to the north. Fazer sold all the production rights and the equipment to a group of employees who did not want to move. The company thus formed, Candeco, produces different toppings for ice cream and cakes. The company also invented a special ingredient called 'hot shots' for drinks. Self-initiated activities created new business.

Unofficial Activity

All creative work contains some degree of unofficial work. This unofficial work may have different forms. Unofficial creative activities can take varying amounts of time. However, it is necessary for the members of the group, or the employees to adopt an experimental approach. Tomoshige Hori's realization at Snowbrand Milk products in Tokyo (Robinson and Stern, 1997, p. 166ff) that he had found a new and revolutionary cheese-making process could not be communicated to the management at an early stage. By developing the idea himself, unofficially, and by writing scientific papers about the physical properties of milk and cheese, he gained recognition and respect for his ideas which could then be officially presented to the dairy industry. This example, together with similar cases, has been the base for companies to make arrangements for employees to promote and support unofficial work. The 3M company was one of the first to encourage people to set aside 15 per cent of their working time as free time to develop their own ideas.

As a part of these innovation studies all of us, senior researchers and PhD students, visited ingredient companies. At one of these industrial visits, to Danisco Ingredients, Århus in Denmark we learned that the staff of the R&D department had to devote 10 per cent of their working hours to unofficial activities. Interviews with these people revealed that they were very proud and happy about this 'free application time'.

The three cases presented in this book are all the result of more or less unofficial work. Both the *ProViva* and the *Oatly* cases started in the university environment where staff are supposed to take initiatives and collaborate in different arenas. Historically this was done only with the purpose of writing scientific papers and making breakthroughs in their disciplines.

However, recently there has been a change at universities regarding collaboration with industry. One reason may be that this has become a requirement for research grants from the European Union (EU) and several other development funds. The Swedish universities have incorporated this policy into their three main goals, namely: education, research and collaboration with industry and society, with the overall aim of making it easier to work with organizations outside academia. This has provided a means of promoting unofficial work and has resulted in researchers setting up companies based on traditional research. Such researchers are now afforded high status in contrast to earlier notions that they were 'selling themselves to industry'.

We now know that this activity, often consisting of multidisciplinary co-operation, has a creative effect in the universities. New research problems are discovered. New combinations of scientific knowledge are made. Researchers get ideas for new, joint research projects. Sometimes also new research departments are founded.

Networks such as the Ideon Agro Food foundation have provided good places for unofficial work. Here, unofficial work suddenly became official by managing working hours and salaries jointly between industry and academia. Ideon Agro Food was the necessary platform for the start of the *Mona Carota* project, starting from a former network project about cooling chains of vegetables managed by Ingegerd Sjöholm. As this first project was pursued in the network of the Ideon Agro Food cluster it was very easy to continue with the new carrot juice project.

In the *Oatly* case the researchers were making unofficial contacts as part of their daily work. The Gang of Four was working in an unofficial capacity in parallel with their official work during the first two or three years, except for the experimental trials which had a financial budget.

Kenneth Andersson from Skånemejerier has been one of the key actors both in the *ProViva* and the *Mona Carota* cases by acting in the area between the university and industry and in different functions. To be able to play on both sides it is important to know the language and have the intention to act in a flexible way. One important ingredient is the common language between all the actors in the two cases. They all have the same education: chemical engineering specialized in food engineering. Both the Gang of Four and Kenneth Andersson are Masters in Food Engineering. Kenneth Andersson is the kind of person who always notices when something new is coming up and is willing to accept turbulence around him: 'You have to allow people to make mischief.' This form of promoting ideas, university research, industrial trials and their combinations is one way to create innovations between academia and industry in cluster innovation projects.

When interviewed, some of the researchers expressed their *satisfaction in participating in cluster innovation projects by saying 'you are free to create new ideas, new applications and just invent things'*. Perhaps we will understand in the future that this 'unofficial work' in cluster innovation projects was necessary to renew the universities in the twenty-first century.

Serendipity

Is it possible to run a company based on luck? Innovators and researchers will of course answer 'no'. But in all descriptions of how successful companies were established and how they have developed the founders or their families are very good at singling out the moment or situation when and how the brilliant idea was born. The story quite often grows with time and all the problems associated with money and lack of support from colleagues are forgotten. In Robinson and Stern (1997), the birth of Teflon and Gore-Tex material is one clear example. In this example the lack of solubility of a component puzzled the researchers so much that they just had to use all their professional knowledge to solve the riddle. In this way they invented both the Teflon coating and the concept of Gore-Tex material, widely used nowadays.

All innovations are made in the context of solid competence. Those who are 'lucky' in innovation processes are successful because they have detailed knowledge, understand what they are looking for, and can interpret unexpected results of experiments. In the *Mona Carota* case, the idea of making a juice was the result of the availability of high-quality fresh carrots, at a reasonable price together with the lack of a healthy and tasty fresh carrot juice on the market. At the time the project was focused on the importance of the cooling chain of fresh vegetables and not at all on the juice market. But as the importance of well-defined and controlled raw material, and the process technology of beverages including aseptic packaging were clear in the mind of Ingegerd Sjöholm it was natural to suggest the juice concept.

The decision to work on the juice concept instead of continuing to work on fresh vegetables for consumers was, of course, based on knowledge in the area for the need to make many investigations in different fields. Ingegerd Sjöholm was also inspired and encouraged by Marianne Härning Nilsson during a telephone call related to the cooling chain of vegetables. Marianne was so enthusiastic about carrots she almost persuaded Ingegerd that carrots could be used for anything.

In the *Oatly* case, serendipity is apparent on different occasions depending on by whom and when the milk concept was invented. Lennart Wikström had it in mind, Sigvard Andersson suggested it once, Rickard Öste arranged a project and started to work on the concept and during the meeting with 'Food from Sweden' another star started to shine. All of these people are playing with the serendipity. The reason why this idea was invented here, in the mind of so many different people, is probably based on the broad knowledge concerning starch, fibre, nutritional aspects and process technology at the university. This basic knowledge was gained over several years thanks to financial support from Cerealia and the Skånska Lantmännen Foundation. A number of PhD postgraduate students have performed much of the research. Serendipity has not occurred without the knowledge base.

Diverse Stimuli

It is important for the creative process to allow employees in companies and researchers to think in new ways. The Ideon Agro Food Foundation is a platform where internal meeting places are set up in order to create new impressions. The project leaders are all skilled in traditional academic research which could be applied to food or raw materials for food in some way. One of the activities at the Ideon Agro Food Foundation is brainstorming meetings together with the member industries in order to formulate new projects. As a result of the brainstorming, impressions are linked together and transferred into project ideas.

When innovation organizations are evaluated one of the questions to be answered is 'How many of the concepts are born in the minds of commercial employees and how many in the minds of university employees?' Such evaluations have shown that the university employees articulate most of the technological breakthrough ideas. Some university researchers then consider the innovation complete. But it is not. In order to make an innovation, the unique technological breakthrough in the product area must be matched with process design competence, insight into consumer needs and market penetration methods. We have illustrated this thoroughly in the previous section on the innovation process. The only point that we wish to make here is that those who make unique technological breakthroughs must have deep and specialized knowledge and an enduring interest in order to be creative and invent something new. Knowledge is the main basis for all inventions. Different kinds of knowledge are needed if innovation projects are to succeed.

Communication

Communication is the basis for a successful cluster innovation project. However, the methods of participating and working in cluster projects can vary widely. In the Öresund region there are 26 different clusters. The objective of each cluster may be anything from general knowledge about fruit or cereals to exporting food products. But all of them are based on the will to belong to a meeting place where communication is possible followed by an activity or a learning process. The activities in the clusters are always defined in statements where the goal and performance are defined in order to present the activities for new members, but also to provide a guideline for cooperation in the same business.

Arenas for general communication are well established at the university; namely internal seminars. Such seminars have been transformed in the different clusters into open or closed workshops. In both the *Oatly* and the *Mona Carota* cases, different people participated in meetings and had the possibility to brainstorm, digest and create visions of what could be created. The clusters are able to work freely without any obligations. They provide a way for people to leave their offices and enter a new environment where they are free to look for new visions.

EPILOGUE: RETURNING TO THE EU PERSPECTIVE

We would like to conclude by focusing on the future of innovation. We will do this by returning to the EU's interest in efficient innovation, starting with the Ceccini report from 1988. There, two aspects of diversity in the single market are highlighted. One aspect is that complexity must be reduced in order to promote the best-practice technology and the highest-quality products. The other aspect is that diversity must be increased in terms of new products and processes (Sloth Andersen and Braendgaard, 1992, pp. 242–243). The EU analysis focuses, however, on the diversity reduction aspect since it is considered difficult to measure the effects of diversity creation; it would require a dynamic analysis which the Ceccini report does not use. The effects of diversity creation are considered to be large and positive. When these effects are written about in the report the need for innovation is stated very clearly:

> Examples of this (meaning diversity creation) include product and process innovation which will modify – upwards – the entire trajectory of EC growth and welfare throughout the 1990s and beyond into the twenty-first century (Ceccini, 1992, p. 104).

We notice that from the Ceccini report onwards, the EU has followed the path of complexity reduction in order to promote its best-research practices. This is now clearly accentuated in the Sixth Framework Programme, where the message to the research and corporate worlds is to form larger consortia, guided by large research organizations and large companies.

When we have investigated innovation processes we have learned that interactions between large and small companies and universities seem to help innovation greatly. We have also learned about the positive aspects of complexity. The innovators need to try many options to find the best technology. We also find simultaneous rivalry and co-operation in the clusters that we have studied.

This makes us wonder if there should not be alternatives to large EU-planned, well-focused research projects. Maybe it is time for the EU to pick up the undeveloped ideas in the Ceccini report; that diversity creation can have large positive effects on innovation.

NOTES

1. We remind the reader of the distinction that we made earlier in the theory chapter between knowledge transfer – using technological knowledge in a new project and knowledge integration – creating something new based on different kinds of knowledge.
2. For more information see www.anoto.com. Anoto is creating a global de facto standard for paper-based digital communication. Endorsing this standard is a wide range of companies within the telecom, mobile phone, personal computer, paper producer and writing instrument industries. Christer Fåhraeus is among Sweden's leading high-technology entrepreneurs, founding his first company, C Technologies while studying for a Ph.D. in neurophysiology.
3. Interview with a brand manager for consumer products.
4. Interview with a Managing Director with experience from many large development projects.
5. The interview was made during the IT boom; these conditions have now changed somewhat.
6. Interview with the Vice-President for Strategy and R&D in a major US food company.
7. R&D manager in a large international food corporation.
8. Major supplier of competence and technology to the same corporation.
9. Statement from the President of a small innovative company who tried to involve a multi-national company in an innovation process.
10. Experienced board member working in innovation companies.
11. University professor renowned internationally in the area of food innovations.
12. Joke of a business area manager at a large retailer.
13. Interview with CEO in a food-producing company.
14. Interview with the Vice-President for Strategy and R&D in large US food-producing company.
15. R&D Manager at a Swedish food-producing company.
16. Product Group Manager in a food-producing company.
17. Marketing director in a retailer chain commenting on a functional foods product.
18. The illustrative example of the prairie comes from Brown and Eisenhardt (1998, p.36)

19, For learning, assimilation and accommodation, we follow the theory of Jean Piaget; see, for example, Piaget (1970).
20. This product was later developed for testing of medical substances in the Pharmavision company.
21. Interview with an experienced venture capitalist in Boston, Massachusetts.
22. This concept was first defined by Karin Jonnergård in a study of leadership in federative co-operative organizations. See Jonnergård (1988).

Bibliography

Afuah, A. (1998), 'The dynamic "diamond": a technological innovation perspective' (with J. M. Utterback), *Economics of Innovation and New Technology*, Vol. 6, pp. 183–199.

Agriculture Canada (1991), *Task Force on Competitiveness in the Agro-food Industry: Growing Together*, Report to Ministers of Agriculture, Ottawa: Agriculture Canada.

Ahuja, G. and Lampert, M. (2001), 'Entrepreneurship in large corporations: a longitudinal study of how established firms create breakthrough invention', *Strategic Management Journal*, 22, 521–543.

Asheim, B. T. and Isaksen, A. (2000), 'Regional Innovation Policy Towards SME:s: Learning Good Practice from European Institutions.' Presented at a workshop on 'The Regional Level of Implementation of Innovation and Education and Training Policies' in Brussels, November 22–24.

Asheim, B. T. (2001), 'Learning regions as development coalitions: partnership as governance in European workfare states. Concepts and Transformation', *International Journal of Action Research and Organizational Renewal*, 6 (1), pp.73–101.

Askegaard, S. and Madsen, T. K. (1995), 'European food cultures: an exploratory analysis of food related preferences and behaviour in European regions', MAPP Working Paper No 26, Aarhus: The Aarhus School of Business.

Askegaard, S., Jensen, A. F., and Holt, D. B. (1999), 'Lipophobia: A Transatlantic Concept?', in Linda Price and Eric J. Arnould (eds), *Advances in Consumer Research*, Vol. 26, Provo, UT: Association for Consumer Research, pp. 331–336.

Askegaard, S. and Güliz, G. (1997), 'Product-country Images: Towards a Contextualised Approach', in Basil G. Englis and Anna Olofsson (eds) *European Advances in Consumer Research*, Vol. 3, Provo, UT: Association for Consumer Research, pp. 50–58.

Bain, J. S. (1956), *Barriers to New Competition*, Cambridge, MA: Harvard University Press.

Barney, J. B. (1991), 'Firm resources and sustained competitive advantage', *Journal of Management*, 17 (1): 99–120.

Becattini G. (ed.) (1987), *Mercato e Forze Locali: il Distretto Industriale*, Bologna: Il Mulino, p. 193.

Bech-Larsen, T., Nielsen, N. A., Grunert, K., and Sörensen, E. (1996), 'Means-ends chains for low involvment products – a study of Danish consumers' cognitions regarding different applications of vegetable oil', Aarhus. MAPP Working Paper No 41.

Beck, U. (1992), *Risk Society: Towards a New Modernity* (Mark Ritter Trans.), London: Sage.

Bergman, E. M. and Feser, E. J. (1999), 'Industrial and regional clusters: concepts and comparative applications', West Virginia University: http://www.rri.wvu.edu/WebBook/Bergam-Feser/contents.htm

Bredahl, L., Grunert, K. and Fertin, C. (1998), 'Relating consumer perceptions of pork quality to physical product characteristics', Aarhus: MAPP Working Paper No 53.

Brink, J. and Kola, J. (1995), 'small Countries with Large Neighbours: Choosing Agri-food Policies to Improve Competitive Performance', Discussion Group Report, XXII International Conference of Agricultural Economists, Zimbabwe, *IEEA Members Bulletin* (13), May.

Brown, L. S. and Eisenhardt, K. M. (1998), *Competing on the Edge: Strategy as Structured Chaos*, Harvard MA: Harvard Business School Press.

Buckley, P. J., Christopher, L. and Prescott, K. (1988), 'Measures of international competitiveness; a critical survey', *Journal of Marketing Management* **4** (2) 175–200.

Ceccini, P. (1988, 1992), *Benefits of a Single Market*, Aldershot: Wildwood House.

CERIA (1988), 'Progress in Food Preservation Processes', Proceedings from the International Symposium organised by Centre for Education and Research of Food and Chemical Industries, Brussels, Belgium, April 12–14.

Chipman, H., Kendall, P., Auld, G., Slater, M. and Keefe, T. (1995), 'Consumer reaction to a risk/benefit/option message about agricultural chemicals in food supply', *The Journal of Consumer Affairs*, **29** (1), 144–163.

Cohen, W. M. and Levinthal, D. A. (1990), 'Absorptive capacity: a new perspective on learning and innovation', *Administrative Science Quarterly*, **35**.

Corney, M., Shepherd, R., Hedderley, D. and Nanayakkara, C.(1994) 'Consumer Acquisition of Commercial and Nutritional Information in Food Choice', *Journal of Economic Psychology*, **15**, 285–300.

Daft, R. (1983), *Organization Theory and Design*, New York: West.

Dawson, J. A. and Shaw, S. A. (1989), 'Horizontal Relationships in Retailing and the Structure of Manufacturer Retailer Relationships.' in Pellegrini,L. and Reddy (eds), *Retail and Marketing Channels*, London: Routledge, Chapman & Hall, pp. 49–72.

de la Motte, J. and Paquet, G. (eds) (1998), *Local and Regional Systems of Innovation*, Dordrecht, NL: Kluwer Academic Publishers.

de Mooij, M. (1998), *Global Marketing and Advertising: Understanding Cultural Paradoxes* (1st edn.), Thousand Oaks, CA: Sage.

Denrell, C, (2000), 'Öresund Food Excellence', Unpublished consultancy report.

ECR Europe (1999), 'Efficient Product Introductions: The development of value-creating relationships'.

Edgell, S., Hetherington, K. and Warde, A. (eds) (1996), *Consumption Matters: The Production and Experience of Consumption,* 'Expelling future threats: some observations on the magical world of vitamins', Oxford, England: Blackwell Publishers, pp.183–203.

Edquist, C. (ed.) (1997), *Systems of Innovation, Technologies, Institutions and Organizations*, London: Pinter.

Eliasson, Å. (2000), 'A competence bloc analysis of the economic potential of biotechnology in agriculture and food production', Working Paper, IBM CNRS, Strasbourg, France.

Eneroth, K. (1997), 'strategi och kompetensdynamik – en studie av Axis Communication', *Lund Studies in Economics and Management, 37,* The Institute of Economic Research. School of Economics and Management, Lund University.

Eneroth, K. and Malm, A. T. (2001), 'Knowledge webs and generative relations. a network approach to developing areas of competence', *European Management Journal,* **19** (2), April.

Enright, M. (1990), *Geographic concentration and industrial organization,* PhD dissertation, Harvard University.

Enright, M. (1994), 'Organization and Co-ordination of Geographically Concentrated Industries', in Raff and Lamoreaux (eds), *Co-ordination and Information: Historical Perspectives on the Organization of Enterprise,* Chicago: Chicago University Press.

Enright, M. (2000a), 'survey of the characterization of regional clusters. initial results', Working Paper, Institute of Economic Policy and Business Strategy: Competitiveness Program, University of Hong Kong.

Enright, M. (2000b), 'The Globalization of Competition and the Localization of Competitive Advantage: Policies towards Regional Clustering', in Hood, N. and Young, S. (eds), *The Globalisation of Multinational Enterprise Activity and Economic Development,* London: Macmillan

Erhvervsfremme Styrelsen (2001), 'Kompetenceklynger i dansk erhvervsliv – en ny brik i erhvervspolitikken', http://www.efs.dk

Eriksson, K. (2000), 'Mumsbitar som är allt annat än skräpmat', in *Aftonbladet*, Stockholm, 8 November 2001.

European Comission (1994) *White Paper on Growth, Competitiveness, Employment: The Challenges and Ways Forward into the 21ˢᵗ Century*.

Falk, P. (1994), *The Consuming Body*, London, UK: Sage.

Falk, P. (1996), Expelling Future Threats: Some Observations on the magical World of Vitamins in Edgell, S, Hetherington,, K & Warde, A: (eds): *Consumption Matters. The Production and Experience of Consumption*, Oxford, UK: Blackwell Publishers.

Fanfani, R. and Lagnevik, M. (1995), 'Industrial Districts and Porter Diamonds', paper prepared within the EU Concerted Action Structural Change in the European Food Industry, presented at the Strategic Management Society 15th Annual Conference, Mexico City, October 15–18.

Firat, A. Fuat and Dolakia, N. (1998), *Consuming People: From Political Economy to Theaters of Consumption*, New York: Routledge.

Flosch, J. (1988), 'The contribution of structural semiotics to the design of a hypermarket', *International Journal of Research in Marketing* (4), 233–252.

Freeman, C. (1974), *The Economics of Industrial Innovation*, London: Penguin Books.

Gabriele, C. (1997), 'Vertical Co-ordination and Competitiveness: The Case of High Quality and Aged Foods', paper presented at the international conference 'Vertical Relations and Co-ordination in the Food System', Piacenza, June 12–13.

Galbraith, J. R. (1982), 'Designing the innovating organization', *Organizational Dynamics*, Winter edition.

Giddens, A. (1991), *Modernity and Self-identity: Self and Society in Late Modern Age*, Stanford, CA: Stanford University Press.

Goddard, J. (1978), 'The Location of Non-manufacturing Activities Within Manufacturing Industries', in Hamilton, F. E. I. (ed), *Contemporary Industrialization*, London: Longman, pp. 62–85.

Grant, R. M. (1996), 'Toward a knowledge based theory of the firm', *Strategic Management Journal*, **17**, Special Issue, Winter, 93–109.

Greco, M. (1995), 'Psykosomatiska subjekt och 'plikten att vara frisk': personligt handlande i medicinsk rationalitet', in Hultqvist, K. and Peterson, K. (eds), *Foucault: namnet på en modern vetenskaplig och filosofisk problematik*, Sweden: HLS Förlag.

Grunert, K. et al. (1996), *Market Orientation in Food and Agriculture*, Boston: Kluwer Academic Publishers.

Grunert, K., Grunert, C. S. and Sörensen, E. (1995), 'Means-end chains and laddering: an inventory of problems and an agenda for research', Aarhus: MAPP Working Paper No 34.

Hamel, G. (1994), 'The Concept of Core Competence', in Hamel, G. and Heene, A. (eds), *Competence Based Competition*, Chichester: John Wiley.

Hamilton, F. (ed.) (1978), *Contemporary Industrialisation*, London: Longman.

Harmsen, H. (1995), 'succesfaktorer i produktudvikling og deres implementering i mellemstore födevarevirksomheder', PhD dissertation, Aarhus, The Aarhus School of Business, Denmark.

Harmsen, H. (1996), 'succesfaktorer i produktudvikling og deres implementering i mellemstore födevareviksomheder', Institut for Markedsökonomi, The Aarhus School of Business, Denmark.

Harmsen, H., Grunert, K. and Bove, K. (1996), *Virksomhedskompetence*, København: Börsens förlag.

Hart, S. and Craig, A. (1993), 'Dimensions of Success in New-product Development', in Baker, M. (1993), Perspectives on *Marketing Management*, Vol 3, Chichester: John Wiley & Sons.

Heasman, M. and Mellentin, J. (2001), *The Functional Food Revolution*, London: Earthscan Publications Ltd.

Heasman, M. and Mellentin, J. (1999), 'swedish oats for heart health', *The Newsletter for Functional Foods, Nutraceuticals and Healthy Eating*, October, pp. 23–24, London.

Hellbom, O. (1996), 'Ny mat på hungrig marknad – Svenska företag exporterar livsmedel som gränsar till medicin', *Dagens Industri*, August 30, p. 17, Stockholm.

Henson, S. and Northen, J. (1997), 'The Role of Quality Assurance in Food Retailer–Manufacturer Relations: The Case of Food Safety Controls in the Supply of Retailer Own-branded Products in the UK', paper presented at the international conference 'Vertical Relations and Co-ordination in the Food System', Piacenza, June 12–13.

Hemlin, S. (2000), 'The organization of new knowledge production. VEST', *Journal for Science and Technology Studies*, **13** (3–4), 73–90.

Henson, S., Loader, R. and Traill, B. (1995), 'Contemporary food policy issues and the food supply chain', *European Review of Agricultural Economics*, **22** (3) 271–281.

Högfeldt, Per (2000), 'Lättprodukterna som kan göra dig tjockare', *Aftonbladet*, Stockholm 21 September 2000.

Ippolito, P. M. and Mathios, A. D. (1994), 'Nutritional information and policy: a study of U.S. food production trends', *Journal of Consumer Policy*, **17** (3), 271–305.

Johnson, B. and Lundvall, B.-Å. (1994), 'The learning economy', *Journal of Industrial Studies*, **1** (2).

Jonnergård, K. (1988), 'Federativa processer och administrativ utveckling', *Lund Studies in Economics and Management*, 3, Institute of Economic Research, Lund University.

Kauffman, S. (1993), *The Origins of Order: Self-organization and Selection in Evolution*, New York: Oxford University Press.

Kilsby, T. and Nyström, H. (1998), 'Utveckling och marknadsföring av nya svenska livsmedel med medicinsk effekt (functional food)', 121, Uppsala: Swedish University of Agricultural Sciences (SLU).

Kirkpatrick, D. (1997) 'Intel's amazing profit machine', *Fortune,* 17 February pp. 60-68.

Kogut, B. (1993), *Country Competitiveness*, Oxford: Oxford University Press.

Kola, J., Hyvönen, S. and Virtonen, T. (1995), 'Agriculture and food industry: convergence between public policies and business strategies?', Paper presented at the 44th EAAE Seminar, Thessalonica, Greece, October.

Kowalski, R. (1987), *The 8-week Cholesterol Cure: The Ultimate Program for Preventing Heart Disease*, New York: HarperCollins.

Kristensen, K., Östergård, P. and Juhl, H. J. (1997), 'The success and failure of product development in the Danish food sector', Aarhus: MAPP Working Paper No 48.

Kristensen, P. S. (1992), 'Product development strategy in the Danish agricultural complex: global interaction with clusters of marketing excellence', *The International Journal of Food and Agribusiness Marketing*, **4** (3), 107–118.

Krugman, P. (1991), *Geography and Trade*, Cambridge, MA: The MIT Press.

Kulman, L. (2000), 'Food news can get you dizzy, so know what to swallow', *U.S. News & World Report*.

Lagnevik, M. (1989), *Ledning och ledarskap i olika företagsformer*, Stockholm: Rabén & Sjögren.

Lagnevik, M. (1996), 'svensk livsmedelsnäring i internationell konkurrens' ('Agriculture, Food & Competitiveness'), LOK-rapport nr 13, Department of Business Administration, School of Economics and Management, Lund University.

Lanciotti, C. (1997), Supply Chain Integration, Category Management and the Italian Retail Sector, paper presented at the international conference 'Vertical Relations and Co-ordination in the Food System', Piacenza, June 12–13.

Landro, L. (2000), 'Web Health Groups Ponder How to Set Universal Standards', *The Wall Street Journal*, New York.

Langhoff, T. (1993), 'The internationalisation of the firm in an intercultural perspective', MAPP Working Paper No 15, The Aarhus School of Business.

Leife, Å. (2001), 'Unikt produktsortiment baserat på havre', *Livsmedelsteknik*, pp. 8–9, Stockholm.

Leonard-Barton, D. (1992), 'Core capabilities and core rigidities: a paradox in managing new product development', *Strategic Marketing Journal, 13* pp. 111–126.

Lloyd, P. and Dicken, P. (1977), *Location in Space*, London: Harper & Row.

Lundvall, B.-Å. (ed.) (1992), *National Systems of Innovation: Towards a Theory of Innovation and Interactive Learning*, London: Pinter.

Mazis, M. B. and Raymond, M. A. (1997), 'Consumer perceptions of health claims in advertisments and on food labels', *The Journal of Consumer Affairs*, **31** (1), 10–26.

McCracken, G. (1988), *The Long Interview*, Newbury Park, CA, USA: Sage.

Mellentine, J. et al. (2001), *International Functional Food Centers. Benchmarking of Best Practices,* London: The Centre for Food and Health Studies. Consultancy report for Scottish Enterprise.

Mick, D. G. (1986), 'Consumer research and semiotics: exploring the morphology of signs, symbols, and significance', *Journal of Consumer Research*, **13** (September), 196–213.

NUTEK (2001), *Regionala vinnarkluster*, Stockholm: Verket för näringslivsutveckling.

OECD (2001), *Innovative Clusters: Drivers of national innovation systems*, Paris. OECD.

Ohmae, K. (1995), *The End of the Nation State: The Rise of Regional Economics. How New Engines of Prosperity are Reshaping Global Markets*, New York: The Free Press.

Pellegrini, L. (1989), 'Consumers' behaviour and producer-distributor relationships in convenience goods markets', in Pellegrini. L. and Reddy, S. K. (eds), *Retail and Marketing Channels*, London: Routledge, Chapman & Hall, pp. 3–23.

Pellegrini, L. (1996), 'Brands vs. Trade Names. Manufacturer and Retailer Missions in the Value System', School of Economics and Management paper series 1996/8, Lund University.

Piaget, J. (1970), 'Genetic Epistemology', Woodbridge lectures delivered at Columbia University in October 1968, New York: Columbia University Press.

Pinochet III, G. (1985), *Intrapreneuring – Why You don't Have to Leave the Corporation to become an Entrepreneur*, New York: Harper & Row.

Piore, M. and Sabel, C. (1984), *The Second Industrial Divide*, New York: Basic Books

Pitts, E. and Lagnevik, M. (1997), 'What determines food industry competitiveness?', in Traill, B. and Pitts, E. (eds), *Competitiveness in the Food Industry*, London: Blackie Academic & Professional

Plichta, K. and Harmsen, H. (1993), 'studies of key success factors of product development success: a reinterpretation of results', paper presented at the 22nd annual Conference of the European Marketing Academy, Barcelona, May 23–28.

Porter, M. (1995) *Competitive Advantage*, New York: Free Press

Porter, M. (1998a), 'Clusters and competition', *Harvard Business Review*, November–December.

Porter, M. (1998b), 'Jon Azua panel', SMS Conference Orlando, Florida, November 4.

Porter, M. E. (1998c), *On Competition*, Harvard Business Review Books.

Porter, M. E. (1980), *Competitive Strategy*, New York: The Free Press.

Porter, M. E. (1990), *The Competitive Advantage of Nations*, London: Macmillan.

Porter, M. E. (1991), 'Toward a dynamic theory of strategy', *Strategic Management Journal,* **12**, 95–117.

Poulsen, Jacob B. (1999), 'Danish consumers' attitudes towards functional foods', Aarhus, Denmark: MAPP 49.

Prokesh, S. E. (1995) 'Competing on customer service: an interview with British Airways' Sir Colin Marshall', *Harvard Business Review, 73(6)* 101–116.

Pyke, F., Becattini, G. and Sengenberger, W. (1990), *Industrial Districts and Inter-firm Co-operation in Italy*, Geneva: International Institute for Labour Studies.

Robinson, A. G. and Stern, S. (1997), *Corporate Creativity: How Innovation and Improvement Actually Happen*, San Francisco: Berret-Koehler Publishers, Inc.

Rogers, R. P. (1980) *Staff Report on the Development and Structure of the Electric Lamp Industry*, Washington, DC: US Government Printing Office

Rosenberg, N. (1997 (1994)), *Den tekniska förändringens ekonomi (Exploring the Black Box)*, Stockholm: SNS Förlag.

Rössner, Stephan (2000), 'Livet är fett', in *Dagens Nyheter*, Stockholm, 21 October 2000

Saxenian, A. (1985), 'The Genesis of Silicon Valley', in Hall, P. and Markusen, A. (1985), *Silicon Landscapes*, Boston: Allen & Unwin.

Schumpeter, J. A. (1934), *The Theory of Economic Development: An Enquiry into Profits, Capital, Credit and the Business Cycle*, London: Oxford University Press.

Schön, D. (1983), *The Reflective Practitioner*, New York: Basic Books.

Simon, H. A. (1991), 'Bounded rationality and organizational learning', *Organization Science*, 2, 125–134.

Sloth Andersen, E. and Braendgaard, A. (1992) , 'Integration, Innovation and Evolution' in Lundvall, B-Å. (ed), *National Systems of Innovation*, London: Pinter, pp. 242–243.

Söderström, H. Tson (ed.) (2001), *kluster.se. Sverige i den nya ekonomiska geografin*, Stockholm: SNS förlag.

Spradley, J. P. (1979), *The Ethnographic Interview*, New York: Holt Rinehart and Winston.

Svensson, M. (1993), 'structure, strategy and competition in the Danish dairy- and pork businesses', LOK report, Department of Business Administration, School of Economics and Management, Lund University.

Szulanski, G. (1996), 'Exploring internal stickiness: Impediments to the transfer of best practices within the firm', *Strategic Management Journal*, 17 Special Issue, Winter, 27–44.

Thompson, C. J. and Hirschman, E. C. (1995), 'Understanding the socialized body: A poststructuralist analysis of consumers' self-conceptions, body images, and self-care practices', *Journal of Consumer Research*, 2 2 (September), 139–153.

Tillotson, J. E. (1999), 'Juices in the 21st century: A futuristic Vision of the Global Fruit & Vegetable juice Industry', International Federation of Juice Producers 22nd IFU Symposium, Paris, France, March 18.

Traill, B. and Grunert, K. (eds) (1997), *Product and Process Innovation in the Food Industry*, London: Blackie Academic & Professional.

Traill, B. and Pitts, E. (eds) (1997), *Competitiveness in the Food Industry*, London: Blackie Academic and Professional.

Tsoukas, H. (1996), 'The firm as a distributed knowledge system', *Strategic Management Journal*, 17, Special Issue, Winter, 11–26.

Utterback, J. (1974), 'Innovation in industry and the diffusion of technology', *Science*, 183, 658–662.

Utterback, J. (1994), *Mastering the Dynamics of Innovation*, Boston MA: HBS Press.

Warde, A. (1997) *Consumption, Food and Taste*. London. Sage

Wennerholm, T., Lagnevik, M. and Göransson, G. (1996), 'scenarioteknik vid strategisk planering: tillämpningar inom livsmedelskedjan', LOK-rapport nr 7, Företagsekonomiska institutionen, Ekonomihögskolan vid Lunds Universitet.

Wernfelt, B. (1984), 'From critical resources to corporate strategy', *Journal of General Management*, 14, 4–12.

Wikström, L. (2000), 'Förnyande företag', *Svenska livsmedel*, 6, 16–17.

Wigmore, B. (1996), 'A milk that can make you slimmer', *Daily Mail*, August 27, (p. 34, London.

Zachrisson, M. and Sjögren, H. (2002), 'Comparing the effect of different financial systems on the financing of high technology small firms in Mjärdevi Science park/Berzelius Science Park, Linköping, Sweden and Silicon Valley, USA', *NUTEK Work in Progress*, p. 83.

Index